THE CIGAR FACTO[RY OF]

ISAY ROTTENBERG

HELLA ROTTENBERG & SANDRA ROTTENBERG

THE HIDDEN HISTORY OF A JEWISH ENTREPRENEUR IN NAZI GERMANY

Translated from the Dutch by Jonathan Reeder

WILFRID LAURIER
UNIVERSITY PRESS

LAURIER

Inspiring Lives.

Wilfrid Laurier University Press acknowledges the support of the Canada Council for the Arts for our publishing program. We acknowledge the financial support of the Government of Canada through the Canada Book Fund for our publishing activities. Funding provided by the Government of Ontario and the Ontario Arts Council. This book was published with the support of the Dutch Foundation for Literature. This work was supported by the Research Support Fund.

Canadä   Canada Council for the Arts / Conseil des Arts du Canada   Ontario   ONTARIO ARTS COUNCIL CONSEIL DES ARTS DE L'ONTARIO an Ontario government agency un organisme du gouvernement de l'Ontario

Library and Archives Canada Cataloguing in Publication

Title: The cigar factory of Isay Rottenberg : the hidden history of a Jewish entrepreneur in Nazi Germany / Hella Rottenberg and Sandra Rottenberg ; translated from the Dutch by Jonathan Reeder.

Other titles: Sigarenfabriek van Isay Rottenberg. English

Names: Rottenberg, Hella, author. | Rottenberg, Sandra, author.

Description: Translation of: De sigarenfabriek van Isay Rottenberg: de verborgen geschiedenis van een joodse Amsterdammer in nazi-Duitsland. | Includes bibliographical references.

Identifiers: Canadiana (print) 20210237279 | Canadiana (ebook) 20210237341 | ISBN 9781771125505 (softcover) | ISBN 9781771125512 (EPUB) | ISBN 9781771125529 (PDF)

Subjects: LCSH: Rottenberg, Isay, 1889-1971. | LCSH: Jews, Dutch—Germany—Biography. | LCSH: Jews, Polish—Germany—Biography. | LCSH: Businesspeople—Netherlands—Biography. | LCSH: Jewish businesspeople—Netherlands—Biography. | LCSH: Cigar industry—Germany—History—20th century. | LCSH: Confiscations—Germany—History—20th century. | LCSH: Jewish property—Germany—History—20th century. | LCSH: National socialism.

Classification: LCC DS135.N6 R68713 2021 | DDC 940.53089/924—dc23

The main cover photo shows the Krenter Werke cigar factory in Döbeln, ca. 1931, from Stadsarchief Döbeln. Photo of Isay Rottenberg from the Private Collection of the Rottenberg and Jacobs families. Cover design by Heng Wee Tan. Interior design by Michel Vrana.

De sigarenfabriek van Isay Rottenberg © 2017 by Hella Rottenberg and Sandra Rottenberg Originally published by Uitgeverij Atlas Contact, Amsterdam

This translation © 2021 Wilfrid Laurier University Press
Waterloo, Ontario, Canada
www.wlupress.wlu.ca

Advance Praise for *The Cigar Factory of Isay Rottenberg*

"Two granddaughters go in search of the hidden history of their Jewish grandfather, and they uncover an amazing story: how he bought a cigar factory near Dresden as the Nazis came to power in Germany, and how he fought defiantly to keep it operating, at the risk of his life. An astonishing portrait of what life was truly like for a Jewish businessman in Nazi Germany, and an exemplary example of how two determined women stripped aside family mythologies and arrived at the surprising truth about the family patriarch." – MICHAEL IGNATIEFF, author of *On Consolation*

"Who wouldn't like to wake up one day to discover a previously unknown family history that illuminates the world events of its day? This is precisely what happened to the highly regarded Rotenberg family of Toronto when the revealing story of their ancestor, Isay Rottenberg, unexpectedly came to light in 2017. Isay's struggle to retain his successful cigar factory in Germany in the early days of the Hitler regime is a detailed and historically valuable microcosm of how quickly violence overwhelmed German society in the early 1930s. *The Cigar Factory of Isay Rottenberg* is also the poignant story of newly discovered ties with living European relatives. And the cherished continuities that bind families together." – ERNA PARIS, author of *Long Shadows: Truth, Lies and History*

"*The Cigar Factory of Isay Rottenberg* is a fascinating story of resilience and survival. Much as their ancestor fought his fight, the Rottenbergs have left no stone unturned to preserve his story. Thank God they did! They write the way you should smoke a cigar—savouring every moment without ever letting the flame go out!" – MARK CRITCH, performer and author of *Son of a Critch*

"The extraordinary story of a determined, inventive man in lethally dangerous times and the legacy of bravery, tenacity, and endurance shared by his widespread family." – ANNA PORTER, author of *The Appraisal* and *Deceptions*

"A remarkable window into the life of a Jewish family, just one among the millions who endured so much, who struggled so valiantly to maintain human dignity in those shadow years of the early 1930s when even the cruelest heart could not imagine a time when murder and industrial slaughter would become the German national pastime. A story of redemption, courage, and honour that leaves one shuddering in awe." – WADE DAVIS

"Two journalist cousins retrieve their grandfather from the silenced history of a factory stolen and a family saved. An enthralling quest."
– NESSA RAPOPORT, author of *Evening: A Novel*

"A powerful and riveting account of a family suddenly discovering their heroic ancestor's past, a story that reminds us of an individual's power to resist the brutal killing machine of the Nazis. In the deluge of fatal statistics from the Holocaust, this book is an example of particular lives impacted, the human stories of families and people that all too often get lost. Now the world can see the brave and unstinting face of Isay Rottenberg." – EVAN SOLOMON, columnist, political journalist, and radio host

THE CIGAR FACTORY OF ISAY ROTTENBERG

TABLE OF CONTENTS

1

ISAY ROTTENBERG

"CLAIMS FOR PROPERTY STOLEN OR CONFISCATED DURING THE Holocaust period. Deadline 31 December 2014," read the boldface announcement in the *Nieuw Israëlitisch Weekblad*. The notice continues with a description of a "Claims Conference" that had set up a fund for "the restitution of Jewish property that was either sold after 1933 under duress or confiscated by the Nazis."* An additional €50 million was available to "late applicants," that is, those who had missed several earlier appeals. Heirs had just one month to submit a claim.

Our cousin Sacha and Hella's brother Menno happened to spot the notice in the Dutch-language Jewish weekly. They remembered having heard something about a factory in Germany that had once belonged to our grandfather, and had been stolen by the Nazis.

We, too, recalled mention of the factory by a parent, but beyond that we knew nothing. Zero, zilch. Not even what the factory had produced, let alone when, why, and for how long our grandfather had done business in Germany.

The notice referred us to the organization's website, officially called *The Conference on Jewish Material Claims Against Germany*, which contains a list of names and addresses of former businesses and their owners. Sacha

---

* http://www.claimscon.org/what-we-do/successor/

1

clicked it open. And there, among the thousands of names, was that of our grandfather, Isay Rottenberg, and next to it: Deutsche Zigarren-Werke, Industriestrasse 2, Döbeln. Just a few words, but unequivocal confirmation, for the first time, of the factory's existence.

The discovery caused a flurry of agitation within the family. We had a month to verify that Isay Rottenberg had been the owner of the factory, that it had been unlawfully confiscated from him, and that we, the seven grandchildren, were his rightful heirs.

We went straight to work, armed with no more than the barest of data. We were eager to submit the claim, of course, but it was mostly out of a burning curiosity. Entering *Isay Rottenberg + Döbeln + Deutsche Zigarren-Werke* in the search engine gave an immediate result. It was a report in *Der Stürmer*, a virulently anti-Semitic German tabloid of the day, informing its readers "with joy" that the Jew Isay Rottenberg was no longer in charge of the Deutsche Zigarren-Werke in Döbeln and that the company had not a single Jewish employee. So now we had the tail end of our grandfather's German story, but not the beginning—and no idea where to start. Our parents were deceased by this time, and nowhere in the papers they left behind were there any hints or leads.

At first our search unearthed little, but once we visited Döbeln months later, we encountered a trove of documentation. The key to this hoard of data was a meticulously documented business conflict: beginning in 1933, rival firms throughout Germany had apparently banded together with the goal of bringing down the Deutsche Zigarren-Werke. But our grandfather doggedly resisted. The fracas did not only involve mayors, civil servants, and ministers of the Third Reich in Saxony and Berlin. The Chamber of Commerce, industry associations, the Nationalsozialistische Deutsche Arbeiterpartei (NSDAP), and the German Labour Front all took sides. The Döbeln trove included letters, memos, reports, photos, and newspaper and magazine articles. But in Berlin, Dresden, Leipzig, and Chemnitz, too, archives provided accounts of the Deutsche Zigarren-Werke and the dispute regarding the factory's future. We could follow a blow-by-blow account of the conflict: Who had the upper hand? Who had pulled a dirty trick? We even found the minutes of meetings where our grandfather crossed swords with NSDAP leaders, city functionaries, and other entrepreneurs.

Finding these memos spurred us to learn more about the men who sat across from our grandfather at the negotiating table; their relationship to him, a Jewish factory owner; and the tug-of-war over the cigar factory. We succeeded. Even the stories of men who orchestrated and executed the theft of the factory in 1935 were painstakingly chronicled.

The conflict also afforded us the opportunity to home in on the workings of a typical German city during the early years of National Socialism. We saw the town's administrative branch change its hue from "red" to "brown."* We met the profiteers, the collaborators, and the victims of the new regime, and we saw how quickly this all became "the new normal" under a veneer of legality. And where interests and ideology clashed, vested interests usually won. Döbeln in the 1930s came to life, and we had a front-row seat.

We also got to know a hitherto unknown side of our grandfather. We had uncovered an episode about which generations of Rottenbergs had assiduously kept mum, but one that, at the time, must have thoroughly upended family life. We saw what a stubborn, wilful, but also intrepid man our grandfather was. We were flabbergasted that he had the nerve to set up shop in Hitler's Germany: he was combative but overconfident, oblivious to danger, and well-nigh reckless.

As youngsters we never really gave much thought to why our grandfather's time in Germany was taboo. So many things were simply not talked about. The pre-war years were cloaked in a haze. And if anything *was* discussed, it was mostly in the form of scattered anecdotes—there was no way to weave it all into a coherent story. Hella's mother, whose knowledge of the details was only second-hand, occasionally alluded to the Nazis having stolen Granddad's factory and putting him in jail. But more than that, she either didn't know or wouldn't say. Hella's father Alfred never talked about it, nor did Sandra's father Edwin.

The notice in the Jewish weekly jogged Sandra's memory. Someone did, albeit briefly, lift the veil on the episode once. This was at Edwin's funeral in 1997 when, in her eulogy, his sister (our Aunt Tini), reminisced about her youth in the 1930s. Her speech had been recorded, and listening to the tape now, we could hear the emotion in our aunt's voice: "Around 1935, not many people bothered about what was going on in Germany. But our family was faced with a great drama. Father suddenly disappeared and we didn't know where, why, or how. We assumed he was no longer alive."

A drinking-straw factory in Amsterdam

Our grandfather, when we knew him, was the director of the Amsterdam-based family business J. Rottenberg & Sons, a manufacturer of plastic

---

* i.e., from communist ("red") to Fascist ("brown").

drinking straws and tubes he had set up after the war on the Nieuwe Keizersgracht, and where both our fathers also worked. He was the boss, and even as children it was clear to us that he was an entrepreneur to the core. Nattily dressed, in a suit and carefully chosen necktie, handkerchief in the breast pocket, gold cufflinks, and elegant Italian shoes, he was self-assured and resolute. His sons, on the other hand, were cut from very different cloth: unkempt hair and ill-fitting suits, disorganized, and wont to launching into rambling stories. They were reluctant businessmen.

Isay Rottenberg's dominant personality was always front and centre. He was like a magnet. Whenever he entered a room, he would stand silently and wait for as long as it took for the attention to turn to him. Only then did he greet those present. He was small and stocky, and had a round, shiny, bald head, a good-sized nose, and large ears. His eyelids were triangles from behind which his dark eyes observed the world with curiosity and amusement.

He left his mark on our fathers, our mothers, and us grandchildren. We looked up to him and were fascinated by him. When we were little, the family got on well. Grandfather was the patriarch, with his children and grandchildren circling in orbits around him. Later, though, there was a falling-out that had to do with the factory. Edwin broke with his father and brother, with Aunt Tini siding with Edwin, and their brother Alfred remaining loyal to Granddad. In addition to our age difference, Hella being somewhat older than Sandra, this bad blood determined the role our grandfather would play in both our lives and how we remember him. Even now, decades later, the rift colours our memories.

For me, Hella, Granddad was a rock. We were next-door neighbours on the Milletstraat in Amsterdam, both on the ground floor. The fence separating the two backyards had been taken down, and we went in and out of each other's house via the kitchen door. From my earliest youth, his rhythm determined my own daily routine. I would go over to his place early in the morning, he would slice a grapefruit in half and we would share it, segment by segment. When he drove off to the factory, I would amble back home. At around one o'clock, lunchtime, I would make sure I was in his front hall as the car pulled up, and when I heard him on the stoop, I would open the front door. "Hello, my *schatzi*," he would say, and together we would wash our hands, mine inside his, with lukewarm water in the bathroom. At six o'clock sharp—he was a punctual man—we'd repeat the ritual. I usually started eating with him and Aunt Agnes, his live-in housekeeper, and would stay until my mother came to fetch me for dinner at home. Then Granddad would come over to our place for dessert.

As soon as I could read, he would pick me up on Saturdays and we would walk to the bookstore. He left me there while he did his shopping, but when he returned, I had still not made up my mind. I took forever to choose a book because my only criterion was that it mustn't be an "I book," one written in the first person.

Later we would do crossword puzzles or play word games. I was all ears when he talked, and he listened intently to my stories. Sometimes my parents were worried that I preferred his company to that of my own friends.

I couldn't get enough of him, and in retrospect I understand why. At home, the sparks flew. Both of my parents were insomniacs: my mother because of nightmares or wartime memories, my father because he had served as a decoder on board a British destroyer during the war and was never able to shake the four-hours-on, four-hours-off regime.

No matter how upbeat my mother tried to be, she was in a permanent state of barely suppressed dread. She was forever poised to make a run for it. The veneer of joviality could crack at any moment, and the panic would come bursting through. This might happen when, for instance, she was in the kitchen and hadn't noticed that Granddad had slipped in through the back door. I can still hear her breath catch in her throat. And every time it happened, she got the fright of her life, *every time* she'd get angry at Granddad, *every time* she begged him to wait until she'd seen him before coming inside, and every so often he would forget. It took her many minutes to pull herself together.

I sought out safe havens so as not to get dragged into her vortex of anxiety. I nagged relentlessly to be sent to nursery school, and when I was three, they gave in and enrolled me. And I had my grandfather.

I felt safe with him. I knew he had been through a lot, that he came from Poland and had lived in Germany, that he had had to flee a few times in his life, and that most of his family was gone, but that it hadn't dented his character or stability. I knew I could always turn to him, no matter what. Whatever cards life happened to deal, he would know what to do.

His alpha personality didn't always sit well with my parents. My mother doted on him as if he were her own father, but if he joined us at dinner and grilled my father with shop talk, she would sigh with impatience. "Father, can't you let Alfred just eat?" she'd ask, and then Granddad would give my father five minutes' respite.

He ate at our place on Friday evenings. The table was set with festive white linen and fancy tableware. Shabbat began with the lighting of the candles, sharing challah and wine, and reciting the appropriate blessings. Granddad stood by and watched. As soon as the last word of the prayers had been uttered, even before we wished one another "Shabbat Shalom," he whisked off his yarmulke and tossed it on the table or behind him. The only time he felt obliged to go to synagogue was for a grandson's bar mitzvah.

Grandfather always had a cigarette in his hand, except during meals. The cigarettes came from flat, yellow boxes emblazoned with an exotic illustration. A supply of cartons was kept in a drawer in his dining room. My first-ever cigarette was one filched from that very drawer. It was an Egyptian brand—Christo Cassimis—and the tobacco was so strong that I was sick for hours.

I never once saw my grandfather smoke a cigar.

When I was in primary school I would sometimes accompany him to the factory during school holidays or on a free afternoon. I would sit at the table with the factory girls, count out fifty straws, and pack them in cellophane. The others would shoot each other knowing glances and watch their words while the boss's granddaughter was around. My father worked in the office, but Granddad was always present in the factory proper, wearing a spotless white coat over his suit, like a doctor or a pharmacist. From the mezzanine he could oversee the works, and would go down to the production floor if a machine jammed or if there was any fuss among the workers. He would call out instructions to the mechanics above the din of the machinery. While overseeing the production line he would mix the coloured plastic pellets in deep barrels. He did this with painstaking perfectionism, as though the factory's future depended on it.

I eagerly took in everything he taught me. He read *Vrij Nederland* from cover to cover, and before passing the magazine to my parents, he would tick off the articles he deemed worthwhile. So from about the age of eleven I was following his recommended reading. Even though I understood just a smattering, it made me feel like I was approaching his level. He always marked Renate Rubenstein's columns and thus sparked my lifelong love of her writing.* I adored my grandfather, and while I was well aware of his foibles, I would never tolerate hearing him ill-spoken of.

He died when I was nearly sixteen. Never had I loved and felt such kinship with anyone as much as him. It felt as if half of me had been amputated. He had promised to take me to his beloved Prague after I graduated high school, but it was not meant to be. A year and a half later, I started studying Russian, and much later I lived in Prague as a newspaper correspondent. These were links to my grandfather: he was by my side and provided me with self-confidence.

---

* Renate Rubenstein: 1929 (Berlin)–1990 (Amsterdam). German-Dutch writer, journalist, and columnist.

I, Sandra, only felt somewhat at ease with my grandfather. I was the young-est of seven grandchildren. I saw Granddad once a week, on Thursdays, when my brother Felix and I ate our midday meal at his house. Our pri-mary school was close by, on the other side of the Stadionweg. He went to the factory every day, even though he was already nearly eighty. Usually we had to wait until he pulled up in his Daf, passing the time by chatting with the incredibly sweet Aunt Agnes and paging through Granddad's photo albums. Vintage pictures of men in tall hats and genteel ladies in wicker beach chairs flanked by men in bathing suits.

"Sandra didn't say anything again!" my older brother tattled to our mother when we got home from school. He was the spokesman, while I dared not utter a peep, especially if anyone I didn't know dropped by unexpectedly.

Who were those people? What did they call him again . . . *Shaya?* What kind of strange name was that? No one ever explained anything. "My grandfather is Russian," Felix used to tell our friends. It sounded cool.

Grandfather served us a luxurious lunch of roast beef sandwiches on white bread, with chocolate milk. We were expected to be quiet and listen to the one o'clock news and the current affairs segment that followed it. After that there was little time left for chit-chat, as we had to get back to school. Sometimes Granddad would do a magic trick for us, like swal-lowing his watch and retrieving it from his sleeve.

Granddad was good-natured and charming, and at the same time aloof and rather impenetrable. He used to blow cigarette smoke lovingly around my face. He had to be kissed quickly on both cheeks, nose, fore-head, and chin, otherwise his head would fall off. When we left, he would give us both a ten-pack of Milky Way bars for the road. They had the unforgettable slogan, "Real chocolate, without ruining your appetite." We gobbled them up after school all by ourselves—you weren't about to share something that special with classmates.

For my birthday I could choose an "expensive" present: new skates or a subscription to the science magazine *Kijk*. But first he had to check it out himself. "Interesting, very good." Or a new desk lamp that my mother had seen in the fancy home furnishings store across the street. "Let's go have a look," Granddad would say. He would give his approval—"Yes, excellent, a really fine lamp"—and then produce his wallet. Granddad had good taste, my mother used to say. He enjoyed going to auctions.

When I turned seven, Granddad showed up with an enormous pack-age. In my recollection the box was as big as I was. Behind the clear plastic window on the front was a large doll in a lacy wedding dress. She had breasts, an hourglass figure, and wore high heels. And this wasn't all: there was an entire wardrobe to go with it, in the latest fashions. Having mostly played with toy cars with my brother, I had never dared dream of such a marvellous gift. However, I could sense my parents' discomfort with the kind of present that ran counter to their modern, 1960s ideas about appropriate toys, so I thought it best to curb my enthusiasm—but it was the nicest thing my grandfather had ever done for me.

A year later, in 1968, came the family rift. His two sons had such radically different ideas about how to run a factory that my father, Edwin, left the company in high dudgeon. He was fed up with his father's authoritarian style, and turned his back on the family business. This meant that Granddad no longer came around to our place, nor were we welcome at the factory. The falling-out between my father and his brother and father was complete. Our lives changed drastically. My father was out of a job, but my mother kept up the morale. The drinking-straw factory and the Milletstraat were synonymous with conflict and family strife.

My grandfather arranged with my mother that he would still get to see us grandchildren. This became the Thursday lunch. My brother and I unwittingly acted as youthful diplomats who minded their Ps and Qs and acted as though nothing at all was amiss.

On the occasion of his eightieth birthday—celebrated, by way of exception, with all the children and grandchildren—each of the grandchildren was given a plastic tube from the factory with eighty *dubbeltjes* (ten-cent coins), *kwartjes* (twenty-five cents), guilders, and *rijksdaalders* (two-and-a-half guilders). He beamed as he handed them out. Additionally, he bought a lottery ticket for everyone, including himself. He was the only winner: ten guilders. To celebrate that win, he organized another party for all the grandchildren. He was exuberant that afternoon, genuinely at ease, laughing and bantering with the older grandsons.

He died a year and a half later, in 1971. I was eleven. Better if you don't go to the funeral, my mother said. She wanted to spare me the family tensions, which were as palpable as ever.

Iwaniska and Łódź

We didn't know much about his life history. He spoke German and Russian, and—to our ears, at least—fluent Dutch. While scouring for details about his life, we came across a single cassette tape with his voice, made at his seventieth birthday party. Everyone is chattering at once, excitedly poring over old family photos. You can occasionally catch his voice, a deep, dark-brown timbre. But with the very first word you can hear the thick German accent, the open, broad vowels, the L at the front of his mouth.

No more than a few details of his life made it to our ears. The rest of the story we learned from the album Edwin had made for his father's birthday. Sandra was familiar with this album because it ended up in their house after Granddad's death. Hella had never seen it until Sandra made her a copy.

Isay came from a large Jewish family of twelve children and grew up in a part of Poland that then belonged to Russia. His passport states his date and place of birth as 13 May 1889 in Iwaniska, a village you'll struggle to find in an atlas. We imagined it as an impoverished hamlet with wooden shacks, a dirt road with pecking chickens and geese, and the occasional wobbly horse cart. How, then, did he become such a man of the world? And how did he manage to create the impression of never having spent a single night in his life in a hovel like that? He never let on. The one time Hella attempted an innocent "Gramps, where do you come from? Tell us something," he changed the subject and pretended not to have even heard the question.

During our college years we cousins reconnected and became instant friends. In 2010 we went to Poland to see if we could uncover anything about the family's history. All we had to go on was the name of that town—Iwaniska—and an address in Łódź that Edwin had mentioned in the album. In Warsaw we sought advice from the Jewish Genealogy and Family Heritage Centre, whose archives include pre-war phone books. One of these, from Łódź in 1937, lists the name of one of Isay's sisters, Genia Rottenberg, with the very same address from Edwin's album: Ulica Narutowicza 47.

An hour-and-a-half train ride and a half-hour street search later, we're standing in front of the house in Łódź. To our astonishment, it is a stately five-storey apartment block, with balconies and tall windows decorated with light-green fin-de-siècle motifs, a double-door main entrance, and a port through which a coach or car could pass. What a worldly and well-to-do impression this house made! A house for the comfortable middle class.

A visit to the Łódź municipal archives is an eye-opener. Yes, our grandfather had been born in Iwaniska, but he lived in Łódź from a young age and attended school there. The civil registry—which, amazingly, had survived—provided indirect evidence: a death certificate, written in Russian, of one of Granddad's brothers, who had died at the age of twelve. He is referred to in the document as the son of "the Rottenbergs, permanent residents of the village of Iwaniska, Radom Governate." This is the civil registry's only mention of the family. The family had presumably already lived in Łódź for many years, but was still registered in Iwaniska, some two hundred kilometres away.

This probably had to do with the regulations of the day. In the Russian Empire, one needed permission to settle in a city, and this was not an easy procedure. If permission was not granted, usually one just moved anyway and arranged matters otherwise, that is, through family connections or by bribing the right official.

Around the turn of the century, Łódź was a boom town. In thirty years the population had trebled: as the European centre of the textile industry, it attracted labourers, capital, and trade. Our grandfather hadn't lived in a provincial village at all, but in a dynamic, industrialized city. The image of the dirt-poor country-bumpkin-turned-man of the world was in dire need of revision. And when, in the course of our research into the German factory, we perused Edwin's album once more, we saw that Isay was initiated into the cigar business at an early age: his father earned his living as a cigar dealer.

Edwin did manage to wrest loose one anecdote about his father's youth, either from Isay himself or a family member. At that time, Russia had set quotas for the number of Jews allowed to attend high school and university: a maximum of 10 percent of the student body. But as some 30 percent of Łódź's population was Jewish, some of these youngsters did not make the cut. So the Jewish parents who could afford it would pay the tuition for ten non-Jewish students, both securing a place for their child *and* raising the total number of students enrolled. The larger the student body, the more Jewish children allowed in.

Tuition was expensive, so some of those non-Jewish students had to drop out after their first, subsidized, year. Szaja (the Polish spelling), as Isay was known to his friends and family, thought this was unfair. The thirteen-year-old collected money for his classmates through book sales, lotteries, bazaars, and theatrical productions. He liked to take part in these performances, with an eye to later becoming a stage director. Isay was rewarded for his initiative: as long as he attended the trade school, he went to school tuition-free.

In 1907 the czarist regime put an end to its "Russification" policy. From one day to the next, classes were no longer given in Russian, but in Polish. But there were no educational materials or qualified teachers. So at age eighteen, Isay decided to drop out of high school. He wisely did not wait around for inevitable military conscription because bloody pogroms could break out in Russia at any time and a Jewish soldier was never completely safe in peacetime, let alone during a conflict. The best way to avoid being drafted was to settle abroad.

Berlin

Isay moved to Berlin. All he needed was a train ticket, Edwin explains in the album—no passport or work permit was required. Via the Alliance Israélite Universelle he contacted the firm Treuherz & Fuss, import-export mercers who were looking for someone to carry out the firm's Russian correspondence. Soon Isay was handling the company's business in Russia, England, and France. In 1912, after a conflict with a colleague, he decided to set himself up as an independent agent. He secured a number of lucrative contracts, including as the representative for a button factory in Lüdenscheid (Westfalen) and a dealer in cigarette papers based in Paris. Additionally he worked as an interpreter for Russian buyers, for which he earned a pretty penny on commissions.

He must have felt quite pleased to be living in bustling Berlin. His business was thriving and there was plenty to do. Isay enjoyed cabaret and the theatre, including that of the famous director Max Reinhardt, who lived on the same street—the Kupfergraben, across from the Museum Insel in the city centre, where Isay rented a room.

Amsterdam

On 28 April 1910, Isay paid his first-ever visit to Amsterdam. Abraham Ptasznik, an uncle on his mother's side, had left Poland a decade earlier, intending to emigrate to America. But Abraham stayed in Amsterdam and, with one of his brothers, he founded the firm Ptasznik Frères, which specialized in the production of cigarette sleeves. Isay's cousin Jos showed him the city and introduced him to his sister Lena, two years his senior. They kept up a correspondence and were engaged the following year, although Isay remained in Berlin.

He and Jos became business partners, and in 1913 Isay became the agent in Germany for the Realgold Bobbins Company, which produced the elegant cigarette holders they called a "cardboard mouthpiece"—a paper tube with a gold-leaf mouthpiece into which the cigarette was inserted.

When World War I broke out in 1914, Isay's landlord warned him that the police had been by, looking to arrest him as a foreign national from an enemy country (Russia). Isay managed to secure proof of "upstanding moral character," and between this certificate and the general confusion typical of the outset of war, he managed to slip away to Sweden. Via Denmark and Scotland he travelled to London, where Scotland Yard, too, kept a close eye on him—he was, after all, a Russian national. Eventually he made it to Amsterdam, his fiancée Lena, and her family. He rented a room in Zandvoort (some thirty kilometres from Amsterdam) because as a foreigner, he was unable to obtain a residence permit within the defence boundaries of the west of the country. But for all intents and purposes, he lived with his family in Amsterdam.

In 1915 Isay was given permission to return to Germany, where in addition to resuming his business in cigarette holders he began dealing in cigars. Curiously, the fact that the country was at war was apparently not enough to hold him back. After a six-year engagement, Isay and Lena were married in Amsterdam on 17 April 1917. He remained in Berlin, however, until mid-1918, and was thus abroad at the birth of his eldest son, Alfred, exactly a year after the wedding. "Abroad" is the word Hella had been told in her youth— no one said it was *Germany*. Isay printed a photo of the baby on cigar bands in lieu of a birth announcement, but regretfully, none of these survived.

The paper business

Would our grandfather, we wonder, have actually preferred to stay in Berlin, but that Lena, being attached to her sisters and parents, vetoed it? Whatever discussions might have taken place, the bottom line is that Isay settled in Amsterdam.

He became part of a family of assimilated Polish-Jewish immigrants. The family name, Ptasznik, was quite a mouthful, but the Jewish and Yiddish given names had been Europeanized: Temerl, Isay's mother-in-law, assumed the chic name Teofile; Hinde, Isay's wife, called herself Helena (shortened to Lena); her brothers Kalman Jozef and Jacob became, respectively, Jos and Jim; her sisters Chane and Sala took the names Anna and Salomea. And out of gratitude for being granted asylum in the Netherlands, they named their youngest daughter, born in Amsterdam, after Queen Wilhelmina, shortened to Willy. Isay, known to everyone as Szaja, kept his first name.

Isay and Lena's family grew. After Alfred came Edwin (1920) and Tini (1923). The parents spoke Dutch with each other, which was logical, in a way. They had no other common language: the fickle language politics under the czarist regime had produced a Russian-speaking Isay and a Polish-speaking Lena.

Isay went into the paper business, opening the firm Papyrolin on the Looiersgracht, where Ptasznik Frères, his in-laws' firm, was also located.

Already having proved himself a successful businessman in Berlin, Isay's Amsterdam enterprise flourished as well. He was able to afford a large, five-storey house on the Valeriusplein in the well-to-do neighbourhood of Amsterdam-Zuid. Being a foreigner was not an issue in the

Netherlands, as long as one was self-supporting and not a nuisance to others. Naturalization was not obligatory and was seldom requested, but when Abraham, Jos, and Jim Ptasznik became Dutch citizens in 1927, Isay followed suit. Two years later, according to documentation in the National Archives, "Szaja Rotenberg*, merchant, born in Iwaniska" was granted Dutch nationality and the invaluable passport that went with it. A few years later it made him feel, in Tini's words, "invincible."

Isay was a generous man and, judging from the photos from those years, he spoiled his family with clothes, gifts, and outings in his fancy car. The boys were dressed in spiffy sailor suits, Tini in a frilly dress, and Lena in a chic ensemble or lavish dress and jewellery. Isay always had a project going. One of these was the subject of decades-long hilarity. He and the children built, in the attic of the Valeriusplein townhouse, a boat in which the family could go sailing. But of course the finished boat didn't fit through the attic door, so the boat ran aground before it ever reached the water.

We knew he lost a good deal of money in the stock market crash of 1929, and that it meant the end of the family's high life. How the 1930s treated Isay and his family, we had only a vague impression. The ingredients: Isay had been imprisoned in Nazi Germany but, after an unknown period of time, was then released; Lena suffered from depression; Alfred had to drop out of school in his last year in order to help support the family, and the Rottenbergs traded the grand Valeriusplein brownstone for a modest rented apartment on the Noorder Amstellaan, now called the Churchill-laan.

Vevey

When war broke out and the Germans occupied the Netherlands, Isay and his family were living on the Noorder Amstellaan; Lena's elderly parents, Abraham and Teofile Ptasznik, lived nearby, as did Lena's sisters and their families. Her two brothers had emigrated to America and the Dutch East Indies. The Ptaszniks were a close-knit family, coming together for

---

* In a letter to his son Alfred, Isay explained why his name was changed from Rotenberg to Rottenberg. Before Isay's naturalization, his name was registered as Rottenberg, with two t's. He used this spelling in the trade registers of Holland, Döbeln and Dresden, as well as in bank accounts. When he received Dutch citizenship, his name was officially spelled Rotenberg, with one t. This, Isay wrote, caused serious problems. Because of the spelling discrepancy, banks refused to disburse cash, certified mail was not delivered, and his signature risked being invalidated. Isay sent a request to the mayor of Amsterdam to officially change his name back to Rottenberg. Isay's wife, Lena, added her own comment in the letter: "Alfred, I like the name with one t much better. Your own mother."

dinner every Friday evening, and the grandchildren grew up together as best friends.

When the *razzias* began and young Jewish men started being rounded up, the family considered fleeing. Two Ptasznik cousins left first, paving the way for Alfred and Edwin. Isay arranged for his sons to be smuggled across the border. In the spring of 1942 they left home several weeks apart, both with the aim of eventually reaching England and joining the Allied forces. After them, two more male cousins escaped. Of Abraham and Teofile Ptasznik's six grandsons, four ended up fighting the Nazis from England, and one as a partisan against the Italian fascists.

Isay, Lena, and Tini fled the country in the summer of 1942. After a journey by truck, bicycle, train, and foot, which they survived by the skin of their teeth, they finally reached Switzerland. In one of her parents' photo albums Hella found a picture of the three of them with mountains in the background. The reverse, in Lena's handwriting, reads: "9 October 1942, for Alfred." It must have been intended as a message that they had reached safety, perhaps sent to the camp in the Pyrenees, where Alfred was waiting to cross the border into Spain.

Isay, Lena, and Tini remained in neutral Switzerland for the duration of the war. They found lodgings in Vevey, on Lake Geneva. As soon as the war was over, they packed their bags and boarded the train back to Amsterdam.

Back in Amsterdam

They resumed their lives as best they could. Not everyone made it back. Abraham and Teofile Ptasznik were deported and murdered in Sobibor. Two of Lena's three sisters were likewise murdered, along with their husbands and one daughter. Among Isay's extended family in Poland, there was hardly a single survivor.

Alfred, Edwin, and Tini married and had children—seven in total—whom their grandmother Lena, having died in 1956, did not really get to know. But grandfather Isay, on the other hand, was a part of their lives until his death in 1971.

Before embarking on our first trip to Döbeln, we asked our brothers and cousins how they would describe our grandfather. Menno said, "Granddad is my beacon." Felix called him "a Jewish-Russian Napoleon." Michael: "The pasha, the patriarch." Fedia answered with a question: "Ever wondered about what he wanted to be, deep down?" and answered it himself with,

"I do. Independent." Sacha backed that up with an anecdote: "Granddad once went with us on a ski vacation. He spent a week, we stayed longer. When the bus arrived to take him back home, the whole hotel turned out to wave him off. Guests, staff, everybody. As he got in, someone remarked, 'You look just like a king.' To which Granddad replied, 'More than a king.' He then fell silent, keeping us all in suspense, and added triumphantly, 'I am a free man.'" It is just the anecdote with which to begin this history.

2
DÖBELN JUNCTION

THE TRAIN JOURNEY FROM DRESDEN TO DÖBELN, BARELY FIFTY kilometres, takes an hour and a half. It is literally a "local" service, stopping everywhere and with a transfer halfway, as there is no direct connection. The route winds its way through a gently undulating landscape. Meadows with cows, fields of solar panels, creeks, steeples, red rooftops, whitewashed farmhouses, clusters of trees, orchards, dilapidated factories, and ancient half-timbered houses roll by.

Döbeln station is on the outskirts of the city. It is a proud fortress, built in 1870. Its two towers exude ambition. Now, however, there's not much life left in it. Tickets must be purchased from a machine, the service windows are closed, the waiting room and the restaurant are for rent. It is a mere shadow of what it must have been, for this station marked the beginning of Döbeln's heyday.

Before Döbeln was connected to the railway network, it was an artisan and cottage-industry town with a wood, grain, and wool market. Its population shrank when the region endured war and pillaging, when the plague crept through its environs, or when fires burned half the town to the ground; and it grew during prolonged periods of relative peace and prosperity. For hundreds of years, Döbeln was home to, at most, between one thousand and three thousand inhabitants. They traded, brewed beer, tanned leather, dyed wool, weaved linen, and made hats, boots, and furniture. Döbeln was not so remote that history passed it by, nor was it carried along on the tide of progress. Thanks to the Mulde River valley and the surrounding hills, the main roads gave Döbeln a wide berth.

With the construction of the railway, modern times came charging into the town. In 1852, the railway line connecting Berlin with Chemnitz was put into service, and sixteen years later came the Dresden-Leipzig rail link. Suddenly, Döbeln found itself at the centre of a railway web, at the junction between the north-south (Berlin-Chemnitz) and the east-west (Dresden-Leipzig) lines.

Manufacturers sensed potential and flocked from surrounding cities and towns to build factories there. What they were looking for was already at hand: a ready means of transport, plenty of room to build, trained artisans, and cheap labour. Capitalism took hold, factories operated at full steam, building and trade thrived. Soon it was necessary to import workers from further afield, and thus the population grew. By 1900, Döbeln had grown to some eighteen thousand inhabitants, two-and-a-half times as many as when the railway was introduced half a century earlier.

Promise beckons

Past the market and through narrow medieval streets, one reaches a large square dominated by the white-stuccoed city hall and its tower. This structure, too, is proof of the progress that Döbelners witnessed around 1900. The municipality had outgrown the old town hall. It had to either be enlarged or replaced with a larger one. It was razed in 1910, and just two years later the new city hall was inaugurated.

The building has two ports. The old one, dating from 1571, was incorporated into the side facade and symbolizes the centuries-old religious world view, with a chiselled god holding up a globe; the new port is the main entrance and is flanked by masculine images representing Reason and Resolve. Everything about this city hall radiates self-confidence and faith in the future: the building's proportions, the height of the tower, the ornaments on the port and in the facade, remembrance of an age-old past, pride in being the jewel of the city.

The city centre stands on an island in the Freiburger Mulde. From a distance, two landmarks stand out: the city hall tower and that of the Church of St. Nicholas, the church steeple just a few metres taller than that of worldly authority. The unruly river, which flows into Germany from the Czech Republic, regularly results in wet feet—or worse. High-water marks on a house on the riverbank show that during the last flood, in 2013, the water reached three metres. Thanks to the floods, Döbeln is in far better shape than neighbouring towns because funds are made available to renovate or repaint local homes. The occasional gust of wind burns the nose with the smell of brown coal, a reminder that Döbeln is situated in what was once East Germany.

Unlike Dresden, which was bombed to rubble by the Allies on the night of 13–14 February 1945, Döbeln escaped the war practically unscathed. Only one or two wayward bombs hit a house. At the capitulation in 1945, Soviet troops took over the city without a single shot being fired. From then on, Döbeln was known as a "golden city," one of the few German towns not half-ruined or riddled with vacant lots. The stately nineteenth-century school buildings and the imposing courthouse, the neoclassic theatre, the restaurants and cafés, the old water mills, the beautiful covered swimming pool—none of it has lost any of its charm.

A mountain of newspapers

We enter city hall. On the uppermost floor, under the collar beams, municipal archivist Ute Wiesner gives us a warm welcome in her office. Ute is about forty, with an open, playful look in her eye; she speaks with a faint Saxony accent and is keen to help us in any way she can. We have already been in touch via email, so she has already done a preliminary search for documents related to the Deutsche Zigarren-Werke, but to no avail. "The reading room is tiny," she says apologetically as she leads us across the hall to a cubbyhole, where she has laid out a large stack of bound newspapers from the 1930s. "I've got time tomorrow for you to fill me in on your grandfather," she says. "That might give us something more to go on."

We open the first heavy ledger to reams of Gothic letters in small typeface, and the hopelessness of our search sinks in. We are gazing into the maw of Nazi-era Döbeln. Page after page of swastikas, uniformed Nazis, and impassioned slogans about the German national awakening. How, in this mountain of "brown," are we to find anything about Granddad and his cigar factory?

We take a ledger of the *Döbelner Anzeiger* from the previous year and page bravely through it. And what do you know? On the date that Ute had put on her list, we spot a small item about the establishment and official registration of the Deutsche Zigarren-Werke. Two hours and hundreds of swastikas later, we're not a whole lot wiser, and we call it a day.

Our lodgings are in a villa up the hill to the north of the Mulde island. It is a four-storey Jugendstil house with a sunroom and terrace that look out over a yard as big as a park. The foyer is spacious and dark, with green-glazed wall tiles and a semicircular wooden bench at the bottom of the grand staircase. The house dates from 1911; its first inhabitant was a German metal magnate. It is still in the family. Did our grandfather live among the Döbeln industrialists? Would he have rented a house like this, or rooms in a swanky villa?

We call the grandson of the first owners, and he enthusiastically tells us about the status the local moguls enjoyed. "My grandparents were Döbeln royalty," he says. "The kind of money they spent is hardly imaginable today." His grandfather had the villa built for him and his four children, plus personnel. During the GDR years, the house remained the property of one of his daughters, but because she could not afford the upkeep, it was used as a daycare centre. After reunification, the grandson restored the villa to its former glory, and later repurposed it as a guest house. We go out for a look around the neighbourhood, strolling down lanes of similarly palatial villas enclosed by sumptuous gardens.

Eleven dossiers

The next morning we share what we know with Ute. This is more than we had written to her because just a few days before leaving for Döbeln, we discovered, in the National Archives in The Hague, the dossier concerning our grandfather's detention in Germany. "Were the minutes of the city council's meetings saved?" we ask. Surely the cigar factory was discussed either at council meetings or by the municipal authorities. The city likely offered the factory some sort of assistance, and surely had dealings with its predecessor, whose name we now know: Krenter Werke. It opened its doors in 1930 or 1931 and must have been the picture of modernity. For Döbeln, establishing a new manufacturing plant in the early thirties was a thing of great importance. It is unimaginable that the council would not have discussed it.

Ute takes notes and promises to have another look though her archive, this time using new keywords. An hour later she returns to the cubbyhole, where we, for lack of anything better, are still glumly paging through the *Döbelner Anzeiger*. "I may have found something," she says. "It's in the attic of another building. I'll let you know when I've got it." We are not exactly hopeful, afraid that it will be some sort of gag gift.

But when we enter Ute's office, we see a row of thick dossiers with yellowed cardboard covers lined up on her table. Ute is beaming. And rightly so, it appears, when we randomly open a dossier. "Look," we call out in turn, "this is Granddad's signature!" "Here, a letter to him from the mayor!" "A city council meeting!" "A letter from the Finance Ministry in Berlin!" "A newspaper article about the factory!"

There are eleven dossiers in total, starting in 1930 and running through 1938. Their title, in thick black letters, reads: "Die Bemühungen der Stadtverwaltung neue Industrien in Döbeln anzusiedeln betr. Krenter Werke," and from 1932 onward, "betr. Deutsche Zigarren-Werke A.G." Thousands and thousands of pages. Letters, reports, documents, photographs, handwritten notes, newspaper clippings. Each one of them about the Deutsche Zigarren-Werke and its predecessor, Krenter Werke. So it's true. Our grandfather actually walked around here in Döbeln. He was undoubtedly in this very city hall, where we now sit with Ute. He had a factory here. For years. And never uttered a single word about it.

He would never have imagined that we, eighty years hence, would unearth a trove of information about his business venture in Nazi Germany. He liked being in control. He was the family's stage director. But, well, now it's out of his hands. We're dying of curiosity, but at the same time we both feel a certain tacit uneasiness.

3

MERCHANT FROM AMSTERDAM

16 AUGUST 1932: ONE ISAY ROTTENBERG, MERCHANT FROM Amsterdam, presents himself to Döbeln's municipal authorities, expressing his interest in taking over and reviving the bankrupt cigar factory belonging to Salomon Krenter. That same day the mayor, Theodor Kunzemann, informs a meeting of his aldermen that there are several candidates interested in Krenter's business: a consortium from Berlin, a foreign cigar manufacturer who preferred to remain anonymous, and since today, Herr Rottenberg from Amsterdam.

Our grandfather was in Döbeln at the time: his four-page letter starts with the heading, "Amsterdam, presently Döbeln." For months, he writes, Krenter has been pressing him to take over the factory. He has considered the offer, and wants to accept it. He has already had contact with the American manufacturer of the state-of-the-art machines Salomon Krenter has leased and taken delivery of. In talks with the Ministry of Finance in Berlin and Dresden, he and Krenter have secured a government promise of leniency regarding back taxes. The ministry is keen "under all circumstances that the company stay afloat, and shall do everything necessary to get it up and running again." According to the deal that he, Rottenberg, has made, the city of Döbeln will not be held responsible for Krenter's back taxes. After supplying additional figures to verify he can arrange for a capital base, he closes by urging the committee to give him permission to operate the factory temporarily. He can provide a hundred people with jobs making cigarillos, which were out of stock and in high demand.

That same day, Salomon Krenter and Isay Rottenberg go to see Curt Reuther, director of the municipal bank and caretaker of the bankrupt business. They ask him to make the factory available immediately—that very day—and Krenter reproaches Reuther on various matters. Mayor Kunzemann hastily joins them, reprimands Krenter, and threatens to end the meeting then and there. Soothing words are spoken; Rottenberg, too, feels that Krenter has gone too far. They part with the agreement that Rottenberg first must present his motivations to the city council.

A week later, permission is granted.

While the factory restarts, the city managers look into the particulars of the Amsterdam merchant. The council had taken a risk with Krenter; it had backfired miserably and cost the city a considerable amount of money. Not only had they offered Krenter generous tax breaks, but they also underwrote the purchase of the factory buildings and grounds. Of course they were keen to restart the factory, but the new owner had to be of solid standing. They received a confidential letter from an unnamed source in Dresden with vaguely worded assurances: "A respectable man. His financial situation does not figure into our assessment."

Fait accompli

Rottenberg was in a hurry. A few machines were up and running, but otherwise nothing else had been arranged. He requested permission to rent the factory buildings from the city (now the owner following Krenter's bankruptcy) for three years with an option for an additional three years, provided he was given the same tax breaks as Krenter. The city council was hesitant, wanting first to determine who would be the most suitable candidate to take over Krenter Werke.

That search did not pan out, and the city council faced a fait accompli. A director of the American International Cigar Machinery Company wrote to Mayor Kunzemann that he had reached an agreement with Rottenberg regarding the lease of the Döbeln cigar machines. The contract was to be signed in Berlin two days later. If the city wanted to put forward another serious candidate, they had better be quick about it. He gave his contact address as Hotel Adlon, Berlin.

Negotiations with the bank, tax officials, and customs office proceeded satisfactorily, and by now, more than four hundred labourers were employed. But the agreement with the city was not yet finalized. Rottenberg pressed

Kunzemann and his deputy, Otto Röher, to move things along. "You are aware, as we made clear from the very start, that not only the planned expansion of the business but maintaining current production relies on immediate financing by the banking firm Gebr. Arnhold. The banking house has repeatedly pointed out to the honorable mayors that extending credit is out of the question as long as the contract with the city of Döbeln has not been signed." He does not hide his vexation, and ends with the threat that he will be forced to bring production to a halt, or close the factory, if the contract is delayed any further. "Everyone's patience has run out."

A few days later, on 25 October 1932, there is finally a rental contract. The cigar factory could step up production to full capacity.

So here we see, for the first time, our grandfather as an entrepreneur in action. He sidelines his competition and forces the city council to make a decision. He plays it like a game of chess: get an overview of the board, plan your strategy, and then move quickly to checkmate your opponent. He never lost a grip on the chance he had grasped in Döbeln.

But what in God's name brought him to Döbeln in the first place? We don't have a clue. There isn't a single letter or memo that sheds light on his motives. The foreign affairs dossier on his detention includes a few letters from our grandmother, but they contain no hint as to why he was there. Our grandfather corresponded regularly with family and friends, and would have had contacts in Germany as well. But not a shred of this personal correspondence has survived. It was presumably destroyed or lost in 1942 when he, Lena, and their daughter Tini fled the Netherlands.

When all we knew was that Isay Rottenberg was the owner of the Deutsche Zigarren-Werke in the city of Döbeln, an intriguing sentence popped up on google.books from a publication entitled *Unerledigte Geschäfte* (Unfinished business). Available via an antiquarian bookseller, it took four long weeks to arrive. The book is a 1998 study by the Swiss financial journalist Urs Thaler. A scandal had spurred Thaler to study the degree to which Swiss cigar manufacturers had profited from the Aryanization of Jewish-owned cigar factories in Germany. In an appendix Thaler lists 109 cigar-making firms that had been confiscated and "Aryanized" during the Nazi era. He devotes eleven lines to the Deutsche Zigarren-Werke, referring to our grandfather as a foreign Jew who saw business opportunities in the early days of the Nazis. Hella takes umbrage at this and writes to Thaler that Isay Rottenberg had taken over the factory in 1932 and could have had no idea that the Nazis would come to power six months later. But Thaler's comment still rankles.

On the eve of Nazism

In the summer of 1932—just when Isay Rottenberg decided to take his chances on kick-starting a bankrupt factory—Germany was in the throes of extremism and violence. Unemployment had skyrocketed, with six million workers relying on state welfare. Even those who did not live in Germany need only read the German newspapers to be struck by the combustibility of the political situation. The newspaper *Vossische Zeitung* wrote on 24 June 1932:

> Shots are being fired in the streets. Every day the wounded,
> victims of the agitators, are brought to hospitals, and there are
> deaths to mourn. It is as though the populace is in the grip of a
> blood rush, even though it has only been a few short years since
> the great carnage came to an end.

It was clear for all to see: the Weimar Republic was on its last legs, and the country was slipping into lawlessness.

It had briefly looked as though the violence would be reined in when in April 1932 the authorities banned the brown-shirted paramilitary Nazi militia, the Sturmabteilung (SA), and their black-clad Schutzstaffel (SS) cohorts. But the federal government collapsed a month later, and the new chancellor, the Catholic aristocrat Franz von Papen, needed the support of the Nazis in order to govern. In return for Adolf Hitler's backing, the ban on the SA and SS was lifted, and elections for the Reichstag were announced.

From mid-June onward, Germany endured an orgy of violence. The SA's ranks had swollen to four hundred thousand, more than four times the size of the German Army as stipulated in the Treaty of Versailles in 1919. People speculated openly on the possibility that Hitler's storm troopers would attempt a coup, or that the violence would drag the country into civil war.

The NSDAP claimed to be the only party that could keep the Communists in check and would put "Germany first." As the Nazis were not yet members of the government, they were free to strew about reckless and even contradictory assurances. They promised radical change and an end to the societal chaos and the impotent flailing of the federal government. In the space of a month, clashes between Nazis and their opponents claimed the lives of 99 people, with another 1,125 injured. This was the climate in which the Reichstag elections were held in the summer of 1932.

Might Saxony, where the cigar factory was situated, have been more stable than the rest of Germany, that our grandfather therefore dared take the plunge?

Germany's "brownest" state

Saxony—the most heavily populated, the most industrialized, and most urbanized state in the federation—was hit harder by the economic crisis than other regions. A good 60 percent of the workforce in "Germany's workplace" earned its income in the industrial sector. Because industry was largely geared toward export, the global Depression meant that as early as 1929, Saxony led the pack in German unemployment figures. In the years that followed, businesses nationwide were falling like ninepins, nowhere as quickly as in Saxony. In 1932 the state tallied a record number of unemployed: 725,000, equal to 40 percent of the labour force. While the situation elsewhere was dire as well, the average in Germany as a whole was considerably lower.

The fact that the Nazis were better organized in Saxony than in other German federal states was mainly thanks to one Martin Mutschmann, a textile manufacturer from Plauen, a lacework town south of Leipzig. His name often crops up later as a player in the tug-of-war surrounding the cigar factory. Mutschmann's anti-Semitism dated from before World War I, when he blamed Jewish immigrants from Eastern Europe for the demise of his business. He joined the Nazi Party in 1922 and established a personal bond with Hitler by visiting him in jail and offering him financial support. His loyalty was rewarded: in 1925 Hitler appointed Mutschmann NSDAP regional leader (*Gauleiter*) for Saxony. The following year, Mutschmann organized a rally in Plauen in honour of Hitler's birthday, one of the first instances of Führer glorification.

The Nazi base in Plauen assisted in setting up local NSDAP chapters throughout Saxony. Gauleiter Mutschmann, a fanatical anti-Semite, was keen to make short work of the Jewish riff-raff. In 1931 he said, "The day of reckoning will come, and the synagogues will go up in flames." The Nazis became wildly popular in Saxony, with so many new members that the state boasted being Germany's "brownest." With eight hundred chapters, by 1932 the NSDAP was represented in every Saxony city and town. The state's Nazi newspaper *Der Freiheitskampf* had a circulation of 107,000 and was Dresden's leading daily.

The Red Kingdom

One reason Nazism was so successful in Saxony is that modern anti-Semitism had taken root there early on. The first "international anti-Jewry congress" was held in Dresden in 1882, and the second in Chemnitz. In

Leipzig, the publisher Theodor Fritsch issued his *Handbuch der Judenfrage* in 1907, a sequel to his *Antisemiten-Katechismus* of 1887. Hitler claimed to have read it in his youth and was much taken with it. "I am convinced that this very book has contributed in an exceptional way to forming the basis for the National Socialist anti-Semitic movement." Later, the handbook became a practical guide for the struggle against the Jews, and in 1944 it had its forty-ninth printing.

Another reason is that right and left were diametrically opposed, without the buffer of a moderate political centre. This situation arose in the nineteenth century, when Saxony was known as the "Red Kingdom." It was the birthplace of the labour movement, with powerful unions and socialist parties whose members were drawn from the legions of machine workers and the textile industry. At the other end of the spectrum was the arch-conservative, antidemocratic business community. The existence of a moderating Catholic centrist party, such as in Bavaria, was absent in Saxony.

This mix of circumstances proved disastrous for political stability. Saxony had already seen a serious crisis back in 1923, when the Communists organized themselves into paramilitary "Proletarian Hundreds," and the extreme-right in turn dispatched goon squads to the streets. The Social Democrats had brought the Communists into the government in the hope that this would ease tensions, but the situation boiled over when a Communist minister announced a plan to arm the Proletarian Hundreds. The central government in Berlin sent troops to Dresden, removed the left-wing administration, and appointed a *Reichskommissar*.

The main beneficiaries of all this upheaval were the Nazis. They played on the antisocialist, anticapitalist, nationalistic, and anti-Semitic sentiments of dissatisfied shopkeepers, tradesmen, and centre-right citizens. With the slogan "Never Again Soviet Saxony" and the promise of a social and political shakeup, they unified the right-leaning electorate and raked in the desperate labourers to boot.

Reichstag elections held on 31 July 1932 gave the Nazis in Saxony a much larger share of the votes than the national average: more than 41 percent. The conservative-right parties suffered a crushing defeat. The parties on the left received more total votes than the Nazis, but the Sozialdemokratische Partei Deutschlands (SPD) and the Kommunistische Partei Deutschlands (KPD) had been at odds for so long that a robust coalition was out of the question.

So the chance that Saxony would be a favourable exception in an increasingly Nazi-run nation—this, Isay Rottenberg could not possibly have believed.

Goon squads

The NSDAP started to flex its muscles in Döbeln, which had become a commercial hub for the region at large. Twice a year there was a fair and a horse market that attracted many thousands of visitors. Döbeln's location made it a favourite venue for rallies of both the left and the right, says Helfrid Piper, author of the book *Ich überlebte Workuta*, in which he recalls his time in a Russian prison. The son of shopkeepers dealing in colonial wares, Piper was a youngster at the time. He describes witnessing an SA rally as a nine-year-old. His father forbade him to leave the house, but he and a friend managed to slip out unnoticed. At the *Hauptbahnhof* they saw extra trains pulling in and ranks of storm troopers parading to upbeat march music. One incident in particular made a lasting impression on him. "Girls in brown blouses were selling NSDAP newspapers. A passing cyclist, who took exception to the Nazi bumf, slapped the papers out of their hands. The next moment, an SA man leapt out of the ranks and punched the man in the face, knocking him off his bicycle."

Communists and socialists also gathered in Döbeln, which often led to brawls with Nazi thugs. Piper recalls driving back to Döbeln with his parents one election day, when a truck full of storm troopers overtook them. Further along, a group of men armed with spades blocked the truck, tipped it over, and started beating the storm troopers, seriously injuring about a dozen of them. "There were more and more frequent attacks on SA men," Piper writes, "but all this did was give more votes to the Nazis."

The run-up to the Reichstag elections of July 1932 was marked by constant scuffles and brawls between the Nazis and their political opponents. Massive rallies were held in Döbeln, with Nazi bigwigs from Berlin and Dresden in attendance. The mayor of Dresden, who had recently switched allegiance from the Social Democrats to the Nazis, held a speech for a thousand-strong crowd about his own experience of the Social Democrats' betrayal of the people and the labourers. Saxony's Gauleiter Martin Mutschmann also campaigned in Döbeln. Storm troopers from the entire region converged on the city, marching a thousand strong and physically assaulting passersby.

These elections resulted in the NSDAP capturing in Döbeln, as in the rest of Germany, the largest single-party share, with 5,364 votes. The combined left-leaning parties were still in the majority in Döbeln, with 4,911 for the Social Democrats and 2,330 for the Communists. A few scraps went, in a poor showing, to the conservative right.

Two weeks after the election, in which the National Socialists, the Nazis, became the largest party in the Reichstag, our grandfather arrived in Döbeln.

Pragmatic city officials

Nevertheless, Döbeln was neither ungovernable nor at the edge of the abyss when Isay Rottenberg bought Krenter Werke. Since 1927 the city had been managed by the competent team of Mayor Theodor Kunzemann and Deputy Mayor Otto Röher, both from the SPD. Kunzemann, an ex-union official, moved to a municipal function in 1925. Röher was a Döbeln career civil servant: he began as an apprentice minute-taker in 1902 and climbed the administrative ladder, running for office when the opportunity presented itself.

Both men were elected in 1927, partly thanks to the KPD. The collaboration was not an easy one, with the Communists willy-nilly accusing the Social Democrats of betraying socialist principles and in fact of becoming "Fascism's left wing."

Internal bickering within the KPD itself led to a schism within the party, leaving one to wonder who the KPD actually represented. The left's scant majority in Döbeln's city council was, for all intents and purposes, a chimera.

In order to reach any kind of consensus and avoid legislative gridlock, the Social Democrats had no choice but to co-operate with their ideological opposites on the right. The stark polarization in Saxony made this no easy task. But Kunzemann and Röher managed admirably, thanks to the fact that the four right-wing parties, too, were often at odds with one another. More essentially, writes historian Christian Kurzweg, who researched the industrial politics of Döbeln during the Depression, "the day-to-day agenda and the economic crisis from the end of the 1920s turned sworn antisocialists and left-wing social democrats into pragmatically minded realpolitikers."

In short, despite the political and economic crisis, the Döbeln city government functioned adequately and got things done. The effect was clear: the Nazis made less headway here than elsewhere. Until late 1932, the NSDAP had only one seat on the city council. The SPD could boast of creating jobs even during the severest periods of the Depression: in 1930, Kunzemann and Röher succeeded in attracting a brand-new, hypermodern, and promising cigar factory, Krenter Werke, to Döbeln. At its peak, operating on triple shifts, Krenter Werke employed some three thousand people. The economic situation in Döbeln was thus a far sight better than in the rest of the region.

At the end of 1931, Kurzweg calculates, there were just sixteen Döbelners per thousand on welfare, compared to twenty-one per thousand in nearby Meissen and twenty-nine per thousand in Dresden. But in the course of the following year, Döbeln too suffered from the Depression. Unemployment grew. Krenter Werke halted production in July 1932, and the number of unemployed jumped to more than 20 percent of the working-age population.

Alert, and yet…

The Nazi ascendance could not possibly have escaped our grandfather's notice when he petitioned the Döbeln city council in August 1932, but it did not scare him off. We got to know him, in the decades following the war, as an exceptionally alert man. For him, following the international news was one of life's necessities. Every day, before driving to the factory, he would listen to the eight o'clock morning news. He hurried home at lunchtime to catch the midday news, and again after work. Anyone in the room had to quiet down as soon as the bulletin's three opening beeps sounded. He had an old radio whose volume would taper off after a few news items, at which point he would get up and give the radio a slap, and the sound would bounce back again for another few news items. In addition to the liberal weekly *Vrij Nederland* he read the Amsterdam daily *Het Parool*; later, when he had a television, he never missed an eight o'clock news broadcast. He read Dutch and German literature and nonfiction, and was quick-witted and inquisitive: the opposite of naive, ignorant, or indifferent.

Was this thirst for news perhaps the result of what he had gone through in Nazi Germany? No—it was too much a part of his character. He must have followed politics closely back then as well. But then, why would someone with a family in Amsterdam—a wife and three school-aged children—buy a factory in Germany in the summer of 1932?

One name that crops up in connection with the takeover of the factory is the tobacco dealer Vincenz Silvan, a Polish Jew who had lived in Germany for many years. We believe that Silvan travelled to Amsterdam—then an important tobacco trading centre—to buy raw tobacco, which he then sold to Krenter. When Krenter ran into financial troubles, Silvan likely tipped off Isay Rottenberg.

Rottenberg already had a connection with the tobacco industry. The Ptaszniks, Isay's in-laws, imported cigarette machines and cigarette paper, and manufactured cigarette mouthpieces. Isay had seen his capital evaporate and his paper company run aground after the 1929 stock market crash. He had always been "in business," but at heart he was an entrepreneur and technician. Perhaps he had visions of running his own factory, of mechanized production, and of technical innovations he would help devise. The offer to take over a brand-new, state-of-the-art factory was just the challenge he had been waiting for. Opportunity knocks only once, and it happened to be in Germany.

Would Isay have consulted his wife Lena? Probably not. He was the bread-winner, the head of the household. Lena took care of the children and saw to the housekeeping. From what we have heard about her, Lena was an outstanding cook and she was prudent, kind, and hospitable. Isay loved and respected her, but decisions on work and investments were his and his alone. Our grandmother likely made her opinions known concerning his new adventure, and maybe even offered some resistance, but she could not prevent him from taking the plunge.

A brand-new factory

We study the Döbeln municipal archive's photos of Krenter Werke around the time it opened. There are seventeen in total, methodically documenting the entire production process. They show a workshop with dozens of women dressed in aprons and white bonnets, seated on high stools at the machines. There are four women per machine, each responsible for one part of the process. Men in overalls keep an eye on the operation floor.

The speed and precision must have been a wonder to behold. Nearly everything that was done by hand elsewhere was executed here mechan-ically: a machine precut strips of tobacco, the filler, after which these were bunched together, cut to size, and set aside. Packing and smoothing the binder leaves was still done by hand, but then the machine took over again, cutting the binder to size and positioning it on top of the filler, then rolling the binder around the filler. This was only a partially completed cigar. Next, a worker laid the expensive wrapper leaf onto a metal plate; the machine then cut the wrapper to size and wound it neatly around the filler. A cylin-der then evened out the cigar's form, and sent it to another roller, where it was wrapped in cellophane. The last photo shows the automated packaging machine, which boxed the product.

When we later visit the cigar factory De Olifant in Kempen, the Netherlands, to witness cigar production first-hand, we are struck by how modern Krenter Werke was. The production process at De Olifant in 2017 hardly differs from Krenter Werke in 1930 and its successor, the Deutsche Zigarren-Werke. Even the machines are practically identical.

No one at the municipal archive can tell us whether the buildings are still there. But a few days later we get word that the factory is abandoned, but probably still standing. We visit Stefan Conrad ("der Conny"), Sophie Spitzer, and Judith Schilling in the Treibhaus, Döbeln's youth centre, housed in a former hotel on the long Bahnhofstrasse. The three, all born in the late 1980s, are the driving force behind a local historical workgroup, which, under the motto "learning from the past, for the future," examines and exposes the city's Nazi past. They trace the fate of Jewish residents, research forced labour and the death marches, have created an app that leads visitors to places associated with the Nazi era, and organize guided tours.

Before we arrive, they have already contacted the current owner of the property on which the former Deutsche Zigarren-Werke stands. The owner is still a cigar manufacturer: the multinational Dannemann, whose headquarters are in Lübbecke, Westphalia. Dannemann sent photos of the building in 1989, at the time of the *Wende*, the fall of the Berlin Wall: a dozen or so Trabants parked in a courtyard; in the background, a wide, tall outer wall with large windows.

Conny tells us that his grandmother worked there for years after our grandfather lost the factory. She was employed during the war and thereafter, when it was a GDR state-run company. She is still alive and lives in Döbeln, but unfortunately won't receive us. Conny remembers hearing from his father that his grandmother smelled deliciously of tobacco when she came home from work.

Off we go, all five of us. The factory must be somewhere on an abandoned industrial estate on the east side of town. We don't have to look for long: across the railway tracks and up the street, the building from the photos appears off to our right. The industrial estate is fenced off, there are floodlamps to illuminate the building at night. All the windows are intact.

The property is easily accessible by cutting through the bushes off to one side. The factory is an enormous, white-stuccoed building, four or five storeys high and with two wings, perpendicular to each other. It takes a good ten minutes to walk all the way around it.

Kestrels—small falcons—swoop in and out of the chimneys and holes in the outer wall. On the side facade, a clock is stopped at 8:10. We peer through the filthy windows. In the semidarkness we can make out machines shoved alongside one another. We can hardly believe our eyes: they're identical to the ones pictured in the archive. There's an axle with spokes, the metal plate shaped like a bent square, and cigar-pressing cylinders. It is as though we've been transported back in time, like in a children's fairy tale.

All we need to do is say "abracadabra" and the machines will start whirring again, our grandfather will appear in his spotless white lab coat. He smiles when he sees us, taps his cheek, which we each obediently kiss, takes us by the hand, and says, "Come, *schatzies*, I'm going to show you how we make cigars."

4
KRENTER'S RISE AND FALL

WE ARE INTRODUCED TO DÖBELN'S *Heimatfreunde* (LITERALLY, homeland friends), a group of local history buffs, in archivist Ute Wiesner's pleasant attic room. It is their regular meeting place; Ute provides them with coffee and cake and is generous with her time. The oldest member is Horst Schlegel, born in 1928 and a lifelong Döbelner. He is a smallish man with glasses and a friendly face.

"That Prince Claus of yours," Schlegel gushes, right off the bat, "the Von dem Bussches, they lived here! On the Bahnhofstrasse!" Apparently there is a link between Döbeln and our Dutch royals, and the Heimatfreunde glow with pride. But as well-disposed as we are, we don't really get their drift, and only after some explanation do we catch on.

Georg Freiherr von dem Bussche-Haddenhausen was an officer in the infantry regiment stationed in Döbeln, and lived near the barracks, on Bahnhofstrasse 22. In 1902 this house was the birthplace of his daughter Gösta, the mother of Claus and grandmother of the current king of the Netherlands, Willem-Alexander. In 1908, having served in Döbeln for sixteen years, Georg was reassigned to Freiberg, forty kilometres away.

The Heimatfreunde are well-prepared for our visit; everyone has found something and starts taking papers out of their bag. Horst Schlegel lays an oblong album on the table. On the cover is an Native American smoking an oversized cigar. The Native American is stylized into a capital K:

Krenter's logo. "Unfortunately," says Horst, "the first page was damaged during a flood." He pages through the album, showing us colourful illustrations of Native Americans accompanied by detailed descriptions of their tribe, attire, headdress, and customs. The illustrations and thoroughly worded captions come from the Ethnological Museum in Berlin.

"I put together this album myself," Horst says. "I started collecting paste-on illustrations as a child, from when I was about four or five." Krenter's "Indian" album was his first. Later in the 1930s, he collected stickers from other tobacco brands, and he still has those albums as well. His collection includes an album from 1936, issued to commemorate Hitler's Olympic Games held in Berlin, with beautifully printed sports photos. And as Germany geared up for war, there were illustrations glorifying World War I and the Wehrmacht. "Ja . . .," he says bitterly. "That's how it was."

May we take pictures of the album, we ask. "No, no," he says as he hands us the book. "Take it, please! It's for you. What am I going to do with it, at my age?" Moved by his generosity, we accept the gift. The Krenter "Indian" album is now in Amsterdam.

Horst cannot recall having ever seen Krenter Werke in operation. The factory was on the edge of town, where a small boy would have no business going. His parents knew people who worked there, but that was hardly unusual: Döbeln, after all, was a "cigar town."

"Walk through Döbeln and you'll find a name on practically every street that had something to do with the cigar industry." He rattles off a list of family names: Sturms, Loose, Stockmann. "The Greek restaurant on the Mulde," Karl Enzmann interjects, "was a cigar factory once. Nobody knows that anymore."

The first cigar factory was established in 1846, just before the railway was built, says Jürgen Dettmer, the youngest Heimatfreund. The statistics he has dug up are impressive indeed: in 1871, eleven factories plus an unknown number of at-home workers produced some fifty million cigars per year. By 1894 Döbeln was home to thirty-two cigar factories. The decline set in around the beginning of World War I. In 1924 there were eighteen factories left, and in 1929 just ten, plus several hundred at-home workers. That was the moment Salomon Krenter came to shake things up in Döbeln and much further afield.

Salomon Krenter

The *Döbelner Anzeiger* ran the following scoop on 1 October 1930:

Yesterday, even before the official press viewing, this newspaper was allowed inside! In a large, hygienically organized workspace served by a special ventilation system that constantly circulates fresh air, nearly forty American cigar machines have already been installed, which are indeed wonders of technology. The perimeter of the factory is defined by enormous tobacco and supply depots. Approximately 1,000 people are already employed. As soon as the expected 70 additional machines are installed, the number of employees will increase to some 3,000. When fully operational, the Krenter Zigarren-Werke will be Europe's largest cigar factory. We cannot see into the future, but it is already clear that the plant is of immense significance to our city and region, as a great many labourers have been engaged and unemployment is declining.

Mayor Kunzemann had run himself ragged in enticing Krenter Werke to Döbeln, and at last, the city was to be the home of Germany's first fully machine-operated cigar factory.

It was only a year earlier that the city council had received a letter from the Bulgaria cigarette factory in Dresden, inquiring about the availability of female labourers in Döbeln. The information was intended for a firm in search of a suitable location for a new cigar factory. The letter was signed Salomon Krenter.

Some years later, the council recalled the lengths it had gone to in securing Krenter's venture. More than one hundred German cities had responded eagerly to Krenter's overtures—small wonder, considering that Krenter had promised to employ six hundred men and women at first, and would quickly expand to a workforce of two thousand.

Krenter had hinted that if Döbeln met his demands, it would be his first choice for the factory. His decision depended on suitable factory buildings, wages, tax breaks, and housing for his personnel.

Eager to meet Krenter's conditions, Mayor Kunzemann and Deputy Mayor Röher went to Berlin and Dresden to press for tax incentives for the new factory. Kunzemann, himself an ex-union man, personally visited the Tobacco Workers' Union to negotiate a lower hourly wage. The union was so pleased with the potential employment opportunities that it was prepared to compromise on wages. Kunzemann took meticulous notes, including of his telephone conversations. He devoted part of nearly every day, as his notes show, to securing favourable conditions for Krenter. Kunzemann left no stone unturned in his quest for premises, artisans, unskilled workers, and permits—all with the goal of attracting the factory to Döbeln.

Once, when Kunzemann and Röher went to Dresden for talks at the office of the new firm, the Americana-Havanna Zigarren Fabrik, they were not received by Krenter, but rather one Isidor Kronstein, who introduced himself as the firm's business representative and economic adviser. Kronstein tightened the screws even further, demanding exemption from local taxes and wages without overtime pay or other bonuses. After another round of negotiations, the council agreed to a three-year exemption from local taxes in return for a guarantee from Krenter to give hiring preference to Döbeln residents and to remain for at least five years.

The deal threatened to unravel yet again when Krenter reneged on the wage agreements made earlier and refused to pay the first year's rent for the factory up front. But eventually the firm announced that production could begin as soon as the machines arrived from America. "We are pleased to take this opportunity," wrote an enthusiastic Mayor Kunzemann, "to wish you all the best in launching your firm in our city, and that it will flourish, thrive, and prosper!"

So who was Salomon Krenter, founder of the Döbeln cigar factory?

Researching his personal history, we see similarities with our grandfather's. Salomon Krenter (b. 1896) was also born into a Jewish family in the Russian Empire, in his case in Novoselitsa, a trading town at the tripoint between Austria–Hungary, Romania, and Russia. His hometown is not far from Chernivtsi, now part of Ukraine. Jews accounted for two-thirds of Novoselitsa's population at the time, but alarmed by the pogroms in neighbouring regions in the early part of the new century, many of them fled, crossing into Austria to start a new life outside Russia. Salomon Krenter was one of them.

Not Berlin, but Vienna became his new home, where he initially made ends meet by working as an egg-packer. Krenter went into business, but unlike Isay Rottenberg, his reputation was soon tainted. An item in the *Wiener Zeitung* on 21 April 1921 reveals that the police sought Krenter for suspected customs fraud. He purchased duty-free tobacco in the free-trade harbour of Trieste and used it to produce cigars and cigarettes in Austria. Rather than exporting them—which would have been legal, as the duty would be paid in the country of sale—he sold them duty-free on the black market in Austria itself. Krenter evaded the police, fleeing to Bulgaria. In 1924 he moved to Dresden, and with the money he had earned in the tobacco trade in Bulgaria he bought an ailing cigarette factory, renaming it the Zigaretten Fabrik Bulgaria, or Bulgaria for short.

Daring advertising

Salomon Krenter had a feel for the zeitgeist, and applied a novel, American-style marketing strategy to the promotion of his Bulgarias. At that time, cigarette brands were hard to tell apart. Packs, regardless of the maker, were decorated with the same Oriental images of camels, pyramids, and belly dancers.

Krenter took an entirely different route. For the logo, he chose a Star of David formed from two interlocking triangles against a white background, with crisp blue, green and red elements, referring to the colours of the Bulgarian flag. That star—would people recognize it as a Jewish symbol? and would it put off buyers?—and the snazzy packaging made it an eye-catcher at the tobacconist's shop. The Jewish Museum in Berlin has in its collection several Bulgaria cigarette boxes and an enamel advertising sign. The museum refers us to an article by the cultural historian Volker Ilgen to explain the surprising packaging design. In it we read that in 1920s Germany, Krenter was not alone in using the Star of David in his logo. Many other Jewish firms did the same, without reservation.

Bulgaria cigarettes became popular with German smokers. Krenter imported high-quality tobacco from Bulgaria, and with his modern mixing machines he was able to produce a cigarette of reliable quality. Production was stepped up. Within a few years Bulgaria had outgrown the factory, and moved to larger, brand-new premises. Krenter himself moved to an imposing villa on Dresden's chic Wienerstrasse.

Another German manufacturer, Reemtsma, shook up the cigarette branch by buying up smaller companies and creating a quasi-monopoly. The remaining smaller firms were left to fight it out, and competition was fierce. Krenter gambled that showy advertising stunts would draw attention to the Bulgaria brand. For instance, he tried aerial advertising and projected lighted ads onto the facade of a futuristic metal pavilion at the Dresden Exposition.

But despite his daring advertising campaign, the company was simply no match for the cartel, and in 1928 Krenter sold Bulgaria to Reemtsma. The sale brought in four million marks, which Krenter intended to reinvest in a new enterprise. His idea was to apply the automatic cigarette manufacturing process to cigars. Cigars were still rolled by hand, a time-consuming and expensive process. Krenter set out to revolutionize the cigar branch, and did not go for half measures.

The official opening of the Krenter Zigarren-Werke—the names "Americana-Havana" and "Deutsch-Amerikanische" had by now been jettisoned—was announced for 1 November 1930. It was to be a spectacle, with regional VIPs in attendance and, as icing on the cake, the landing of the famous airship *Graf Zeppelin*.

The event was a washout. Two days prior, Kunzemann told Krenter the festivities had to be cancelled, as Chancellor Heinrich Brüning would be visiting Dresden that same day and all of Krenter's high-placed invitees would be attending the chancellor's function instead. The landing of the *Graf Zeppelin* had already been scuttled due to inclement weather. But it was seen only as rotten luck, not as a bad omen.

"The Indians are coming"

Krenter spared no expense when promoting his cigars, planning a bold media campaign to introduce his brand, the "Indianer," to Dresden smokers. The public's attention was to be whetted with advertisements in daily newspapers and cinemas; Dresden was plastered with posters sporting the Krenter logo and the slogan "The Indians are coming." A few days later, delivery trucks emblazoned with the text "The Indians have arrived!" drove through the streets. Department stores set up small exhibitions about Native Americans, and tobacconists hung Native American outfits in their shop window. Men dressed in Native American costume hit the shopping streets, handing out cigars wrapped in colourful foil. There was even an "Indian" ditty:

> Wir rauchen nur „Indianer", die der Krenter fabriziert.
> Bill'ge Marken liefern kann er, weil er selber importiert.
> Ob „Sioux" oder „Texas", alle Sorten sind „eins – a"
> Fur die Verwöhntesten etwas. Freuet Euch: Die Indianer sind da!*

The modernity of Krenter's approach was borne out by the effectiveness of its subconscious influence. Fritz Feller's book *Psychodynamik der Reklame* (1932) praises the "Indianer" campaign as an example of Freudian strategy. The logo's image of a cigar-smoking Native American, says the author, evokes nostalgia for a man's carefree childhood, when he used to play Cowboys and Indians. And, of course, we can see the cigar as a phallic symbol. "Zigarre = Phallus," Feller writes. Even the colours on the boxes are given Freudian approval. To sublimate the guilty feelings about the unhealthiness of smoking, the author suggests that Krenter include something extra

---

* "We only smoke Indians, produced by Krenter / He delivers fancy brands, he imports them himself. / Whether 'Sioux' or 'Texas,' these are first-class cigars / for the most discerning smokers. Enjoy: the Indians are here!"

for the smoker's children. Did Krenter heed Feller's advice? We don't know, but he did introduce the collectible paste-in picture album, which now, eighty years later, Horst Schlegel has bequeathed us.

While Krenter's marketing strategy might have excited the consumer and the Döbeln city council, it did not exactly win him friends within the industry. His refusal to play by the rules angered his competitors. Krenter's aim was to manufacture and distribute cigars as he had done with his Bulgaria cigarettes. In other words, to mass-produce standardized-quality cigars at a fixed price, and to make them widely available for purchase. In doing so, he became a threat not only to the hand rollers and smaller manufacturers, but also to the tens of thousands of corner tobacconists. It was, after all, their job to offer personal advice to the client wanting a hand-rolled cigar: the tobacconist knows his customer's taste, follows the trends, and keeps a close eye on the quality of individual suppliers. Compare the introduction of the mass-produced cigar with the rise of off-the-rack clothing, and the effect of Krenter's bombshell becomes clear.

Add to the equation that the smaller shop owners had pinned their hopes on the Nazis, and rushed to join organizations allied with the NSDAP. Krenter, in their eyes, was the prototype brash, capitalist Jew out to snatch food from the mouths of honest, traditional, modest, hard-working Christian Germans. *Der Freiheitskampf*, the Nazi newspaper in Saxony, called for an immediate boycott of Krenter's cigars and of the shops that stocked them.

Every machine operator employed by the "Eastern Jew Krenter," *Der Freiheitskampf* claims, will cost three manual workers their jobs. "The Indian cigars are manufactured using American machines, by a Jew who immigrated from the East after the war. Anyone wanting to rob German workers of their livelihood should buy these cigars!"

In another issue of *Der Freiheitskampf* is a photo of a tobacconist's shop window in Dresden, decked out as an anti-Krenter protest. "Deutsche Handarbeit bringt Brot, Amerikanische Maschinarbeit mehr Not,"* reads the slogan spanning the entire breadth of the shop window. Below that is a drawing of a fur-hunter shooting his rifle at Native Americans. On 9 December 1930 *Der Freiheitskampf* devotes three full pages to the anti-Krenter campaign, with the headline "Fight the Indian Jew!"

Nor were the Marxists at all enamoured with Krenter. Although they cared not whether someone was "a Jew or a Christian, a capitalist is a

---

* "German handwork brings home the bacon; American machines mean Germans forsaken."

capitalist," they could not help remarking that after all, "the Jews are a lot more wily than Hitler's bunch."

Döbeln first

In Döbeln, too, trouble was brewing. Smaller cigar manufacturers and other businessmen felt it was unfair that this foreigner with his American machines was getting preferential treatment from city leaders. The established cigar makers threatened that if they got edged out by the newcomer, they would leave. Erhardt Tümmler, the powerful owner of a Döbeln metalworking plant, member of both the city council and the board of directors of the Reichsverband der Deutschen Industrie (Reich Association of German Industry, brought his indignation to the Verband Sächsischer Industrieller (Association of Saxony Industrialists). According to the minutes of the meeting, "Director Wittke urges the union to intervene posthaste, because the Krenter case is simply outrageous." The entrepreneurs argued that inaction would be a slippery slope. Government subsidies should be resisted, especially if the stimulus money "benefits foreign firms who use such privileges to decimate German industry."

The result was an angry letter to the city of Döbeln. It was the city's responsibility to support existing businesses, and not just any newcomer. The association of industrialists, in fact, was in principle opposed to government subsidies, as these disrupt the free market. The city would be better off creating favourable conditions by lowering corporate taxes, offering discounts on energy rates, and—as with Krenter's employees—providing living quarters for workers brought in from elsewhere. It was folly for the city to base its policies, they argue, on attracting new factories during this profound economic crisis. Krenter's plant is a fluke. Conclusion: Döbeln first!

Of those local business concerns, Tümmler's was the largest. His riverbank factory—an enormous complex with three tall chimneys, its likeness immortalized on postcards and stationery—was, until Krenter arrived, the city's largest, with thirteen hundred employees. It was one of the first modern factories to be built in Döbeln. Erhardt's father, the Leipziger Robert Tümmler, built the plant in 1878. In its wake, dozens of metalworking factories, large and small, came to Döbeln and helped the town flourish.

Of course, the city suffered during World War I and the postwar economic crisis, but judging from the number of businesses and employed labourers in 1925, Döbeln appeared to have recovered admirably. Industry and trade provided jobs to some six thousand workers. In addition to metalworking, there was a large factory that produced agricultural machinery, there were chemical factories, a chocolate factory, a sugar mill, and a plant that made industrial filters. The city also produced furniture, fire hoses, silver cutlery, and, of course, cigars. Many of these goods were either luxury items or export products, so the 1929 crash severely impacted these businesses, many of which went bankrupt or only barely survived. It was therefore not surprising that local industry was put out by the favours the city bestowed on Krenter.

Mayor Kunzemann ignored the industry association's letter, waiting several months to reply. Only in the spring of 1931, once Krenter's factory was operating at full steam with some two thousand personnel, did he respond with a brief note to Tümmler and his fellow petitioners: "Like you, we are opposed to subsidies of any kind to the private sector, whether from national, state or local government. However, this principle cannot, in this exceptional time of unheard-of economic malaise, always be observed."

Krenter's factory drove a wedge into local politics. His preferential treatment brought about a rupture between the SPD and the conservative-right members of the city council, who sided with the local businesses and pulled further to the right. Kunzemann did his best to quash the anti-Krenter propaganda. At his insistence, the government in Dresden forced the Nazis in the Saxony parliament to stop harrassing Krenter. But *Der Freiheitskampf* did not let up, spreading rumours that the cigar factory employed only fifty labourers. Krenter gave as good as he got: he demanded that the Döbeln employment office provide an official report that he had already hired 1,132 unemployed workers, and took out an advertisement for it; other newspapers reported that his "Indianer" cigars were selling like hotcakes; he solicited political support in resisting the Nazis. The SPD parliamentarian Paul Hertz raised the issue in the Reichstag in Berlin. Hertz had visited Krenter's factory the previous day and presented him as a man who invested his money in Germany, despite being a "Romanian Jew." It was, Hertz asserted, a positive exception amid all those German entrepreneurs who were safely investing their money abroad.

Temporary setback

Production grew steadily and the factory soon outgrew its premises. Franz Richter, a manufacturer of farm machinery, had unused factory space, but was unwilling to rent it out. Afraid of losing Krenter, Kunzemann tried everything he could to cajole Richter. Enticements to Krenter were streaming in "from all corners of the German fatherland," according to a city council report two years later. "We felt it was our duty to keep Krenter for Döbeln, and thus also for Saxony. Our mediation resulted in a sales contract between Krenter and Franz Richter."

Krenter purchased, for 360,000 marks, two large buildings and the accompanying land. But he did not pay up front. His business was growing and he couldn't afford to siphon money from it, he said. So the city council, hungry for employment opportunities and trusting Krenter's business acumen, negotiated a loan and even offered itself as guarantor for the entire sum. After much hesitation, the Leipzig district government authorized the deal, but was not—rightly so, in the end—at all enthusiastic about it: if a company has to ask for such a deal, it is not a sign of fiscal wellness. Döbeln, in Leipzig's view, was taking a big risk.

Why they did so is easy to explain. In the above-mentioned report, the city authorities note that Krenter's company grew by such leaps and bounds that by the summer of 1931 he was employing some three thousand workers, spread over three shifts. "The Krenter factory provided a crucial economic boost to the city. It paid out 60,000 marks per week in wages, which flowed almost immediately back into the local economy." The Döbeln council voted thirty to one in favour of underwriting the loan, with the factory land and Salomon Krenter's luxury villa in Dresden as collateral.

A week after purchasing Richter's large premises—these were the buildings we found more or less intact at the industrial park in East Döbeln—Krenter requested a partial production halt and the layoff of six hundred labourers and fifteen other personnel. It was a temporary measure, he assured the authorities, that would be reversed once the new machines had arrived from America.

In the Bundesarchiv in Berlin-Lichterfelde is a report in which Krenter describes what went wrong, and how he attempted to turn the tide. He may have been a marketing genius, but in launching the machine-made cigar, he overlooked one thing: the taste of the German smoker. The German likes a dry cigar. He is not used to the moist cigar that the American machines produce. Well, then, we'll dry them, Krenter must have thought, and installed drying rooms. The pitiful result was a withered cigar, unsuitable for sale.

Krenter called in the assistance of the International Cigar Machinery Company, and American engineers wasted no time in sailing to Germany. They advised Krenter to switch to a different model machine. This being a huge investment, they offered to buy shares in the business, eyeing Döbeln as a springboard for the rest of Europe. If they succeeded in cornering the German market, then the rest of the continent would be theirs.

Krenter's in-laws objected to the American investment, wanting to keep the business in the family, and took control of 60 percent of the shares. With this capital, Krenter ordered another 150 new machines. But they did not arrive in the promised ten weeks, but only five months later. Hundreds of workers needed to be trained to operate the new machines, and sales slumped. A newspaper reported that the "Indianer" cigars "have lost their draw." The cigar revolution had stalled.

Now in dire financial straits, in 1931 Krenter requested deferral of payment. A temporary setback, he insisted. He was still confident of his project, and even made plans to purchase yet more machines.

The city of Döbeln, however, was worried. Mayor Kunzemann went to Berlin at the end of November to beg the Ministry of Finance for assistance. If Krenter sinks, he argued, Döbeln will be dragged down along with him. And then those who believed in the enterprise and took risks on behalf of the city will be called to account. Kunzemann and his deputy Röher, bracing for the worst, took a drastic measure. In December, with salvage operations in full swing, the SPD mayoral duo called snap elections, a year before the end of their current term. The move had to be ratified by the city council. There was opposition from the right-wing parties and the Communists alike.

But when it came to a vote, the measure passed by seventeen votes to sixteen, thanks to a defector from the right—a council member, in fact, who was also employed by Krenter. The conservative bloc was furious. They stormed out of the meeting and boycotted the rest of the sitting. The *Döbelner Anzeiger* was outraged that the Social Democrats pushed through early elections. But by Christmas, Kunzemann was re-elected for another six-year term, until 1939. Röher requested, and was given, a double mandate, meaning that if all went well he could stay until 1945.

Early in 1932, Krenter Werke's situation worsened, but the owner did not give up. He feverishly made new calculations and envisioned a breakthrough via a new distribution network and a deal with Dutch buyers. The municipal authorities, still determined to keep Krenter Werke afloat, went in search of funds to buy into the Krenter distribution company. But by now the SPD was Krenter's lone supporter on the city council. Krenter sent one plea after another to his creditors, but in vain. By August there was no saving the sinking ship. With his expensive American-style advertising campaigns and hasty expansion, Krenter had been overambitious. He made the mistake of introducing a moist rather than a dry cigar. Corner tobacconists refused to sell his "Indianer" and Krenter's other quality cigars. And, the city council reported in retrospect, "the factory's management, in our opinion, was nonchalant and not very frugal." The Krenter

Zigarren-Werke, which had burst with such bravura onto the German market, shut down after less than two years.

Bankruptcy

Halfway through August, creditors opened bankruptcy proceedings. But there was no verdict because the courts would not act on the case as long as there was no sign the lawsuit's costs would be paid and Krenter ignored summonses. Döbeln put the enterprise into receivership and seized the factory, the grounds, and Krenter's villa in Dresden, hoping that by auctioning the properties they could recoup their loss of 360,000 marks, plus interest. It could not have come at a worse moment. Germany's unemployment had risen to six million, there seemed no end to the crisis in sight, and there was no interest in any of the properties up for auction. The villa had been stripped of all its valuables, right down to the gold-plated faucets. Krenter had moved to Berlin, and would leave Germany a few months later. Was this because of Hitler's rise to power, or to flee his business fiasco? In any case, he gave both the Nazis and his creditors the slip.

In Dresden we meet the historian Christian Kurzweg. He has come specially from Berlin to talk to us. His doctoral thesis on the political and economic dynamics of the Krenter Zigarren-Werke dates from 1995, but the subject still excites him and he is eager for new sources. "Krenter wasn't a bad entrepreneur," he says. Krenter himself was partly to blame, but circumstances also played a role in the debacle. And there was the relentless boycott from the cigar retailers. He knows the anti-Krenter slogan by heart: "German handwork brings home the bacon; American machines mean Germans forsaken." "Krenter was ahead of his time. He was a pioneer. He failed, but the modernization he introduced was unstoppable."

Isay Rottenberg learned his lesson. "Cigars, as far as the Germans are concerned, were hand-made," says Kurzweg. So Rottenberg called his product "cigarillos," which helped somewhat, but not enough, because the retailers continued their boycott of the "American cigars" from Döbeln.

When we tell him about how our grandfather ran the drinking-straw factory in Amsterdam—walking around the factory floor in his suit and spotless white lab coat, mixing the colours himself, forever conferring with the head technicians, applying his technical know-how, focused on innovations in manufacturing—Kurzweg exclaims, "But that's just it! It's precisely the way a business is run here. Hands-on. Not like Krenter, who was much more a modern manager and an advertising man, distancing himself from the work floor."

A patriarchal, caring attitude toward labourers, technical personnel, and office staff "entrusted to him"—that, says Kurzweg, is typically Saxonic. Rottenberg's working methods were more accepted and appreciated inside and outside the factory than Krenter's. "It must have helped him."

5

THE **NAZIS** IN **POWER**

ISAY ROTTENBERG REGISTERED HIS NEWLY PURCHASED COMPANY
at the Chamber of Commerce on 4 October 1932. He chose the name
Deutsche Zigarren-Werke, borrowed from the name Salomon Krenter
had originally intended: the Amerikanische Deutsche Zigarren-Werke.
Mindful of the German nationalistic spirit, Rottenberg dropped the
"Amerikanische," but even then, the name raised some hackles. Before
year's end, the regional Chamber of Commerce in Chemnitz had brought
a lawsuit against Rottenberg over the name.

On 6 November there were again new elections for the Reichstag, and
local voting a week later. The Nazis pulled out all the stops, including in
Döbeln, holding a stream of propaganda-laden campaign rallies in which
they presented Hitler as the savior, and the Jews the bane, of the nation.
Julius Streicher, who saw to it that the slogan "The Jews are our misfor-
tune" appeared on the front page of every issue of *Der Stürmer*, travelled
to Döbeln to rail against the Jews. City council elections were held on
13 November. The SPD, the Social Democrats, remained the largest party,
with twelve seats. But the NSDAP became the second largest, with eight
seats, up from just one in the previous council.

The Nazis, meanwhile, attempted to take control of the Chamber of
Commerce in Chemnitz, under which Döbeln falls. They did not succeed,
but the industrialists were nonetheless taken by surprise, and realized that

49

to hold onto power, the Chamber and its leaders must adopt a Nazi-style nationalistic approach. A lawsuit contesting the naming of the Deutsche Zigarren-Werke was as good a vehicle as any.

The Chamber presented a long list of objections. The term *Deutsche* was misleading because it suggested a firm that serves the entire German Empire. "Moreover," argued the Chamber, "we have been informed that the director of said enterprise, Mr. Isay Rottenberg, a Russian national, lives alternately in Germany and Holland. The production of his cigars is carried out nearly exclusively with American-made machines. Taking all these facts into account, one cannot possibly call the factory 'German.'" They likewise objected to the term *Werke*. Only "a large-scale industrial enterprise with many employees and machines, and considerable mechanical, transport and other facilities" could legitimately be called a "Werke." Furthermore, a Werke had to have more than one factory building, at separate locations, to be able to use the term. The Chamber of Commerce could not fathom how the name Deutsche Zigarren-Werke could be registered as such and demanded the name be changed.

Was Isay Rottenberg surprised by the swift resistance to him—a foreigner and a Jew—and his factory, the most state-of-the-art in all of Germany, with its fully-automatic, American-made cigar machines? Or did he think, overconfidently, that Krenter just took the wrong approach and thought to himself: leave this one to me?

On 10 January 1933, at the new city council's first sitting, the eight Nazi members showed up wearing their brown *Sturmabteilung* uniforms. Mayor Kunzemann addressed the new council in sombre terms. "The past year has seen the economic crisis deepen at all levels of society. Once again, the self-reliant among us are being swept along in the maelstrom. For many of our citizens, a modest income today can turn into welfare tomorrow." A year earlier he had spoken of a "foreboding" time but also of his trust in a speedy recovery. Now, alas, he had to conclude that this was false hope.

Poverty among unemployed artisans and manual labourers was especially severe. The city did what it could to ameliorate their situation, but had little means at its disposal. Now, said Kunzemann, assistance for those in need must come from voluntary donations. This "winter relief"—the infamous safety net during the German occupation of the Netherlands, but which apparently already existed in pre-Hitler Germany—would be less generous than the previous year, so Kunzemann called on the business community to contribute. Döbeln is fortunate, Kunzemann reminded the council, in that its city authorities and civil servants applied themselves without falling prey to partisan friction. Elsewhere in Saxony this was not the case. But the Döbeln civil servants did not have it at all easy: it must "be bitter for them to be falsely criticized and at times physically threatened" by citizens who, "in these unsettling times, lose sight of goals and boundaries."

Kunzemann tried to boost his and the council's morale with terms like "self-preservation" and "resolve," and quoted respected economists with talk of the crisis having reached its nadir. The national government's employment stimulus program might hopefully bear fruit. "Work must be created because work is the redemption that will liberate us from this malaise." He concluded his lengthy speech with the hope that the actions of the city council in the year to come will be governed by "a sense of justice and social good." His wish was in vain. It would be the last time Kunzemann addressed the city council.

On Monday, 30 January 1933, the day President Hindenburg named Adolf Hitler chancellor of Germany, Kunzemann and Röher were also officially confirmed for their new terms as mayor and deputy mayor: Kunzemann for six years, Röher for twelve.

The next evening, Döbeln SA members met at their headquarters on Bahnhofstrasse 8. Joined by members of the SS and the veterans' organization Stahlhelm,* they all marched, carrying torches, to the very city hall where we now sit thumbing through the archives on the topmost floor. Looking out the window, we see the square, the Obermarkt, where the march ended and where long-time Nazi Hermann Groine euphorically addressed the mass of brown- and black-shirts about the power now in Hitler's hands.

This Groine, with whom our grandfather would have many more encounters, was thirty-five at the time, and had a long history of violence and fanaticism. He was barely eighteen when he was drafted to fight in World War I. He served for three years, first on the Russian Front and then on the Western Front. Like so many other soldiers, he refused to acknowledge the German defeat and the collapse of the empire, regarding it as a "stab in the back" by the Social Democrats. He joined the Deutsche Schutz- und Trutzbund (the German Nationalist Protection and Defiance Federation), an organization that had become popular in the 1920s and quickly amassed some two hundred thousand members. The federation's

---

* The term *Stahlhelm* refers to the distinctive German steel helmet design used since World War I. Here, *Stahlhelm* refers not to the object but to the name of the Bund der Frontsoldaten, a paramilitary organization during the Weimar republic made up of former World War I front-line soldiers.

manifesto was simple: get rid of the Jews and abolish the Weimar Republic. Notable members included the fanatic Nazis Julius Streicher and Reinhard Heydrich, and it was here that their ideas took root.

In 1923 Groine joined the NSDAP, then in its third year. He slowly climbed the party ladder, working as an electrical engineer until being given a full-time position as Döbeln district leader in 1931. The portrait printed in the *Döbelner Anzeiger* is of an earnest-looking man, someone deeply conscious of the profound responsibility placed on his shoulders. His hairline is receding, with a razor-sharp part running over his scalp.

Helfrid Piper, the shopkeeper's boy, was nearly twelve years old at the beginning of 1933. He still vividly remembers the torchlit march and the mass of Nazis thronging the square in front of city hall. He was surprised by those who suddenly turned out to be a party member. "Many of our teachers came to school in an SA uniform."

Whether Isay Rottenberg was in Döbeln then, we cannot say. Nor do we know if he saw Hitler's regime coming and was shocked by it, or was simply occupied with his own worries. What we do know, however, is that the family back in Amsterdam was following the situation closely. Sandra's father Edwin recorded a video of his recollections of the war and the years preceding it as part of a worldwide Holocaust testimonial project initiated by Steven Spielberg. Edwin says, "I remember reading the news items from January and February 1933 in the *Algemeen Handelsblad* from beginning to end. The family was gathered around the table and I read out all the articles. The *Algemeen Handelsblad* had good journalists. Their stories were very thorough, right down to the last detail. I can still see the font."

Was there any discussion of whether Isay Rottenberg should remain in Germany under these circumstances? His son Edwin doesn't say. If it had been discussed, then he, as a boy of twelve, was probably excluded. Children were not supposed to hear about this sort of thing.

The Reichstag fire

Once Hitler became chancellor, he set out to tighten his grip on power while keeping up the pretense of legality. His first goal was to command a sufficient majority in the German parliament—with the support of the Deutschnationale Volkspartei, if necessary—to amend the constitution in his favour. But he did not have a majority in his current cabinet, and he immediately abandoned talks with the Catholic Deutsche Zentrumspartei, forcing yet new elections for the Reichstag. These were set for 5 March 1933.

Despite their provocations, intimidation, and violence, the Nazis were not guaranteed a victory. But then, less than a week before the election, the Reichstag in Berlin went up in flames. Arson—but who was behind it? The Nazis were quick to blame the Communists, accusing them of plotting a coup. The fire was to be their signal for a revolt. The next day, President Hindenburg issued emergency measures, curtailing civil rights. Freedom of the press and assembly were suspended; postal privacy and the sanctity of one's home and property were rescinded. Communists and other opponents of the Nazis throughout Germany were arrested.

In Döbeln as well.

On 3 March, fourteen members of the KPD, the Communist Party, were arrested and charged with "illegal assembly." On 22 March, another twelve Communists were detained, and a week later the police arrested four more KPD members whom they accused of making cyanide poison to be used against Nazis. "The Döbeln Communists' plans went so far as to have party-approved confidants who would cunningly administer the 'sugar' to the selected victims," the *Döbelner Anzeiger* reported. To nip all such nefarious activities in the bud, Döbelners were urged to immediately report any suspicious behaviour to the police, confidentiality guaranteed.

Later that year, during the trial of the chief defendant in the Reichstag fire, Marinus van der Lubbe, the Döbeln Communists were portrayed as his accomplices.

The day before the elections—4 March—the Nazis again held a torchlit march and blared a speech from Hitler through loudspeakers on the Obermarkt, at the doors of city hall. Despite the election merry-go-round that had been going for more than a year without even once delivering a functioning government, the Döbeln voters were raring to go, with a turnout of 95 percent. The conservative right suffered a devastating defeat. And, for the first time, the Nazis outpolled the Social Democrats, with 6,456 votes to 5,171. Undeterred by the spate of arrests nationwide following the Reichstag fire, 2,381 Döbelners still voted for the Communists, as many as in July 1932. Döbeln's city council makeup—whether it would tip right or left—hung by a thread. Once the votes were tallied, the *Döbelner Anzeiger* boldly announced that "Döbeln is no longer red, but national," meaning Döbeln had rid itself of the socialists in favour of the Nazis.

Heimatfreund Horst Schlegel was still a boy in 1933—he was born in 1928—but he still remembers the 1930s as though it was yesterday. Fighting back the tears, Horst says, "In Döbeln there were a lot of unschooled labourers. They were the first to lose their job. I can still see the lines where they stood waiting for a measly hunk of bread. A girl, Marianne, used to come by our house. Her parents were so poor that she had no lunch to bring to school. So my mother would give her a slice of bread with jam or fat." His voice breaks. "The poverty, the poverty, it was so extreme. That's why people voted for Hitler."

Helfrid Piper, too, described the dire hardship in the pre-Hitler period. The already meagre unemployment benefits were slashed again in 1932, he writes. Winters were freezing cold, and coal was expensive. "Classrooms were set up as public warming places, people collected kindling in the woods. Many families went hungry. And always those bloodstained demonstrations."

The elections of 5 March snuffed out democracy. The Nazis' 44 percent of the Reichstag seats did not give them a majority, but it hardly mattered. A few days later the KPD was banned, and on 23 March, President Hindenburg signed the Enabling Act, giving Hitler and his cabinet permission to override parliament. The state of emergency abolishing most civil liberties became permanent. The dictatorship of the Third Reich was a fact.

In Saxony, the National Socialist revolution was implemented with an iron fist by two long-time Hitler disciples: Gauleiter Martin Mutschmann and SA leader Manfred von Killinger, a former marine officer who had carried out political assassinations in the early 1920s and had been involved in the murder of Walther Rathenau, the liberal Jewish minister of Foreign Affairs. Three days after the elections, they ordered raids on buildings used by their political opponents throughout the state, and the arrest of Social Democrats and Communists. That same day, 8 March, Hitler named Killinger as Saxony's police chief, and two days later, as prime minister.

Upheaval

Döbeln's administration unravelled on 9 March. In the municipal archive we find a dry but chilling record, no more than two typed pages, of Mayor Kunzelmann's expulsion from his post by the Nazis. It must have happened two floors down in the very building where we sit reading the report.

Döbeln City Hall, 9 March 1933

Today, shortly after 8:00 p.m., the following gentlemen appeared at the office of Mayor Kunzemann:
Councilman Saupe
District leader Groine
Council members Damme, Schomburg, Uhlemann, Braun and Thiele.

Herr Groine addressed Herr Mayor Kunzemann thus:
"On orders from a higher organ, I hereby dismiss you as mayor of
the city of Döbeln. Councilman Saupe will temporarily assume
your duties."

Kunzemann: "Dismissed? On whose orders?"
Groine: "No, not dismissed, but given a leave of absence for an
    undetermined period."
Kunzemann: "Are you authorized to take these measures? I plan
    to remain at my post as a civil servant as long as those who
    have installed me, that is, the city council, the district leader-
    ship and the ministry, grant me the mandate to do so."
Groine: "I am acting on behalf of a higher organ. I have been
    charged with informing you of your leave of absence."
Kunzemann: "What kind of higher organ?"
Groine: "I already told you: a higher organ."
Kunzemann: "Mr. Saupe, as councilman, what do you think of
    this?"
Saupe: "It is none of my business."

*Meanwhile, police chief Rönneke, recently appointed head of the
police, was called in. Herr Groine repeated his message and pointed
out that he had been in Dresden that afternoon and that he had taken
orders from Herr Killinger, the Reichstag representative from Saxony,
to grant Mayor Kunzemann a leave of absence.*

Kunzemann: "Herr Killinger did not appoint me; his only
    responsibility is to the police force. The only directorates
    relevant to me are the city council and the ministry. I was a
    soldier and will remain at my post. Mr. Groine, does your
    communiqué mean that you intend to use force to prevent
    me from executing my function?"
Groine: "Yes, it does."
Kunzemann: "Police Chief Rönneke, may I ask what you are
    planning to do about this?"
Rönneke: "There is nothing I can do to change it."
Kunzemann: "I hereby formally object to these measures. I
    expressly assert the rights which are contained in the terms
    of my engagement."
Groine: "You are entitled to submit an objection."
Kunzemann: "Then I relinquish my post under explicit protest.
    I will go only under duress, and accept the consequences

thereof. I do so also in the interest of maintaining peace in
our city."

At the bottom of the report is Theodor Kunzemann's signature. It is not
clear whether Kunzemann himself or a secretary recorded the exchange.
In any case, the report was duly filed in Kunzemann's permanent dossier.

Fritz Saupe is, at the time, a forty-eight-year-old entrepreneur, the
owner of a factory that makes industrial filters. In a photograph we find
in Chemnitz Chamber of Commerce's archive he is a handsome, distin-
guished-looking man in a tailored suit, looking self-confidently straight
into the lens of the camera. In his curriculum vitae, drawn up in 1935, he
emphasizes his time as an officer in the Imperial German Navy, which he
joined in 1902 and in which he served during World War I as a submarine
commander. He lists his various military distinctions up to his retirement
from the navy in 1919, when he went to work in his father's business. He
was first elected to the city council in 1924.

Saupe fails to mention that for eight years he served on the city council
for the conservative, nationalistic German National People's Party, part
of a right-wing coalition that enjoyed a reasonable working relationship
with the socialist SPD and Mayor Kunzemann. He claims to have sat on
the council "for the far right" and "from that moment on, waged a struggle
against Marxism in Döbeln." In February 1932, he writes, he applied for
NSDAP membership, and was admitted on 1 May. At the next election, in
November 1932, Saupe stood on the ballot as a Nazi, and won.

You have to hand it to him: he accurately gauged the zeitgeist and was
rewarded for it. Now that Kunzemann had been ousted, on 9 March 1933,
the NSDAP entrusted Saupe with its power grab in Döbeln.

Fritz Saupe wasted no time in moving into Kunzemann's office and
getting down to business. He clearly enjoyed his new role. The very next
morning, at 8 a.m., he summoned the entire corps of civil servants to the
council chambers. He informed them that from now on, he was their boss,
and demanded loyalty. Anyone who did not wish to serve the government
of "national awakening" should step forward. No one budged. Saupe then
required all those present to place their hand on their heart and recite:
"Sieg Heil! For Adolf Hitler as the redeemer of Germany!" Three "Sieg
Heils" later, everyone returned to his desk.

This is how easy it was. Try to imagine the scenario described here, and
one can understand that all of Döbeln's civil servants obediently stayed at
their jobs. Whoever refused to serve the Nazis would be fired. And then? It
was the Depression, and one would rightly doubt the new administration
would make welfare payments to someone who had openly opposed it. The
Nazis had yet to show their true colours, but it was clear they would show

no mercy to challengers. Civil rights had already been abolished, it was open season against Communists, and even the mayor himself had been unceremoniously ousted.

The new order in Döbeln

Saupe's meeting with the civil servants in the council chambers was meticulously notated. As with other documents dating from that year, it was filed under the category "The national awakening in the year 1933." When Ute Wiesner became Döbeln's archivist in 1991, two years after the Wende, this was part of a large collection of sensitive dossiers kept in the "closed archive." Ute rescued these files from the repository, and now they are free for anyone to read.

We are fortunate that Döbeln hardly suffered any damage during the war, and that the takeover by the Red Army was reasonably orderly. Elsewhere in Germany, entire archives were burned by the fleeing Nazis. And what did not perish in the last days of the war still faced an uncertain future: Moscow decreed that Nazi documents found in eastern Germany be brought to the Soviet Union. Some of them have been returned, some not.

Nazi-era dossiers, newspapers, and archives that remained in the GDR were kept under lock and key. The State Security Service, the Stasi, had a particular interest in the documents, as they could come in handy in keeping citizens with a Nazi past under their thumb. Many local archival materials were therefore transferred to centralized Stasi repositories. In Döbeln, however, the municipal archives from the war years are quite complete, allowing us to follow the Nazi city leaders, and to form a picture of the men from whom our grandfather would later seek support in keeping his factory running.

The first days of Saupe's tenure as mayor are painstakingly recorded, nearly hour by hour. We know that after addressing the civil servants, he summoned his predecessor to turn over the keys to the safe, two cashboxes, and a silver box. He asked his Nazi superiors in Dresden whether he should continue to pay Kunzemann his salary. But rather than put in a good word for him, Saupe stabbed him in the back with the comment, "Herr Kunzemann is a member of the Social Democratic Party and not a career civil servant."

Dresden instructed Saupe to fire all the Social Democrat and Communist aldermen and councillors, twenty-two in total. Only ideologically pure Nazi sympathizers could remain on the city's payroll. Everyone, regardless of his position, must produce a signed statement within two days swearing allegiance to the government and that he or she has no further connections with Marxist (i.e., social-democratic or Communist) parties or persons.

Otto Röher, deputy mayor in the previous administration, likewise submitted a floridly handwritten pledge of allegiance. Unlike Kunzemann, he had not been fired on 9 March. He immediately quit the SPD and was reappointed to a paid function within the city government, which, thanks to Saupe's intervention, was approved by the higher-ups within a month. Röher, wrote Saupe, was indispensable, being an "extremely capable and hard-working civil servant, who in a neutral, non-partisan manner managed the finances of the city of Döbeln, despite the obstructionism of the Marxist members of the city government." While Saupe understood that Röher's long-time membership in the SPD disqualified him from the position of deputy mayor, would No. 3 in the hierarchy, second deputy, be a possibility? Saupe requested a speedy decision on this matter.

Nowhere do reports, correspondence, and personnel dossiers indicate that Röher so much as lifted a finger on Kunzemann's behalf, notwithstanding years of close-knit teamwork. Nor did he do so later, when Kunzemann had been reduced to poverty and had to beg for the small pension he had a right to, but was denied him.

During a short break in his first busy days of the National Socialist revolution, Saupe penned a brief letter to the last emperor of Germany, Wilhelm II, who was living in exile in the Netherlands.

> To Your Imperial Majesty
> I report in all servility that, following my installation as mandated first mayor of the district city of Döbeln, I issued an order for the portrait of Your Majesty, which until 1918 adorned the council chambers, to be replaced to its original position, effective immediately.
>
> I beg Your Majesty's indulgence in accepting this notice.
>
> Your devoted and grateful servant,
>
> Fritz Saupe, Imperial Lieutenant Commander and mandated first mayor.

Apparently Saupe hoped that the "national awakening" would also include a glorious revival of the monarchy. To underscore his zeal, alongside Wilhelm II he also hung the portrait of the last king of Saxony. The only thing to add to this episode is a thank-you letter from Saupe to Wilhelm for the photo the ex-Kaiser sent him, which brought "inexpressible joy" to him and his family.

While Saupe was busy consolidating his power within city hall, Groine was establishing the new order in the public sphere. On the evening of 9 March, war veterans and brownshirts marched from their clubhouses on the Bahnhofstrasse, wielding torches and accompanied by music, to Döbeln city hall. A long swath of cloth—the black-red-gold German flag—was hurled from the tower. Later, it was consumed in flames. The crowd cheers, orders were barked. The next day, the *Döbelner Anzeiger* reports: "To the sound of music and deafening cheers from thousands of voices, a massive swastika banner was unfurled from the top of the tower, illuminated by floodlights, and red Bengal flares putting it in a magical light." In one fell swoop, the usual businesslike tone of the newspaper has been replaced by swollen Nazi bombast.

Groine addressed the crowd from the balcony. The *Anzeiger* quotes him: "For years, national [i.e., National Socialist] Döbeln has lived under the yoke of political and economic terror. Those days are over, once and for all." Well aware of the makeup and sentiments of the local populace, Groine propagandized that Hitler has the best interests of the workers at heart. Just look at the first measures taken by the government: health insurance premiums have been lowered. And that was only the beginning. The rally closed with a triple "Heil!" for the Führer and the "Horst Wessel Song." The city hall tower, with its new banner, was photographed for posterity and placed in the archive as a momentous historic milestone. The photo caption reads: "On the day of national revolution."

The next day, Friday, fearing resistance in Döbeln, Groine called up paramilitary reinforcements from the region. The storm troopers hung Nazi banners, patrolled the streets, and positioned themselves in front of Jewish-owned businesses. The *Döbelner Anzeiger* reports that the militiamen did not impede customers: anyone who wished to do so was free to enter the shops. It was calm in the city, writes the newspaper, only to report in the next sentence that the police were kept busy with scuffles and other gatherings, and that the windows of the union buildings had been smashed. The item ends with a stern reminder of the revolution that has taken place. "No one will be the least bit harmed as long as order is maintained."

The new overlords have been instructed to be vigilant and to nip every protest in the bud. Dresden's missive reads: "Unscrupulous persons have circulated rumours of an imminent general strike." Mayor Saupe invited those council members who had not fallen from grace to a gala conference at city hall Sunday morning. NSDAP members were to wear their Nazi uniforms, the civilian members a black suit with top hat. Once all were gathered in the council chambers, a motion was introduced to make President Hindenburg and Chancellor Hitler honorary citizens of Döbeln. The motion passed unanimously. Why not rename a few streets and squares, while they're at it? The Obermarkt at once became Hindenburgplatz; the street named after the murdered Jewish Weimar politician Rathenau was renamed—adding insult to injury—Adolf-Hitler-Strasse; and the memory of the poet Heinrich Heine, Jewish-born, after all, was to be erased. His street was renamed after Albert Leo Schlageter, a Nazi bomber and martyr executed in 1923 during the French occupation of the Ruhr region. Döbeln wasted no time realigning itself.

Boycott

For Döbeln's Jewish population, the situation quickly became grim. Municipal services were given the directive on 13 March to discontinue all business dealings with Jews, and civil servants were more or less ordered to no longer shop at Jewish stores. To which concerns did this directive apply, the aldermen asked the mayor. A few days later he provided them with a list of twelve businesses: a shoe store, a bedspring supplier, a merchant in oil and grease, a haberdashery, a second-hand shop, two department stores, a needlecrafts shop, a ladies' clothing store, a woman pediatrician, a metalsmith, and lastly, the Deutsche Zigarren-Werke.

The Nazis were particularly suspicious of Hugo Totschek, the Jewish owner of the men's clothing store on Breite Strasse 17. Saupe had the post office tap Totschek's telephone. "Specifically, all telephone calls to Leipzig must be notated verbatim, and communicated here forthwith."

In 1933 there were twenty-nine Jewish residents of Döbeln. Most of them were originally from Eastern Europe and only recently had settled in Germany. In Leipzig, Dresden, and Chemnitz, home to some 90 percent of Saxony's Jews, Jewish life thrived. But not in Döbeln. Once a week, a rabbi came from Leipzig to instruct Jewish children. Aside from not attending church like their Lutheran neighbours, there was not much outward difference between the groups. Most of Döbeln's Jews were not religious, and their shops were open on Saturdays, just like the rest.

As soon as Hitler came to power, Julius Streicher, publisher of *Der Stürmer*, demanded that the Jews be "got rid of." The Nazi leadership felt this was rather hasty. Europe and America were growing uneasy with the recent rise in anti-Jewish violence in Germany. Jewish organizations abroad held large-scale demonstrations, calling for a boycott of German products. When the London *Daily Express* printed the sensational headline "Judea Declares War on Germany," Streicher grabbed his chance to (as he described it in Nuremburg in 1946) "show worldwide Jewry that we would no longer tolerate the smear campaign against the new Germany."

Hitler himself held a speech on 24 March, the day the *Daily Express* headline was published. The speech is available on YouTube. Hitler is standing on a round stage, surrounded by supporters. He gesticulates wildly, theatrically. "The struggle between peoples or mutual hatred is fuelled by certain interests. It is a small international clique without roots that is instigating strife between peoples. These are people who belong nowhere, who have no place they call home, but live in Berlin today, Brussels tomorrow, Paris the day after, or in Prague, Vienna, or in London, and who think they belong *everywhere!*" His listeners know exactly who he is talking about. "Jews!" they shout, and then he continues, "These are the only people one can truly call 'international elements,' because they can do business *everywhere*."

Within a week, Streicher organized, with Hitler's backing, a nationwide boycott of Jews. The boycott was to last until the crusade against Germany stops.

On Friday, 31 March, the *Döbelner Anzeiger* published an announcement with swastikas and a black border. "To protect the German people, NSDAP party leaders have called for an economic boycott of Jews living in Germany, in response to the appalling scare tactics propagated by their racial brethren abroad." The text refers to the horror stories about German soldiers during World War I that made the rounds among foreign Jews at the time, according to the Nazis. Those same Jews were now unleashing a campaign of lies against Hitler's Germany.

The *Döbelner Anzeiger* warns residents: "Whoever brings his custom, starting on Saturday 1 April at 10 a.m., to a Jewish shop, does business with a Jew, or consults a Jewish doctor or lawyer, turns his back on the struggle of the German people and is a traitor to the fatherland." Under the notice is a list of Jewish-owned businesses in Döbeln. Now there are just nine— the list no longer includes Isay Rottenberg, which in itself is not strange, as he does not sell retail. The notice advises shoppers to be aware of where they do their shopping, as a Jewish business might have been unwittingly omitted from the blacklist. When in doubt, consumers are advised to consult the Nazi Party office on the Bahnhofstrasse.

On the Saturday of the boycott, most Jewish businesses stayed shut. (The fact that the national boycott commenced on a Saturday shows the extent to which German Jews had assimilated.) However, the *Anzeiger* reports that they opened as usual, but had to close down later in the day because of the effect of the boycott.

Despite the triumphant tone of the *Anzeiger* article, there are false notes to the story. "Rubberneckers" had to be shooed away by the police, and those who protested against the SA's placing of signs with the text "THESE SHOPS OPEN ONLY FOR TRAITORS TO THE FATHERLAND" were hauled off to the police station.

Hugo Totschek, owner of the haberdashery on the Breite Strasse, would not allow himself to be intimidated by the storm troopers. The men who installed themselves at his front door got a swift kick in the pants and were sent packing.

Helfrid Piper remembers Hugo Totschek. "My parents were good friends with several Jewish families," he writes. "They paid us visits, and we them. We saw a lot of Uncle Hugo. He lived with his housekeeper and his handicapped son, Hansi. His other son studied law in England and became a professor. [. . .] If the housekeeper had chores elsewhere, they would ask me to play with Hansi. Uncle Hugo paid for a sandwich and a bottle of chocolate milk every day for the approximately forty handicapped children at the Pestalozzi School."

Piper describes Totschek's altercation with the SA paramilitaries. He is mistaken about the date—it was 1 April 1933, and not late in the year— but he does recall the details clearly. Totschek was a large, strapping man. When two young SA fellows took up their post outside his door, armed with placards, he went outside and said, "If you two are still here when I come back in ten minutes, I'll give you a thrashing." Ten minutes later, says Piper, Totschek was true to his word, and off they went, tail between their legs. Just before closing time, they returned with another six men and forced their way into the shop. Not two minutes later, the whole gang of them tumbled out onto the street, "at least two of them with a bloodied head." Someone called for the police, demanding to file a complaint of trespassing. The police refused. "The whole city was in stitches over the incident," Piper writes, satisfied. "They tried to cover it up."

That evening, NSDAP leader Hermann Groine spoke on the Niedermarkt, just behind city hall, about the Jews contaminating Germans with foreign blood. He warned that the Nazis are not to be toyed with: "In this defensive struggle, anyone who attacks Germany behind its back is an enemy of the people." The next day the Nazis called for a "time out" of several days, threatening that if the slander did not subside, then the Jews would see the true meaning of "furor teutonicus." But on Tuesday, 4 April, the government decided to call off the boycott because, they say, England and America were so taken aback that they withdrew their sanctions against Germany. In truth, though, the boycott was simply a failure. The response from abroad was withering. Foreign orders were cancelled because companies did not wish to do business with *this* Germany. And, moreover, the boycott did not sit well with ordinary Germans.

And so it was in Döbeln too, according to Helfrid Piper. After all, "the whole city was in stitches" over the humiliation of the SA men in front of Totschek's clothing store. The Jewish shops only did more business than ever, says Piper. Perhaps Döbelners were showing their distaste for the Nazi strong-arm tactics, or at least most were not easily cowed into shunning Jewish-owned shops.

Another resident wrote down his recollections. He will remain anonymous here, in keeping with the conditions under which his diaries were kept at the Döbeln municipal archives. Like Piper, he was a boy in 1933. He often went to the popular Wohlwert department store, opened in 1930 by the Jewish businessman Georg Kariel. For children, the store was a cornucopia, and they would pass through it on their way to school. He still remembers the layout of the various departments—the shoes, the kitchen utensils, the textiles. And, of course, the toy department. Wohlwert was a *"standard price"* variety store where one could buy quality but relatively low-cost housewares.

Starting in 1933, he recalls, the Nazis launched a smear campaign against the owner, Kariel. Unsuccessfully, it seems, because in 1935 the store was still going strong. This is confirmed by advertisements in the *Döbelner Anzeiger* by Wohlwert and other Jewish businesses in the months and years following the boycott.

For Hugo Totschek, however, the boycott proved fatal. His defiance would be his undoing. About six months after the boycott, he was arrested and accused of molesting or raping his female shop assistants. The case was used as nationwide Nazi propaganda. *Der Stürmer* wrote of "the haberdasher-Jew Totschek, the rapist of Döbeln," delving back to before the Nazis came to power. A single example out of "hundreds" was used to illustrate Totschek's devious ways: "Else D. was fourteen when she became an apprentice with the Jew Hugo Totschek. Her parents did not suspect that they had sent their innocent daughter to the devil's lair." Totschek supposedly smothered the girl in flattery, took her on motorcar outings, and imposed himself upon her. Else's father took action and filed charges. The judge, however, found Else's story implausible. He sent the girl to a reformatory and acquitted Totschek. The accompanying cartoon shows Lady Justice allowing herself to be bribed by corrupt Jews: no one dared stand in the Jew's way. But once the Nazis were in charge, Totschek was once again fair game. "The Jew Hugo Totschek has usurped, raped, and poisoned. He has done what the Jewish book of laws, the Talmud, instructs them to do," claimed the article's anonymous author. The accusations against Totschek were used to incriminate Jews nationwide and to call for an end to the "racial disgrace" of sexual relations between Jews and non-Jews. Underneath the article, *Der Stürmer* placed a new demand for a boycott of Jewish businesses. "Whoever buys from the Jew is a traitor!"

By the time the article appeared in April 1934, Hugo Totschek was already dead. The day after he was arrested, he hanged himself—at least, so claimed the Nazis when they announced his death. He carried out his own sentence, wrote *Der Stürmer*.

The Breite Strasse, in Döbeln's city centre, is now a pedestrian shopping street. Stephan Conrad and Sophie Spitzer, our guides from the history club, take us to number 73, Hugo Totschek's former residence, and to number 17, his former clothing shop. In front of the house, three small square brass plates have been cemented into the sidewalk. These are *Stolpersteine*, or stumbling stones, which since 1992 have been placed throughout Germany and elsewhere in Europe in front of a house or place of business to remind modern passersby of the expelled or murdered Jews who lived or worked there. The plates read: "Here lived Hugo Totschek," "Here lived Margarete Totschek, née Grünthal," and "Here lived Fritz Rudolf Totschek," each with their birth and death dates and a few words about their fate.

Conny and Sophie tell us that Hugo was born in Silesia, Poland, and opened a men's clothing store in Döbeln in 1911. He and Margarete had two sons: Carl (1908) and Fritz (1911). The younger son had Down's syndrome. The couple divorced and Margarete moved first to Erfurt and later to Berlin, whence she was deported in 1942 to the ghetto in Piaski, Poland. Her trail dead-ends there. Carl had already moved to England to study law and medicine before the Nazis came to power. He later emigrated to Israel, where he became a university professor. Fritz (Helfrid Piper remembers him as "Hansi") was brought to an asylum after the arrest and death of his father, and as a disabled person was the victim of "euthanasia." In February 1941 he was sent to the infamous Sonnestein asylum in Pirna, south of Dresden, and gassed. Totschek's clothing store was taken over in 1934 by one Karl Damm.

Breite Strasse 17 is now home to an optician. Karl Damm is no longer there. But Conny points to an attractive building a stone's throw away. "Gaber & Damm," the sign reads, in large letters. It is a men's and women's clothing store. "Same family," Conny says.

The factory occupied

We have no idea what our grandfather did during the first weeks of Hitler's regime, let alone how he felt. Hitler's speech about the "rootless clique" must have stung, immigrant merchant that he was. He must have been unsettled by the boycott, despite his factory being left off the list.

He did not settle in Döbeln, but in cosmopolitan Dresden, where there were theatres, cafés, and restaurants in abundance. We found two addresses. The first is a pension on the Beuststrasse, a street once lined with grand townhouses, the English Church, and the Russian consulate. The street is within walking distance of Dresden's main train station, from which there is a direct line to Amsterdam. He presumably took the train to and from Amsterdam, but probably commuted the fifty kilometres to Döbeln by car. There is nothing left of the Beuststrasse now, we discover when we visit Dresden: it was destroyed in the Allied bombings of February 1945.

A letter from our grandmother Helena Ptasznik, from the prison dossier at the Ministry of Foreign Affairs in The Hague, tells us that Isay was not exempt from the consequences of Hitler's takeover. Her letter, dated 22 September 1935, is addressed to Johan Steenbergen, the Dutch consul in Dresden. On two and a half single-spaced typed pages, she lays out the Deutsche Zigarren-Werke's backstory plus any other information she knows. Steenbergen translated the original, no longer extant, into German for Rottenberg's local lawyer. An excerpt from the letter reads as follows:

> In the spring of 1933, shortly after the installation of the Third Reich, a group of SA men suddenly occupied the factory. Both directors [Isay Rottenberg and tobacco buyer Vincenz Silvan] were suspended from their posts. They searched the bookkeeping accounts and dossiers, and even private correspondence. My husband remained in Dresden, but Silvan, who was an Auslandsdeutscher [a German citizen living abroad], chose to flee to Amsterdam, fearful of being taken into preventative custody, something that nearly every Jewish Auslandsdeutscher could expect in those days. After the search, which took several days but did not uncover even the slightest irregularity, my husband was rehabilitated and restored to his function.

The Amsterdam municipal archives reveal some details of Vincenz Silvan's escape. Silvan was named codirector of the DZW at its inception and later worked for the firm from Amsterdam as a tobacco buyer. His registration card states Cologne as his place of residence. He was born in Kalisz, formerly part of the Russian Empire but belonging to Poland since 1918. On

14 May 1933, Silvan went to Essen to request a new Polish passport, which he used to travel to Prague. There, he applied for a Dutch visa, which was issued on 22 August. Once in Amsterdam he was given a temporary residence permit. Nowhere does it say he is an Auslandsdeutscher, but this is probably accurate. He presumably had dual nationality and was reluctant to cross the border with his German passport out of fear of being detained, and therefore used a Polish travel document.

Isay Rottenberg sat things out in his pension in Dresden. Unlike Silvan, he had a Dutch passport and felt safe, as we heard from our Aunt Tini, as though he were protected by the Dutch lion itself (the lion being the heraldic motif of the Low Countries since the twelfth century). He was not about to be chased away, nor to abandon a factory that now employed 670 people and operated at full steam. Our grandmother's letter shows that he was "rehabilitated" within a few days and could resume his task as director. Who put in a good word for him? Did he have to make a deal of some sort in order to stay on as owner-operator under the Nazi regime?

6

THE **MACHINE BAN**

ROTTENBERG DODGED THAT BULLET, FOR NOW. BUT THE NEXT ONE came soon enough. On 15 July 1933, the regime announced a ban on—of all things—the machine production of cigars, encouraging handwork to combat unemployment.

Ironically, the machine ban provided us with the first foothold in piecing together the story of our grandfather and his Werke. From the few sentences the Swiss journalist Urs Thaler devoted to the Deutsche Zigarren-Werke in his book *Unerledigte Geschäfte*, we learned that the factory, with its American-made machines, was a highly streamlined workplace and, Thaler wrote when we contacted him, "one of Germany's most modern factories." Although his research dated from more than fifteen years earlier, he remembered the Deutsche Zigarren-Werke clearly, and promised to send us the documents still in his possession. This was some thirty pages of letters regarding the DZW, and the imposition of a machine ban that to us, at this point, made no sense. The source was the Bundesarchiv in Berlin-Lichterfelde, the repository for Third Reich documents. Thaler seemed to us a thorough researcher, and would have found, we assumed, everything having to do with the DZW.

Just to be sure, we requested the dossier numbers and went to the Berlin archive ourselves. It is a large complex located in a massive barracks on the edge of town. A whole slew of microfilm rolls was waiting for us.

We had expected to have to spend endless hours poring over the microfilm materials in order to stumble across something having to do with the factory. Not so: the microfilm was bursting with documents about the Deutsche Zigarren-Werke in 1933, 1934, and 1935. We left with more than three hundred printouts. What was so special about the cigar factory that Third Reich ministers and top-level civil servants spent so much energy on reams of memos and correspondence?

The answer was quick in coming: the Deutsche Zigarren-Werke was not *one of* the most modern cigar factories, as Urs Thaler thought, but *the* most state-of-the-art and efficient in all of Germany. And because of it, rivals did their best to sideline it. Thanks to their lobbying, Hitler even issued a decree to block the fully automatic production of cigars in Döbeln.

It was a life-or-death battle for the Deutsche Zigarren-Werke. The warring parties included cigar manufacturers (who were also active NSDAP members) throughout the country; Nazi governors and civil servants and party leaders in Döbeln, Saxony, and Berlin; and a Jewish owner-operator with a Dutch passport: our grandfather, who to our amazement never gave up.

Handcrafted vs. machine-made

"Dear Party Member Ender!" writes Ernst Deter, member of the NSDAP and the board of the Reichesverband Deutscher Zigarrenhersteller (the Association of German Cigar Manufacturers), six weeks after Hitler's takeover, to Reichstag MP Herbert Ender. "You might recall that, when Krenter Werke was established in Döbeln, we [the Reichesverband Deutscher Zigarrenhersteller], backed by the party, began a strident campaign against machine production in the cigar-making industry." A similar ban had failed two years earlier, but it must now be reintroduced, and soon, Deter writes, if the small and mid-sized cigar-making businesses are to survive. Some 58 percent of the hand-labourers in the cigar industry were unemployed. Shutting down the machines, says Deter, would allow most of them to return to work. He asks Ender to put the matter on the Reichstag Party agenda.

Ender was himself a Saxony factory manager and a good friend of NSDAP Gauleiter Martin Mutschmann, and, like Mutschmann, hailed from the same city, Plauen, where Nazism began its triumphant march in Saxony.

The machine ban was not aimed solely at Krenter, the DZW's predecessor. Indeed, Krenter's hypermodern American machines, his American marketing strategy, and the widespread distribution of brand-name cigars was a jolt to the industry. But even before Krenter appeared on the scene, long-suffering cigar makers were already mulling a machine ban.

Like the cigarette industry, the cigar branch flirted with automatization at the beginning of the twentieth century, but the first attempts failed. It was technically much more difficult to mechanically produce a cigar—the leaves were far from uniform and market tastes varied—than the standard cigarette. Therefore, the cigar industry and its consumers still favoured artisan cigars.

During the Depression, cigarettes—one could still buy them individually—were more affordable than cigars. And the cigars that one did buy (in the early 1930s, Germans still purchased a hundred cigars per capita per year!) were, by necessity, the cheapest ones.

The only way to offset the shrinking income yet remain competitive was either to lower wages or streamline the production process. The cigar rollers' wages could not be cut back any further. Historian Christian Kurzweg demonstrates the disparity in wages in Döbeln at the time: metalworkers earned seventeen reichsmarks per week, labourers in Döbeln's chocolate factory twenty, and in the corset factory as much as twenty-eight reichsmarks. The handworkers in the cigar factories earned the least: just thirteen marks per week.

But few businesses had the capital to invest in automation. The small-scale operation of the cigar industry is illustrated by W. Reinmann in his doctoral dissertation entitled "Mensch und Maschine in der deutschen Tabakindustrie." In 1931 there were more than five thousand cigar makers in Germany. Of these, three thousand were just one-man operations. Most of the others employed less than ten workers. Only twenty-six firms had more than five hundred employees.

Faced with the example of the cigarette industry, the cigar makers' future looked bleak indeed. Of the more than one thousand German cigarette manufacturers pre-1914, only a few megacorporations were left in 1933. This is what would happen to the cigar industry, they thought, if a few capital-flush magnates were allowed to mechanize production. Slogging ahead with hand-rolled cigars and hoping for a better economic conjuncture offered the best chance of survival.

A successful lobby

For the Reichsverband Deutscher Zigarrenhersteller, which had repeatedly petitioned successive Weimar administrations in vain, the Nazis were the answer to their prayers. The guild immediately lobbied for a ban on

cigar-making machines. "The highest political, social and economic mandate of the day is: to prevent, wherever possible, that diligent human hands
are rendered jobless, to enable idle human hands to return to work," reads
the well-nigh religiously worded request to the government in Berlin and
published on 18 April 1933 in the members' magazine.

One merit of the cigar industry, the organization felt, was that anyone
"who had learned the trade and was thrifty and diligent" had the opportunity to work his way up the ladder from labourer to foreman to independent
producer. This had to be preserved. The group painted a doomsday scenario of a future where the rise of automated production would not be held
in check. Except for cigar rolling, there was little else to augment one's
income in towns where agriculture did not thrive. If these people were to
lose their livelihood, they would migrate to the cities and become a burden
on the municipal and federal governments. "Hopelessness and poverty will
be their fate."

The Nazis were open to these arguments and, more importantly, to the
needs of the social groups now pleading for protection. After all, they had
always claimed to be the guardians of industrial handworkers, shopkeepers, and small-scale businesses. They couldn't leave them out in the cold,
not now. Creating jobs was the Nazis' top social priority.

The ban became law, but not without resistance. German industrialists
were worried about a machine ban. At a meeting of the Reichsverband der
Deutschen Industrie, the German machine manufacturers protested that
"a total ban will force companies that produce the cigar-making machines
to fire their highly-trained workers and engineers. It will make the export
of these machines impossible. It will undermine the development of a
national cigar-machine industry."

A ban, moreover, would harm the entire machine-manufacturing
industry, wrote the Verein Deutscher Maschinenbau-Anstalten two weeks
later in a protest letter supported by statistics and a thorough analysis.
Once a machine ban goes into effect in one branch, they argued, then
other branches of industry will press for a ban in their sector, and con-
sequently no German factories will dare invest in new machines, for fear of
a ban. The organization warned of a "brain drain" and dwindling expertise
among engineers, who were already struggling to find work. "Do we want
to further encourage engineers and skilled labour in the German machine
industry to take their first chance to emigrate, only to become the German
economy's greatest competitors?"

Here and there, tensions rose. A leader of the Nazi labour union wrote
to a Reichstag member on 24 May 1993 that his phone was ringing off the
hook with concerned labourers, anxious about the machines. There is a

"storm brewing in the country," he wrote. If the ban is not imposed soon, then "I know that the labourers will take the matter into their own hands and destroy the machines."

Targeting the Deutsche Zigarren-Werke

Isay Rottenberg kept mum during the run-up to the machine ban. In any case, we have not uncovered any memos or letters indicating he was worried. Perhaps he was unaware of it, or thought it wiser not to get involved at this point.

The machine ban went into effect on 15 July 1933, signed by Hitler and his ministers of economy and finance. Their arguments come straight from the Reichsverband Deutscher Zigarrenhersteller and are given a nationalistic wording. "It is essential to curb a development that will soon uproot many of our *Volksgenossen* who feel attached to their native soil."

But the government also took the arguments of the machine industry into account. There would be no blanket ban: only the use of new machines would be forbidden; factories that already operated with machines may continue to do so, but their production must not exceed the levels of 1932; the ministers of Finance or Economy have the right to lower the production quotas of these factories; machines that mechanically assist handwork—for example, cutting and stripping machines for tobacco leaves—may still be used; and—crucially for the machine builders themselves—there is an exception for German-made machines. These may be set up in factories as test models for export. To soften the blow, the government will free up two million reichsmarks as compensation for factories whose machines must be put out of service. Estimates are that the measures will create five thousand jobs.

Contrary to the fears of the machine builders, the ban in the cigar sector did not usher in a new set of similar bans in other sectors. It remained an exception, a concession for small businesses and shopkeepers, a gesture of great symbolic value at relatively little expense. The aim of the ban was to slow down the modernization of the cigar industry, the chief target being the only fully automatic cigar factory in Germany: the Deutsche Zigarren-Werke.

For our grandfather, the machine ban would be a boulder that had suddenly rolled down the hill and blocked his way. If he were to remain and rescue his factory and investment, then the law must be revoked or declawed. Impossible, absurd, our instinct says. Did he plan to push that boulder back up the mountain, like Sisyphus? How did he think he could take on the Nazi regime and his German rivals?

Back in Amsterdam, Lena Rottenberg, aware of the general situation in Germany, will have anxiously followed the developments. Vincenz Silvan was a regular visitor, so she knew he considered the situation in Germany alarming enough to flee to the Netherlands. She also knew of the boycott and the paramilitaries' raid on the factory, and had surely heard about the machine ban from Isay.

Isay occasionally returned to Amsterdam to see his family. He would stay a few days and then return to Germany. He is not pictured in any of the family photos from that time. We do find him once on a soundless home movie at a party for his in-laws Abraham and Teofile Ptasznik's fiftieth wedding anniversary. The whole family is gathered in the yard. Our fathers and aunt, and their cousins—young teenagers—are rambunctiously jostling one another. The boys are all in suit and tie, the girls in flowered dresses with puffy sleeves. Isay is among the adults, standing proudly with his hand on his hip, clearly joking with the others.

"I didn't see much of Uncle Szaja," says Theo Franken, the youngest of the Ptasznik cousins. He knows next to nothing about the German cigar factory, even though the family lived nearby and socialized frequently. "I was there every day, or Tini was at our place. We were only three months apart in age. Uncle Szaja was mostly away on business, in Germany or wherever. Aunt Lena was a second mother to me, and Tini like my twin sister. But with him, I didn't have much contact."

Theo does remember that his father, Abraham Franken, and Isay clashed over the situation in Germany. "My father was England-oriented, and Uncle Szaja leaned more toward Germany. They sometimes had words over it. I don't remember what about, exactly, but I think my father objected to Uncle Szaja doing business there with Nazis. My father loathed Germany." Ironically, though, Abraham Franken hated his first name, and signed letters with "Abraham Franken, who goes by the name Adolf." "People knew him as 'Dolf,'" says Theo. "Later, of course, that turned out to be an unfortunate choice. Alas, it didn't help him."

No discussions concerning Isay's enterprise in Nazi Germany made their way into family recollections. No one talked about it. But whether the objections were ethical or business-related, our grandfather was impervious to them. He does not appear to have ever considered abandoning his project.

7

A COMPLAINT FILED WITH THE GESTAPO

AS SOON AS THE MACHINE BAN IS IMPLEMENTED, ISAY ROTTENBERG takes action. On 24 July 1933 he sends an express letter to Kurt Schmitt, the minister of Economic Affairs in Berlin, and similar letters to any and all authorities he can think of: ministers in Dresden, the Chamber of Commerce and Industry in Chemnitz, the NSDAP district leaders in Döbeln, the unions, etc.

If the law is applied to the letter, he writes, then he must pull the plug on his machines within two weeks and close down the factory. After all, the 1932 levels were far lower than normal, due to Krenter's bankruptcy and the production hiatus before Deutsche Zigarren-Werke could reopen several months later, and even then only at lower levels. In 1932, the factory produced just twenty-two million cigars, a number they will already reach in two weeks' time. "The consequences," Rottenberg writes, "in no way reflect the aims of the law's drafters. Our employees, numbering ca. 650 labourers and other personnel, will be out of work at once." He suggests adjusting the production quota to Krenter's output in 1931 and the factory's healthy months in 1932. And he requests an answer by the end of the month (thus within a week).

In a following letter he assures the authorities that "we are not soliciting exceptional treatment contrary the law, but rather asking that the law be applied in accordance with its true aims."

73

Rottenberg tries to seduce the Döbeln municipal authorities into join-ing his lobbying efforts. He underscores the urgency by informing them he has already requested permission from the Ministry of Social Affairs in Dresden to shut down operations. Could the city support his requests to the authorities, post-haste?

His appeal has the desired effect. The very next day, Mayor Herbert Denecke, recently named to replace interim mayor Fritz Saupe, submits a floridly written personal letter to the minister of Economic Affairs in Berlin. "The city places great store on preserving this concern, which is unique both in Germany and Europe." Denecke points out that this auto-mated factory cannot simply switch to hand labour because there are not enough skilled artisans in Döbeln and the region. "A well-run factory would be brought to ruin, without compensating the workers with employment in another sector. Moreover, the city where the factory is located would be hard hit by its closure."

The Döbeln municipal archives do not reveal whether there was any discussion before the city's decision to back Rottenberg. If all they did was to tally up the numbers and regard ideology as background noise, then this was the only logical conclusion. Döbeln profited from the Deutsche Zigarren-Werke, the city's second-largest employer. The 670 employees on the payroll did not have to turn to the city for financial support, and their wages meant that money circulated. Additionally, the DZW provided the city with income via taxes and rent. Döbeln was no longer exposed to investment risks because Rottenberg had not been given the kind of subsidies or tax breaks that had been afforded Krenter. These had cost the city dearly, and closing the factory now would only compound its losses. Keeping it open was by far the best option.

Praise from a Nazi

Then we find another letter, dated 29 June 1933, some two weeks before the machine ban was to go into effect. It is a letter from interim mayor Saupe to Georg Lenk, the Saxony minister of Economic Affairs. Saupe had per-sonally discussed the matter of the Deutsche Zigarren-Werke with Lenk a few days earlier. The letter recaps the meeting and includes passionate praise for the fully automated cigar factory. Saupe uses arguments we did not find in our grandfather's correspondence, but were apparently aimed at convincing the Nazi leadership.

Handworkers in the cigar sector are mainly women, Saupe writes, and isn't it the Reich's aim to get women to return to homemaking? A machine-operated factory employs mostly men, whose job is to operate and maintain the machinery. The machine operators earn higher wages than the average labourer—8 percent higher, in fact, by which Saupe suggests that handwork tended to be underpaid. Machine production negates the need for working at home, which was performed solely by women and whose "many social disadvantages go without saying." In addition to social progress, factory hygiene is superior, as Minister Lenk surely knows. Machine-made goods benefit the consumer as well, for he can afford a decent, reasonably priced cigar, "which is, and will be, impossible to match with artisanal production."

On behalf of the city authorities, Saupe asks the minister to wield his influence in Berlin to ward off a machine ban. In closing, he extends an invitation to Lenk to come visit the Deutsche Zigarren-Werke, so that he can witness "truly flawless manufacturing of cigars."

Saupe's letter shows that our grandfather had indeed been quietly lobbying for some time. And it indicates that the Nazi Saupe—and with him, Döbeln's bureaucrats—were determined to keep the Deutsche Zigarren-Werke open. The fact that the owner was Jewish and that the SA had occupied the factory just a few months earlier was of secondary importance, even for diehard Nazis.

By this time Isay Rottenberg had compromised on one point to placate the Nazis and their base somewhat. We gather as much from a letter to Rottenberg from the local Kampfbund des gewerblichen Mittelstandes, the Nazi union of shopkeepers. "Based on documents we have been shown, and on the grounds of statements made by our informers," they write, "we are satisfied that you reject supplying [your product to] department stores, fixed-price shops, and other businesses in such a way that would disadvantage independent shopkeepers."

Rottenberg is forced to distance himself from Krenter's sales plan and to rethink his own marketing strategy. Whether he did so because of the shopkeepers' threats or the SA's occupation and demands, we do not know. The SA and Gestapo archives in Saxony were lost in the Dresden bombardments. But the letter from the Kampfbund suggests that his opponents made it clear that promoting his cigars as quality mass-produced items and selling them in nonspecialty locations was out of the question.

Mayor Denecke wants to avert at all costs a shutdown of the Deutsche Zigarren-Werke. Two days after his first letter regarding the machine ban, he travels with an entire delegation (including Isay Rottenberg and his legal adviser, Arndt Oehmichen) to Dresden so they could plead their case. They aim straight for the kingpins, but Gauleiter Mutschmann, by now promoted to *Reichsstatthalter* (Reich governor) of Saxony, is unavailable or unwilling to meet with them. The first reactions do not bode well. Saxony's minister of Economic Affairs informs them that sooner or later, the DZW will have to switch from machine production to handwork. Denecke suggests that Rottenberg allow the group of between sixty and eighty skilled artisans in his employ to start hand rolling cigars. But this proposal doesn't stand a chance. "Apparently Herr Rottenberg is resistant to this idea," the mayor notes dryly.

Denecke remains a mystery to us. In the municipal archives he comes across as a dependable and correct government civil servant. Nowhere in the reports or memos do we discern any passion for his work—as with his predecessor Kunzemann—or personal zeal akin to Saupe's adoration of the exiled emperor. His language is civil, and his conduct, as far as we can tell, is purely managerial. He has rounded, regular handwriting and always signs his missives with "Dr. Denecke." He is, of course, a member of the NSDAP, a given for the replacement of the ousted SPD mayor Kunzemann in 1933. But we imagine him more as an experienced manager, perhaps as mayor of another city prior to Döbeln. If he wanted to continue in this career, he had to join the Nazi Party. We cannot find any photographs of him. We picture him with the looks of a starched jurist, smooth-shaven and bespectacled, his hair combed back.

Only three-quarters of the way through writing this book did we come across an account of his inauguration in the *Döbelner Anzeiger*. It describes his entrance into the council chambers, accompanied by acting mayor Saupe. Both are dressed in brown SA uniforms. Denecke takes his oath and delivers a fiery speech. For "the petty bourgeoisie and aristocratic Communists" he has borrowed a quote from the Nazi propaganda film *SA-Mann Brand*: "Gentlemen, we cannot take your nerves into account."

This sounds more like a hard-liner than the modest civil servant we had envisioned. In the accompanying photo we see a man in his forties, no glasses, with dark, sharply parted hair. The Döbeln register indeed lists him as a jurist, with "Dr. Jur." after his name. He lived on the Adolf-Hitler-Strasse. What made this man join the SA and become a Nazi functionary? His forced departure from Döbeln several years later only adds to the intrigue.

Eventually we do get our hands on a dossier over Denecke's career. He was an upstanding sort, from a well-educated Dresden milieu. After serving in World War I and having spent time as a prisoner of war, he studied law and passed the stringent state exams with flying colours. A commendation praises him as "a conscientious, diligent, competent, and trustworthy jurist" and someone of "irreproachable character." He then began a career as a judge. He joined the NSDAP as early as 1931—a staunch Nazi, after all. After the party took control on 9 March 1933, he was named interim mayor of the Saxony town of Aue and moved on to his Döbeln post three months later. A passport photo in the dossier shows an ostensibly decent citizen: the irreproachable civil servant of the commendation. But look closely at the photo and you'll see a small round pin on his lapel. With a swastika.

With the danger of closure looming, Rottenberg did not need to urge the authorities to lobby more actively on his behalf. The authorities in Dresden came up with an emergency plan. They temporarily reset the tobacco quota, whereby the factory could continue operating, but reduce its operation times by half. But Damocles's sword is still hanging over the Werke.

The employment office sounds the alarm, there is a flurry of telephone calls, delegations, letters to the ministries in Berlin. Rottenberg, together with second deputy mayor Walter Nitzsche, appears at the regional customs office to wangle the highest possible tobacco quota.

In 1933, Döbeln had fourteen hundred welfare recipients. If the Deutsche Zigarren-Werke were to shut down, that number would rise by 50 percent, a burden the city could not possibly accommodate, argues Nitzsche. Surely this cannot be the aim of the new law. Rottenberg calculates that under normal operations, the DZW would produce 219,000 cigars per day, or 67 million annually.

Meanwhile, rival cigar manufacturers have begun a campaign against the Deutsche Zigarren-Werke, lobbing all manner of accusations against the factory and its owner-operator, in the hope that the machine ban will lead to a complete shutdown of the DZW. What the accusations were exactly, we do not know, but they were serious enough for Mayor Denecke to come to our grandfather's defence. He wrote to Rottenberg personally on 12 August 1933: "I regret to have been informed that certain parties have launched an attack on you, with obvious motives and by unacceptable means, with the apparent goal of bringing down your firm. If it should come to our attention that an irresponsible smear campaign is waged against you, then we shall see to it that those persons are prevented from doing so." And he asks Rottenberg to name names, should he know who is behind it.

Did he do so? He must have felt that Döbeln's Nazi authorities had his back. Our first reaction to Denecke's letter is disbelief. A Nazi mayor asking a Jewish businessman to finger his enemies? The next moment we burst out laughing at the absurdity of it all. Then comes the worry about what our grandfather was prepared to do to safeguard his factory.

Sandra is not entirely surprised that he considered the possibility of co-operating with local Nazi authorities. He proved it was possible. He, the Jew Rottenberg, commanded respect because he showed respect for the professionalism of those he worked with. For him, the ideological side of the matter was apparently secondary to commercial interests.

Misgivings

Six months after their first visit, Hella returns to Döbeln, this time to dig deeper into the municipal archives and to photograph the documents contained in the eleven dossiers pertaining to the factory and related matters. Up until now, we have used only excerpts from that material for our radio documentary, but for this book we need a more thorough selection. I, Hella, hole up for days on end in that tiny attic room in city hall. Ute Wiesner gives me white gloves with which to handle the archival papers, and a key to the toilet. The day after my arrival, on 11 October 2015, the Dutch broadcaster VPRO airs our radio documentary under the title *Niet bang te krijgen* (*Undauntable*).

Unlike our grandfather, I am "dauntable," and am wary of what I might find in this archive. The documentary elicits a wave of positive emails from friends, acquaintances, and strangers. Their words contain no misgivings, only awe and admiration for a Jew who did not let the Nazis run him out of town. "Your headstrong, bold and tenacious grandfather," writes one. "Despite all the trouble he went through, your granddad made me really happy with his recklessness and courage, persistence and energy," writes another. "What vitality!" While I'm pleased with the reactions, I find it hard to banish my own misgivings. That grandfather from my youth was my role model, my rock. He knew everything, he understood everything. I never gave his principles much thought, but assumed them to be virtuous. Am I now being forced to abandon my childish view of him, let go of the admiration that turned him into a demigod in my eyes? Is this what is giving me pause?

Germany was a tainted country during my postwar upbringing. When I was young, the family's precepts were strict: driving a German car was seen as cozying up to the enemy; buying German appliances was "not done"; you didn't cut through Germany on the way to a vacation destination in Switzerland or Italy. Later, the rules were relaxed, and we took the German autobahn on our way to Switzerland. But those principles still meant that the Germans were not going to earn a cent from us: no stops for food or drink, no overnights along the way, just straight through, eight hundred kilometres from home to Basel in a fully packed French compact car. To be in Germany, to talk with a German, my mother emphasized, always meant wondering *Where were you? What did you do in the war?*

For us, whether one was "right" or "wrong" in the war was a cut-and-dried matter. You were either "right"—that is, you were in the resistance or you helped hide Jews—or you were "wrong," a collaborator or profiteer. We had little time for those in the middle, people who had simply tried to "make do" under the occupation. As a child I could scarcely imagine what it was like to be one of them. Someone who just stumbled through the war or tried to make the best of it—this category had no name, no address.

Granddad read German books and spoke German with German-Jewish friends who had fled, but for him, too, all things German were taboo. The fact that he had lived there among the Nazis, that he had run a business and earned a living, all this went unspoken in the family. How much embarrassment or discomfort was there for Granddad's German venture? Did that Swiss journalist Urs Thaler put his finger on it when he called our grandfather a foreign Jew who saw business opportunities in Nazi Germany?

People on the outside are completely understanding. How could your grandfather have known what was coming? Or: he was just a businessman. Or: these things happen so gradually. How could he undo what he had started? His work was in Germany, he had a family to support. He showed spirit, that grandfather of yours. And so on. And if I say I'm wrestling with it, a friend asks, "But did he do anything *wrong*?"

Labourers to the rescue

Then there is a new attack for Rottenberg to parry. Alongside the rival factories, now the tobacconists have joined the bandwagon in shunning machine-made cigars. The promise not to supply department stores is not enough; they are dead set on quashing the mass-produced cigar once and for all. The retailers' union puts out a call to boycott DZW cigars. To counter the campaign, Rottenberg mobilizes his own workers, or at least "the foreman of the company cell" of the National Socialist Factory Cell Organization (NSBO). Compared to the recently banned socialist and Christian trade unions, the NSBO had once been inconsequential, despite the strident propaganda and intimidation the Nazis used to coerce labourers to join, but now it was Germany's last remaining trade union. All the country's other trade unions were abruptly and violently disbanded the day after National Labour Day on 1 May 1933. In an orchestrated nationwide onslaught, union offices were broken into, union and strike funds blocked and confiscated, and their leaders arrested.

The Nazis set up a new organization, the Deutsche Arbeitsfront (German Labour Front), which did not defend the rights of the labourer versus his employer, but lumped employers, personnel, and labourers into a single nebulous and toothless entity. Strikes were forbidden. The Deutsche Arbeitsfront's primary value was as a propaganda machine. After 2 May 1933, the NSBO was the only union left and was absorbed into the Deutsche Arbeitsfront two years later.

"Most esteemed fellow party member!" begins the indignant letter of 19 August 1933 from the Deutsche Zigarren-Werke's NSBO cell leader to the chairman of the Hamburg retailers' association. The letter points out several fundamental flaws in the boycott's reasoning. Contrary to the association's claims, the DZW has agreed not to market branded cigars. Moreover, the boycott is aimed solely at the DZW, even though there are still forty-six other cigar factories in Germany that use machines. Even a close associate of Robert Ley, leader of the Deutsche Arbeitsfront, has vowed to do everything in his power to protect a firm where "650 German labourers have found bread and work." "It is unacceptable, is it not, for your association to call for a boycott which aims to accomplish exactly the opposite." The association is barking up the wrong tree, he says, because the DZW is a model factory with excellent relations between management and the workforce. "A year ago, in fact—thus, long before the national awakening—the owners proclaimed that there was no such thing as labourers and employees, but *colleagues*. [. . .] No personnel are paid below the standard wage; in fact, a great number of them are paid an above-average wage."

The DZW is not being attacked on ideological grounds, the NSBO foreman believes, but out of opportunism. He wonders whether the association of retailers has been egged on by "one of the leaders of the old *Kampfbund* [of shopkeepers], namely the gentleman who has unleashed a new smear campaign against us and who is the representative of a cigar factory himself." If so, then this is "once again a case where certain parties feign 'idealistic motives.'" As though he has the authority to take the association to task, he closes by requesting confirmation that the boycott of the DZW will be rescinded, and that this be communicated in all the association's periodicals. "I thank you in advance and greet you with Heil Hitler!"

Mit deutschem Gruss

Having pored through the documents in Döbeln's municipal archives, we know that Isay Rottenberg, in his struggle to keep his factory afloat, received support from city authorities, the union cell and, so it seems, the powerful Deutsche Arbeitsfront. His firm, lambasted in Nazi periodicals as a textbook example of a ruthless capitalist concern run by a foreign Jew, is at the same time praised by Nazi administrators and leaders as a model company.

Rottenberg's rivals belong to the cigar sector: producers and tobacconists. They have the ear of the federal government, which on their urging decreed the machine ban, and of government departments at both the national and regional level. It is still unclear to us where the NSDAP stands in all this.

The entire autumn of 1933 is taken up with bickering over the tobacco ration to be allotted the DZW. This takes place in all earnestness and with mind-boggling exactitude. The first official decision is published on 19 September. After pages of calculations and argumentation, the customs office in Meissen fixes the maximum allowable cigars per year at 53,311,953. It then calculates how many cigars the DZW may produce between 1 August 1933 and 31 March 1934: precisely 32,981,311 cigars.

Rottenberg has the right to appeal. And he does so. A week later, he submits his petition, followed by additional appeals in October and November. He now talks of "at least 70 million cigars" per year in order to operate at a profit.

Sometime in August or September, in the heat of the struggle to keep his factory going, there is a change in how Rottenberg signs his correspondence. Until then it was always "respectfully yours" or "your devoted." Now, suddenly, the words "Mit deutschem Gruss" appear at the bottom of his letters.* Was this his idea, or the advice of a well-meaning Nazi? In any case, he appears to have thought "when in Rome . . .," and to close with the German salutation.

Deceptively normal

Within just a few months, the National Socialists wiped out the old institutions and norms. The pre-1933 pluriform society no longer existed; political parties and unions were dissolved; "degenerate" or "anti-German" literature went up in flames, politically unwelcome; Jewish civil servants were fired; and the Nazification of organizations and clubs was nearly complete.

But looking at the behaviour of the government, it appears that while the revolution spread like wildfire throughout the country, the bureaucracy itself was still just sitting at its desk, following its own rules and culture

---

* Written communications during the Nazi period typically closed with the salutation *mit deutschem gruß* ("with German regards").

as it always did, only now taking a different rubber stamp out of the carousel, one where the Weimar eagle had been replaced by the Third Reich swastika.

Döbeln's annual reports look as reliable as previous years, with categories such as social welfare payments, health care, homeless shelters, public health, finances, police, crime, education, and elections. Municipal services were asked to draw up year-end reports so that the annual report could be published promptly at the beginning of January, as always.

What has also remained is the endless initialling of documents, the courtesies, the hierarchy, the decisions made only after thoroughly weighing the legal aspects, and the self-indemnifying. You see it in the correspondence surrounding the machine ban, in the dozens of letters and countless memos about fixing cigar production quotas for the Deutsche Zigarren-Werke. It looks deceptively normal, legal, above board. And the men who executed these decisions probably thought it was just that. Go with the flow, learn a few new terms and symbols, and get on with it.

Formally, the authority to fix the tobacco quota lies with the regional customs office. After receiving an appeal, it is up to the Saxony minister of Finance to make the final judgment. But the decision on Rottenberg's appeal is suddenly held up by the federal Ministry of Finance in Berlin. The minister, or whoever signs the papers on his behalf, is keenly interested in the case and asks Dresden to first clarify its standpoint.

The documents do not reveal who brought the case to Berlin's attention. It wouldn't have been Dr. Kolbe, a top civil servant at Finance. Shortly after Krenter's downfall, he told city leaders he was glad "the plague" was over, the plague that had Germany's tobacco industry in such an uproar, because Krenter's business would have put "hundreds of thousands of labourers" out of work. Might the American embassy have put in a good word for the Deutsche Zigarren-Werke, with its American-made machines? We came across a reference to the visit of a leading American diplomat to the ministry in Berlin. But would this have been enough?

Dresden explains its position to the higher-ups in Berlin: according to paragraph 3.1 of the law, it is not possible to allow the DZW to produce more cigars than in 1932, making Rottenberg's appeal therefore ungrounded. But because Berlin has put such great store by the case, Dresden did its own research and came to the same conclusions as owner-operator Rottenberg: namely, that the factory would only make a profit with a production of seventy million cigars annually. But then the civil servant takes pains to indemnify himself against being the one who encouraged bending the rules, for in the very next sentence he says, "There is, however, no legal means to do so. On these grounds I cannot grant a request to increase the quota, and ask you for a decision." He passes the buck to Berlin.

To the Secret State Police

The ban on the purchase of new machines resulted in the vast majority of Germany's 190 cigar manufacturers shutting down their mechanical operations and applying for financial compensation. By late October, 185 factories had relinquished their machines—sometimes only a couple of them. The owners played it safe and accepted a cash payment rather than risk a forced decrease in production.

The Reichsverband Deutscher Zigarrenhersteller is angry that five factories are still stubbornly using machines, and the government is turning a blind eye. During the negotiations for the law, says the Reichsverband, there was no doubt whatsoever that the minister of Economic Affairs would order a decrease in the production of machine-made cigars and in effect would force the shutdown of the machines. The Reichsverband repeatedly warned its members of this danger, so many companies voluntarily abandoned their machine-assisted production. Of the five remaining factories defying the order, "the primary one is the Deutsche Zigarren-Werke in Döbeln, which has some 120 machines in operation. The chief shareholder and director is the Dutchman Isay Rottenberg. The machines the factory uses were made in America." The association is outraged that a foreigner, using foreign-made machines, is given preferential treatment. This must be halted at once.

It does not stop at an irate letter to the ministry.

To the Secret State Police, Dresden.
During a visit today to the firm of Paul Lungwitz, two gentlemen—Mr. Karl Schaedler of Rotterdam, trader in raw tobacco, and Mr. Hans Biehl of Frankenberg, likewise trader in raw tobacco—told of their visit to the Deutsche Zigarren-Werke in Döbeln. The chief shareholder of this concern, Mr. I. Rottenberg (of non-Aryan origin), came to discuss the results of the elections of 12 November. The following is a literal quote from Herr Rottenberg:
"In case you don't know it already, I am a Jew. As a pariah, however, today I provide work for 650 Christian labourers. In the previous election the National Socialists won, with great effort, 48 percent of the votes. In the most recent election, 92 percent

of the citizens became National Socialists. This folk is just like a whore: offer her a pittance and whoop! She's already lying on the sofa."

As a long-time party member I feel it is my duty to hereby file an official complaint. The above-mentioned witnesses, as well as myself, are prepared to swear under oath at any time to the veracity of the incident reported above.

Heil Hitler.

The man who signed this complaint on 17 November 1933 was Ernst Deter. We have encountered him earlier, when in March 1933 he argued for a machine ban to his NSDAP comrade and Reichstag member Herbert Ender. Deter is on the board of the association of cigar manufacturers and has a factory in Frankenberg, not far from Döbeln. That he carries a grudge against Isay Rottenberg and feels quite at home in the Nazi Party is clear from the start. Only later do we realize how dangerous he was. The Dresden state archive has a postwar dossier on Deter, who was prosecuted for crimes against humanity. In the witness statement, one Mrs. Fischer tells that her husband was beaten to death while in custody on 10 May 1933. She was told her husband, who had been arrested five days earlier, had hanged himself in his cell. But his body, which she was allowed to see, showed signs of severe torture. The culprits were, she believes, three SS men from Frankenberg. She points to Ernst Deter as the man responsible for the murder. He had frequent work-related conflicts with Fischer, an active Social Democrat, member of the Tobacco Workers' Union, and a lay judge in civil court. Deter had, said Mrs. Fischer, threatened her husband with the words, "when the Third Reich has finally been established, you'll be the first one to hang." On 10 May, Deter told the workers in his factory, "Well, Fischer is dead," even before Mrs. Fischer herself had been informed.

Deter's complaint against Rottenberg is filed in the archives of Berlin, Leipzig, and Dresden. Deter sent annotated copies to countless NSDAP offices in the hope that someone would finally take action. As far as the literal contents of the complaint, we do not doubt that our grandfather could have said something of the sort. It's rougher language than we were used to, but not atypical for him to use such a graphic metaphor. Stupid and reckless, of course, to insult the Nazis and the German people like that. But certainly a sign that he felt invulnerable.

8

GERMAN VIRTUE

WE SIT IN OUR CUBBYHOLE IN THE ATTIC OF DÖBELN'S CITY HALL, where municipal archivist Ute Wiesner has installed us with the eleven newly discovered DZW dossiers. If you stand up and look out of the small window, you can see the red rooftops of the old city, and down at street level, the bumpy cobblestone paving. We have already spent hours paging through the letters, memos, and reports about the Deutsche Zigarren-Werke when we stumble across a series of densely typed pages. We go through these again from the beginning, attentively this time. It reads like the script of a play. The cast of characters and their actor is listed at the top. Each paragraph begins with the speaker's name, underlined. Here and there are stage directions such as "stands up," "makes as if to walk off," "interrupts," or "raises his voice."

It must be a verbatim transcription of a meeting. We recognize most of the names: Mayor Denecke; his deputy Nitzsche; corvette captain Saupe; Nazi district leader Groine; factory owner Ernst Deter; Taubert, the lawyer for the Reichsverband Deutscher Zigarrenhersteller; members of the Chamber of Industry and Trade in Chemnitz; and our grandfather, accompanied by his legal adviser Oehmichen, foreman Georg Berns, and two other DZW employees. Place, date, and time of the action: City hall, 22 February 1934, from 10:00 a.m. until 2:45 p.m.

The meeting must have taken place in the very building we are in now. Our grandfather, meeting with Nazi bigwigs and city officials, cigar industry rivals, and the man who reported him to the Gestapo, Ernst Deter. Would we be able to locate the room where they met?

We go two flights down, knock on the door of the mayor's secretary, and explain who we are and what we're after. She confirms that the main rooms and chambers of city hall have kept their original function.

She leads us into the mayor's chambers. No, that table is too small for the group that met in 1934. Is there perhaps a conference room? Of course, she says, and opens the door behind the mayor's desk, revealing a large conference table that stretches the length of the boardroom. The old oak tabletop is clad in green leather; around it are about sixteen old-fashioned wooden armchairs. The walls are wood-panelled, and a pair of double doors leads to the shallow balcony overlooking the square. We let the scene sink in. This must be where they met. The furnishings, the floor, the fixtures—it all seems to be frozen in time. Only the wall decorations have been updated: the swastikas and portrait of the Führer have been replaced by innocent city panoramas and pastoral landscapes. We take our time walking around the table, running our fingers over it, looking out of the windows, overwhelmed by the historical experience.

We are tempted to take the "script" and perform it as if it were a play reading. It might help put us in Granddad's shoes, how he sat here in this conference room under the watchful eye of the Führer, across from men in brown shirts and black boots, and men who were civilian on the outside, Nazi on the inside.

The pressure mounts

The meeting in the conference room behind the mayor's chambers had been called, we later conclude, because the DZW conflict had started to include ever more offices, organs, and authorities, and because the Reichsverband Deutscher Zigarrenhersteller had continued to fan the flames. The number of parties involved is mind-boggling: the federal ministries of Finance, Economic Affairs and Labor; the Saxony departments of Economic Affairs, Finance, and Social Affairs; the Deutsche Arbeitsfront; the Chemnitz Chamber of Industry and Trade; NSDAP chapters in Berlin, Dresden, and Döbeln.

Ernst Deter's complaint to the Gestapo against Rottenberg and the copies he sent to party members could not be ignored. Herbert Ender (the Reichstag MP whom Deter had earlier lobbied for a machine ban in the cigar industry) demanded that the Ministry of Economic Affairs in Dresden take action against the Deutsche Zigarren-Werke. The DZW, he wrote, was flouting the machine ban, and moreover was the successor to Krenter, whose machines had endangered the entire artisanal sector and thus necessitated the ban in the first place.

> The non-German Jew Rottenberg, resident of Döbeln, in no way deserves the right to pursue his dirty business. You will also see in the attached report to the Secret State Police that the man is also clearly a political activist. I beg you to intervene. Heil Hitler.

Ender signed it as the "economic adviser to the NSDAP for the *Gau* Saxony," a function used mainly to defend the interests of small- and mid-sized businesses and, soon thereafter, for designating Jewish businesses for Aryanization.

Dresden's economic affairs department was jolted awake by Ender's letter and approached Döbeln's city managers with probing queries. In a thorough reply dated 11 December 1933, Mayor Denecke did his utmost to present Isay Rottenberg and his factory in favourable terms. The fact that the man is a Jew need not, in this case, be an insurmountable problem.

> We are aware that the director and chief shareholder of the Deutsche Zigarren-Werke Rottenberg is a Jew. Rest assured he will be treated accordingly should he behave in any way contrary to Germany's interests. Until now he has acted with the utmost decency and has always endeavoured to provide work and bread for his workforce.

Our grandfather, Denecke's letter indicates, enjoyed much goodwill with the municipal authorities because he hired not only unschooled persons, but those not entirely fit for work and therefore difficult to employ elsewhere. Mayor Denecke, member of the Nazi Party and the SA, even goes as far as to dismiss the complaint as nonsense: "We must therefore regard the incident described in the complaint, as long as there is no evidence to support it, as rival manoeuvring." In addition, he reminds the ministry that Rottenberg is a Dutch citizen, and warns that prosecuting Rottenberg without an ironclad case could create serious problems between the Dutch government and the German Reich. The Dutch envoy, after all, has already raised the subject more than once with Berlin, and the American embassy has likewise questioned the tobacco rations applied to the Deutsche Zigarren-Werke.

But pressure came not only from Ernst Deter, who had personally filed the complaint, but from the Reichsverband Deutscher Zigarrenhersteller as well. The DZW, it protested, was the only cigar manufacturer to flout the machine ban, and moreover, its owner and director was a Jew (this is the first time the association uses this fact so explicitly in its objections to the factory) and operated American-made machines. The Ministry of Economic Affairs in Berlin advised the other ministries that the Deutsche Zigarren-Werke case was in dire need of a solution.

The ministry was being forced into a corner from two sides: on the one hand, the demand for action by the cigar branch, a prominent Nazi, and a Westphalian leader of the Deutche Arbeitsfront; and on the other, American and Dutch diplomats beseeching the minister to leave the DZW alone.

The Ministry of Finance in Berlin finally broke the stalemate. On 4 January 1934 it stipulated a maximum production for the DZW, accepting Rottenberg's argument that as the previous owner went bankrupt in 1932 and the factory lay dormant for several months, the year 1932 could not be taken as a standard. Further, the ministry took into account that the factory would break even with a monthly production of six million cigars and only beyond that would turn a profit. The ministry considered an annual production of sixty-two million cigars "defensible."

Perhaps the ministry was just trying to placate both parties. With sixty-two million cigars, some five million per month, the business could barely break even, let alone make a profit. But it did probably prevent the factory from closing altogether and thus saved 670 valuable jobs. So the upshot of months-long haggling is that the maximum quota imposed earlier went up by almost ten million.

Counteroffensive

No sooner had the decision been made than there arose a counteroffensive from an unexpected corner. Robert Ley, the boss of the Deutsche Arbeitsfront, made a strong case *for* the use of machines. During a visit to a cigar factory in Westphalia he held a speech in which he lambasts the notion that machines are the enemy of mankind. "Life without machines is unimaginable. Destroy the machine and you revert to the cultural level of a caveman." The labourer should be able to enjoy a cigar or an automobile, too, he said. Marxism had sown despair in the working man. We want to give him hope and confidence. Production must not be reduced, but rather, consumption must increase, for this will create more jobs. The machine plays an essential part in the process.

Ley makes mincemeat of the "mechanoclasts" and of their stance that machines automatically lead to overproduction. Machines, in fact, can insure optimal production for the normal consumption of the German people and will put an end to "war wounds, Versailles, and a fourteen-year Marxist-liberal hybrid economy." He guarantees that the machine ban be applied exclusively to cigar manufacturing, and that all the other branches of industry, including tobacco processing such as cigarettes, will be spared. He stops short of openly calling the machine ban in the cigar branch a mistake.

But our grandfather takes Ley's words to mean just that, and sends a copy of Ley's speech, published in the *Vereingte Tabakzeitungen*, to Mayor Denecke. The tone of his cover letter is triumphant:

> We respectfully ask you to take the time to read this article in full. The leader of the Deutsche Arbeitsfront, Herr Ley, defends the opinions of current influential persons in Germany in regard to the use of machines in general, and specifically to their use in the cigar industry. Opinions we have always stood by and which are based on common sense.

He is happy to present Robert Ley, whose opinions correspond to his own and strengthen the position of the Deutsche Zigarren-Werke, as an authority. Apparently Rottenberg is not bothered that Ley is a long-standing Nazi and, moreover, a fanatic anti-Semite. Ley's tirades in the late 1920s and early 1930s against Jewish department stores and against "the Jewish financial powerhouse" were often characterized by a blind fury. We doubt that Isay Rottenberg was unaware of this.

The definitive establishment of the cigar quota means part-time work is replaced by full shifts and a forty-eight-hour workweek. Good news for the DZW, but it does not signal the end of the conflict. The day after the announcement that the DZW could remain in operation, Ernst Deter submits a new complaint, this one many pages long, to the chief liaison of the NSDAP in Berlin. A copy is sent to the federal Ministry of Finance. But the ministry has had its fill of these shenanigans, and sends Deter a curt reply with a formal explanation of the law. And to put paid to this muckraker once and for all, the ministry asks Dresden to check whether Deter's "remarkably detailed knowledge of the firm's workings" in any way contravenes the laws of tax confidentiality.

Deter, however, pushes on tirelessly with his campaign to bring down the Deutsche Zigarren-Werke. He spreads a new rumour that Rottenberg had bribed the head of the customs office. Other manufacturers, too, chime in that the DZW's special treatment must be stopped. Will it never end?

The defence

Paging through the dossiers, an eight-page typed document with DZW letterhead catches our eye. *Darstellung*, it says at the top, "draft." It is a "brief overview of the creation and evolution of the firm Deutsche Zigarren-Werke." The document is dated 29 January 1934. Our grandfather must have felt the need to defend himself, from start to finish, against the many claims made against him.

He presents the factory's backstory and analyzes Krenter's mistakes. In the wake of Krenter's bankruptcy, he emphasizes in great detail, there were no German candidates to be found. The company's new name—still disputed by the Chemnitz Chamber of Commerce—was deliberate.

> The choice of the name, which took place ca. six months before
> the national awakening, was intended to show publicly that
> the factory would be run on German principles, all the more so
> because the chief shareholder, despite his Dutch citizenship, has
> for decades had an extremely strong bond with Deutschtum.

We also get a glimpse into the firm's hiring policy. It appears that Rottenberg had to defend himself against accusations that he hired opponents of the Nazi regime, and refused jobs to NSDAP followers. He writes that in his hiring policy, "only proven achievements" counted.

> When the slander campaign from without began shortly after
> the factory's opening, crucial posts such as head of bookkeeping,
> the telephone switchboard, foremen, etc. were given to NSDAP
> members.

It is not clear when this all happened. Is he talking about the SA raid in the spring of 1933, and are these the concessions he had to make in order to keep the factory? Put Nazis in key posts so that they could keep tabs on the business?

He paints a rosy picture of the work climate and contractual terms. Working at the DZW is pleasant. When the firm changed hands, the personnel was called together and addressed by a member of the new management, who told them it would succeed only if everyone gave it their all. The speaker disavowed the principle of the class struggle and ended his address (to general applause) with the words "We have no employees and workers, we have only colleagues."

What our grandfather says here fits seamlessly into Nazi ideology: he renounces Marxist class struggle and replaces it with the harmonious ideal of a "community." Curiously, though, the DZW opened in the fall of 1932, when the Nazis were not yet in power. Was their ideology already so mainstream that it influenced the internal workings of the company? Not very likely because their labour union was unpopular, especially in socialist Döbeln. Did Isay Rottenberg make this all up, or predate it to show how virtuously German his management style was?

Wages, he writes, were, where possible, above average and were paid out even during brief periods of shutdown. The canteen always served decent meals. The firm, keen to boost community spirit, encouraged its personnel to join a nonaffliated civic sporting club. Narrative literature was distributed cheaply or for free among the workers to further their intellectual development.

Morale was restored. If a person was caught stealing, he or she was not fired, but rather, appealing to their conscience, was asked to pledge never to do so again. To forestall temptation, a limited number of cigars could be enjoyed at breaktime, free of charge, and workers could purchase more at a discount. Not too big a discount and not too many cigars because of course one had to think of the local shopkeepers. Rottenberg offered rewards for suggestions from the lower-ranked workers to improve production methods.

All these measures contributed to a noticeable improvement in working conditions.

Rottenberg also counters the accusations of upending the market. From the word go he endeavoured to establish friendly relations with the shopkeepers, jettisoning Krenter's mass-marketing approach. No more overblown advertising campaigns, no brand-name cigars, no wholesaling to department stores. No price dumping. Most of his competitors, he says, behave decently; "only a small number of firms persists in spreading ugly rumours about us."

Shutting down the machines in Döbeln would result in fewer rather than more jobs because there are no unemployed cigar hand rollers in the region. In support of this argument, he points to Robert Ley's recent speech. Lastly, he lists the foreign visitors who have been to witness the DZW in action, and their favourable impression of both the factory and Germany itself.

He's paying lip service to the Nazis, that grandfather of ours. He uses the terms *Deutschtum* (Germanness or Germandom) and *national awakening*—in other words, Hitler as the saviour of the fatherland! How did he manage to utter these words, we wonder—for, knowing how he ran his postwar factory in Amsterdam, we assume he dictated this to his secretary, pacing the floor of his office. True, he's not a German himself, we think, but almost. He makes no disctinction between higher-ranked personnel and labourers;

he runs the factory like a community project, the way the Nazis want. His factory, a model company, can serve as an advertisement for Nazi Germany.

He might not have had any choice if he wanted to save his business, but unlike German Jews, he has a Dutch passport and can leave whenever he likes. He is in Döbeln of his own free will. Going home would mean only a loss of capital. German Jews, incidentally, could still leave if they wanted, and many did. Of Germany's 525,000, 37,000 had already fled by 1933. Our grandfather, however, continued working and earning a living under the Nazi regime.

Confrontation

So there he is, in the city hall conference room, three weeks after setting his factory's history and business model to paper. It is Thursday, 22 February 1934. Around the large oak table sit thirteen men and Miss Ringler, the DZW stenographer our grandfather brought with him—he might need to recall later what was said, and by whom.

After all the letters, memos, lobbying, rumours, complaints, and reports, the adversaries are finally sitting face to face. Ernst Deter, the Nazi factory owner who had complained to the Gestapo and had levelled charge upon charge, is now sitting at the same table as Isay Rottenberg. Since the literal transcript of the meeting survives, we have front-row seats, as it were, and can watch our grandfather in action.

Mayor Denecke calls the meeting to order. It has been organized at the request of the economic adviser to the NSDAP's Saxony district, Herbert Ender—the one who only recently urged the government to prevent "the non-German Jew Rottenberg" from pursuing "his dirty business." The goal, Denecke says, is to allow the Reichsverband der Deutschen Zigarrenhersteller (RDZ) to negotiate directly with the Deutsche Zigarren-Werke in converting its operations from machine- to handwork.

Tensions rise right from the start when Taubert, lawyer for the RDZ, says that no matter what the outcome, he will remain "cocked and loaded" to put Rottenberg's machines out of commission. Of the previously 190 companies in Germany with machines, there are just four left. Three of these operate just a single machine. Only the DZW is disrupting the market with its mechanized assembly line.

Captain Saupe, as he is consistently addressed—factory owner and now, following his brief stint as acting mayor, city council chairman and board member of the Chamber of Commerce—wonders out loud if there is any point negotiating like this. "We are here to determine whether technically sound arguments can be exchanged between the producers of handmade and machine-made cigars that will lead to a compromise. Otherwise this is a waste of time."

This opens the door for a less belligerent, more businesslike tone. Rottenberg passes around a document summarizing his arguments, explaining:

> We shall demonstrate that although the will to do so is by all means there, converting to handwork is, in our case, impossible. Last year, when the law was passed, we considered this issue at length, made calculations, and came to the conclusion that transitioning was not feasible. Herr Gasch, present here, took great pains to find fifteen people within the company with any proficiency at all in hand rolling cigars. Gasch was completely dissatisfied with their work.

He emphasizes that "our firm cannot be compared to any other in Germany." [...] "If 80 percent of the workforce is already hand rolling, it is naturally easier to transition than in our case, where there is no handwork whatsoever." Curtly, as one in uniform does, Nazi district leader Groine concurs. "That is evident and needs no explanation."

Meanwhile, Taubert has read through Rottenberg's arguments, and concludes there is no point in negotiating any further. "Waste of time," he says and gets up to leave. Saupe intervenes again, reminding him of the NSDAP district leadership's demand for results. He nearly reaches for the telephone to call Dresden; Taubert backs down and the meeting continues.

Rottenberg suggests going through his calculations one by one, and answering any queries that may arise. First they discuss the availability of trained artisans, who could be put to work should the Deutsche Zigarren-Werke transition to hand rolling. He has consulted all the employment agencies in the region, coming up with very few unemployed artisans. He sums up the results: in Döbeln there are twenty female and three male cigar rollers available. Further afield there are another twelve female and twelve male artisans who might be recruited. If more were needed, they would have to be brought in from outside Saxony.

"Perhaps Herr Deter could say whether my information is correct in the case of Frankenberg (where Deter's factory is located) and its environs." Deter is forced to admit that "there are no unemployed cigar rollers in the Frankenberg area." Rottenberg continues: "I would like to pause at each figure and give Herr Deter, who, after all, is a professional cigar manufacturer himself, the opportunity to comment." "Is this number correct?" he asks each time, or, "Is this estimate too high, or too low?" Should Deter occasionally disagree with the statistic, Rottenberg defers to Deter's figures. Calm, systematic, and well-prepared with his figures as well as his arguments, Rottenberg forces Deter into a corner. Together they come to the conclusion that transitioning the DZW away from machine-made cigars would cost at least 138,000 reichsmarks, in addition to the outstanding sum owed for the machines themselves. In total, a loss of 700,000 reichsmarks, which would mean the factory's ruin.

Rottenberg would switch if he *could*; he would like nothing more than to do so, "if only not to be curtailed in production and most of all, not to be constantly in the [competition's] crosshairs." But alas, as Deter too must now see, it is simply not possible.

Deter does not see. If all those other factories could shut down their machines, then so can the DZW. And besides, if the DZW should have to close its doors, then sixty million cigars would be produced by hand elsewhere, which would mean jobs for a good thousand labourers. Rottenberg counters that if existing companies were to take over the production, this would not add any new jobs.

Nazi district leader Groine, who until now has kept silent, seconds Rottenberg's argument with the authority of his function and SA uniform: "I can confirm that if a crisis forces a company to shut down, then no new one will be established to take its place. The resulting unemployment will only create more unemployed. It goes without saying that the lost production would be absorbed by other companies."

Saupe and Denecke agree. In his defence of Rottenberg, Groine then brings out the heavy artillery: Saxony's most powerful Nazi. "I am here as district leader on behalf of Reich Governor Mutschmann. He has instructed us to see to it that more jobs are created. It is my duty, in the interest of employment goals, to strive to find a way not to lay off a single worker."

Alfred Schneider, a member of Rottenberg's delegation, endorses Groine's argument by repeating that to transition to handwork would mean the loss of 670 jobs. He trumpets the harmonious work environment at the DZW, which should be an example to other businesses. "Our priority is to keep *this* business operating because we cannot imagine a more positive partnership. The management, personnel, and labourers enjoy the most agreeable relationship imaginable."

Once all the arguments have been exhausted, only Taubert and his colleague Apitzsch of the Chamber of Industry and Trade in Chemnitz are still on Deter's side. Apitzsch refuses to be taken in by all those figures and calculations and holds his ground.

It is impossible to speculate what will happen if the DZW's machines are shut down. It has never been tried! Pity that the opposing party had not provided their figures earlier. Besides, you can prove anything with figures. In any case, I am not convinced that the DZW cannot make the switch.

The reason for his defiance becomes evident later, when he tells the meeting that the members of the Chamber of Commerce demand action. "There is outrage within the German cigar industry that one firm has still not shut down its machines."

Deter dismisses the general conclusions of those present, and announces that this week or the next he will travel to Berlin to see to lowering the DZW's tobacco rations. But he also feels obliged to defend his position:

> You cannot imagine the kind of personal attacks we have had to endure because of our supposed inaction regarding this case. We at the Bond [the Association of German Cigar Manufacturers] are accused of protecting Herr Rottenberg. The DZW's products do not interest me in the least. It has nothing to do with a rival manoeuvre in order to bring down the DZW.

It is not much of an argument. District leader Groine demands that Deter desist at once, accept that transitioning to hand rolling is out of the question, and inform his members accordingly. As far as the accusations against Deter himself are concerned, he must take no notice because Groine, too, "has been accused often enough of protecting Rottenberg." The elephant in the room—the word *Jew*—has not been uttered.

For his part, Rottenberg hastens to say that today "is in fact the first time since I have been in Döbeln that I have had the opportunity to see Herr District Leader Groine in person."

Dr. Apitzsch, of the Chamber of Commerce, asks Rottenberg for a concise and clear calculation of projected losses, should the operation have to switch to handwork. On the basis of these figures, the Chamber of Commerce will formulate its standpoint. Then Saupe addresses Deter: "I would ask Herr Deter not to travel to Berlin, but to await the Chamber of Commerce's next step." "All right, you have my word," Deter capitulates.

They met for nearly five hours. Our grandfather can be satisfied. Not only the city administrators, but the Nazi honchos as well, see job creation as the highest priority. Quelling anger in the cigar industry, appeasing the shopkeepers, chasing off a Jewish entrepreneur—these are all minor issues compared to the greater goal of providing jobs for Döbeln's workforce.

9

ARBEIT UND BROT*

WHEN THE NAZIS CAME TO POWER, UNEMPLOYMENT STOOD AT SIX million, one-third of the working-age population. Jettisoning democracy was one thing, but they had to legitimize their regime. They did so with the promise of work, income, and public order.

So in 1933, they at once began printing money in order to finance the infrastructure necessary to get people back to work, and at the same time to rebuild Germany's armed forces. For ideological (but mostly practical) reasons, the Nazis encouraged women to leave their jobs and return to homemaking. A woman who married would receive a state-sponsored "dowry" provided she gave up her job in favour of an unemployed man. They also tried to force employers to sack younger workers and then rehire them in so-called "voluntary (i.e., unpaid) employment." Their salaried jobs could then be taken over by family men.

On the municipal level, including in Döbeln, the Nazis also encouraged, and often coerced with the threat of loss of welfare benefits, unemployed workers to join the nation's Volunteer Labour Service, where they were put to work on public land and construction projects.

---

* "Work and Bread" was one of the many simple slogans used by the Nazis as propaganda for its ideology. The Nazi Party portrayed itself as the only political party capable of creating jobs and putting food on German tables.

Shortening the workweek was another device for combatting unemployment. Companies that had to curtail their output because of the Depression and lack of materials were not allowed to lay off employees. Instead, they were to cut their hours, often to as little as half-time. We see the Deutsche Zigarren-Werke do this in the second half of 1933 as well, since the factory—in this case, because of the machine ban—had to decrease production. The effect of these measures was dramatic: by the fall of 1933, the ranks of the unemployed had shrunk by some two million.

However, the Nazis still worried about the mood among labourers. This group accounted for nearly half the country's workforce, and Hitler's regime needed their support.

In the once-socialist city of Döbeln, things were kept under close watch. More than half the workforce were labourers and worked for local industries. In October 1933, deputy mayor Nitzsche discussed the matter with the director of the employment office, thoroughly analyzing the figures and statistics. At that point, Döbeln had 2,273 unemployed, of whom more than 1,500 received welfare assistance. Nitzsche noted that the industrial firms in the city were employed to capacity and that this would not change substantially in the near future. But in the countryside there was a shortage of some 300 agricultural labourers. Say we were to send the women who had left the rural areas to work in Döbeln's factories back to the farms, Nitzsche postulated. The employment office director expanded on this idea, noting that two-thirds of the 600 working women were married, and might be nudged into quitting their jobs, which could be filled by unemployed men.

Most of Döbeln's businesses had already agreed to accept only local job seekers. Only two firms, which were not members of the local industry association, had not yet committed to doing so. One of these was the Deutsche Zigarren-Werke. Isay Rottenberg was immediately summoned to Nitzsche's office. He made two promises: unemployed Döbelners will receive preference in hiring, and out-of-towners will be the first to be laid off.

Crusade against unemployment

On 21 March 1934, against the backdrop of the construction of a new stretch of *Autobahn* and a throng of ten thousand supporters, Hitler calls for a new "work offensive." Work across the country stops for the duration of the Führer's speech. "We must pursue the crusade against unemployment this year with even greater fanaticism and with yet more determination than before. To arms!"

Döbeln follows these words like military orders. The very next day, the city administration calls a meeting of Nazi leaders and the directors of the six largest factories in the city, including Fritz Saupe, manufacturer of industrial filters, and Isay Rottenberg. Hermann Groine, the Nazi district leader, complains that too few young men have joined the Volunteer Labour Service and asks the factory directors to draw up a list of the men twenty-five and under in their employ. They are also to look into which women and girls in their firm were originally from rural areas. A few factories "guilty" of hiring workers from outside Döbeln are "named and shamed." The DZW is one of them.

The campaign is energetically launched in the newspapers and via the employment agencies. "Girls! German agriculture needs you! You are aware of the great value the Führer places on agriculture, and how crucial it is for Germany's revival!" Or do the girls want German farmers to "resort to bringing in foreign labourers to take our German money abroad with them"? Not only do the advertisments appeal to their patriotism, but they offer the promise of speedy placement on a farm and of sisterhood under the wing of the Bund Deutscher Mädel (the League of German Girls, the female branch of Hitler Youth).

The authorities also used threats to try to staunch the farm-to-town exodus. Employers in Döbeln's building and stone industry were warned that "all the agencies will keep an eye out for the hiring of farm labourers." If businesses needed masons or carpenters, they were to take on young, unschooled, and unemployed Döbelners and train them. Disobey, and "appropriate measures" would be taken.

The appeals and threats, however, are not enough. Businesses are in a strong position. The local chapter of the Verband Sächsischer Industieller reports that Döbeln businesses employed, in total, 311 young men under twenty-five, but that only fifty of these at most could be replaced by unemployed twenty-five-plus men without endangering production. Firms give the city a list of names of women and girls who hailed from the provinces. There are fewer than twenty, of which four work at the DZW.

A few are let go, but instead of sheepishly reporting to the employment office, they go to the Deutsche Arbeitsfront for legal assistance. Under no circumstances do they want to return to the farms, which are even more impoverished than the towns. Everyone, employers and labourers alike, has invented an excuse. One might expect that the authorities would be more forceful in carrying out their orders, but they judge the appeals one by one, with almost juridical precision.

"My parents are innkeepers in Rittmitz," one Hildegard Heinrich writes to the city. "After leaving school I helped with the housekeeping and at the inn. At the age of seventeen I went to Döbeln to work at Köberlin [a silverware manufacturer], where I have been employed ever since. I have never worked on a farm; I am more an industrial labourer. Thus it is not a matter of my having left farming." Hildegard argues further that an unemployed welfare recipient must first be trained to replace her, and ends with a loyal "Heil Hitler!"

On 15 May, two months after the declaration of the second "work offensive," deputy mayor Nitzsche throws in the towel. He tells the local party and employment campaign leaders that the city has done its best these past weeks and months to recruit young men for voluntary labour and to convince girls to return to the farms. "The bottom line is that unfortunately, for a wide variety of reasons, the campaign has not had its desired effect. Therefore the municipal authority sees no reason at this time to pursue further measures."

Combatting unemployment at the municipal level is an uphill battle. No additional funds have been made available for the second work offensive, and the subsidy for local work programs is reduced. Every *pfennig* goes to nationally needed infrastructure and—secretly—to the arms industry.

Discontent

Between March and September 1934, the German economy found itself in deep trouble. The downward spiral of shrinking export, currency shortage for imports, and a scarcity of raw materials was felt throughout the country. Civil industry had difficulty keeping afloat, and small businesses were struggling and angry that measures promised to rein in department stores and fixed-price outlets had not materialized. For labourers, life was harsh.

The Gestapo issued weekly reports on the general mood. "The workers complain of inadequate protection against layoffs, of substandard wages, excessive rent, and the high cost of daily necessities. Nothing has changed regarding mass layoffs, two-income households, and poor hygiene in the factories. Attendance at personnel gatherings has dropped considerably," the Saxony Gestapo reported to the Ministry of Economic Affairs in Dresden. There was a shortage of margarine, and the price of bread had gone up. "The *Gau* is rife with speculation concerning the economy."

Rumours of a new depression, price hikes, hoarding, and Reichs ministers who have fallen out of favour were clear indications that something was amiss.

The Gestapo asked the police to report on the exact nature of the rumours, who was spreading them, and from which political faction they originated. The Döbeln police "can ascertain that one such rumour monger is a Jewish textile merchant, who claimed to live in Leipzig and once ran a large-scale business there, but had to sell it in the aftermath of the national awakening and the hostilities against the Jewish race, so that he is now relegated to the straitened life of a market hawker."

Reports from later that summer do not hide the fact that the jubilance surrounding the national awakening was beginning to wane. "The mood of the labourers is not as it was directly after [the Nazis] came to power. The most common reason for discontent are poor wages and the high cost of living. Shortened working hours, and thus lower income, render a large portion of the community unable to make ends meet."

Persistent unemployment, slave wages for those who have work at all, the high cost of food, shortages of milk and butter, and resentment of Nazi bigwigs who flaunt their privilege—it is a dangerous mix. The Gestapo reports that workers "continue to draw attention to the fact that few party leaders stick up for the labourers. Discontent is particularly high regarding the Deutsche Arbeitsfront." And yet, Hitler remains widely popular. This is a recurring theme in the weekly and monthly Gestapo reports: "Workers assure us that they still stand completely behind the Führer, as he understands the needs and worries of poor people."

So it is not surprising that Döbeln's municipal and party leadership were more interested in keeping the DZW open than with following anti-Semitic ideology and placating the cigar industry.

Back at the negotiating table

In April 1934, two months after the meeting at Döbeln city hall that was supposed to have resolved the situation, the flood of correspondence against the Deutsche Zigarren-Werke begins anew. Cigar makers throughout Germany protest to the authorities in Dresden, Berlin, and Döbeln that the DZW is the only machine-operated cigar factory in all of Germany, and is allowed a far too high production quota. It is the same old song. Why is Rottenberg being given special treatment? demands the rival cigar manufacturer Wieprecht & Hauschild, from the city of Gera. "No other firm can demand or expect this, let alone one that works with American cigar machines and has a foreign Jew as its director, but still calls itself a 'German' cigar factory."

We come across the DZW in one of the Saxony Gestapo reports (of which only about ten from the year 1934 survive). "There is widespread resentment within the cigar industry that the Jewish cigar manufacturer Salomon Krenter, at present the Deutsche Zigarren-Werke in Döbeln, received approval for the increase of the quota for machine-made cigars, from fifty-one million to sixty million per year." The Gestapo erred on the low side: the DZW may produce *sixty-two* million, but the part about the resentment is accurate.

While the cigar manufacturers persist with their campaign, the Chemnitz Chamber of Commerce (which had earlier objected to the name Deutsche Zigarren-Werke) has changed its tune. A month after the meeting at city hall, the Chamber of Commerce admits that the city authorities and the NSDAP were right: the DZW cannot possibly be called a market disrupter because it accounts for just 1 percent of the total cigar production in Germany. "We are obliged to withdraw our proposal to lower production quotas and force a partial shutdown, and only advise against raising the allowed quota." The Chamber requests that this about-face be treated with confidentiality, so as not to upset its relations with its own members.

For Mayor Denecke, enough is enough. Addressing those cigar makers who have once again lodged a collective protest to all and sundry, he is blunt: "The Reichs Ministry of Economic Affairs has, to the best of our knowledge, dismissed the call to take any action against the Deutsche Zigarren-Werke. We implore you to accept this decision and not, through continued attacks that present nothing new, to endanger economic harmony."

Denecke resolutely refutes the suggestion that the city has given the DZW special treatment just because the buildings bring in rent income. "Our priority is safeguarding the jobs of 670 employees."

The Saxony cigar manufacturers refuse to give in. The Chamber of Commerce, faced with a flood of angry letters, does not waver either. Another investigation into supposed price dumping by the DZW brought nothing untoward to light, so as far as they are concerned, the case is closed.

The parties hope a new meeting will put an end to this tug-of-war once and for all. It has been going on for a year now. The date is Friday, 20 July 1934; the venue is the Döbeln city hall conference room; the time, 2:30 p.m. The transcript of this meeting is eighteen pages long. Mayor Denecke is there, as is Saupe, another NSDAP economic adviser, and now three representatives from the Chamber of Industry and Trade. NSDAP district leader Groine, having been transferred, has been replaced by Rudolf Behr. The most important man present (he is listed first on the transcript), Behr is there to see to it that the meeting proceeds according to the party's wishes. Not Ernst Deter, but another manufacturer on behalf of the rival firms, is present, as well as Emil Stockman, a cigar maker from Döbeln who had been a vocal opponent of Krenter. Rottenberg has brought with him his legal adviser, Arndt Oehmichen, the foreman Georg Berns, and one other employee. The DZW's Miss Hucek is the stenographer.

The plan, says Halber, vice-chairman of the Chamber, is that those present inspect the factory together and that the cigar makers jointly issue a concrete proposal as to "which machines can be shut down, and how this factory can, immediately or gradually, transition" to handwork.

Before that, Emil Stockmann takes the floor and launches into a denunciation of the Deutsche Zigarren-Werke's unfair advantage. The firm can sell its cigars more cheaply, he claims, presenting a series of figures, so a normal factory is no match for it. In a dramatic speech, he outlines the fatal role of DZW and its predecessor Krenter. "The moment Krenter Werke opened," says Stockmann, "marked the death knell for the cigar industry."

> It was the beginning of a life-or-death struggle. Small and mid-sized businesses went belly-up. According to my information, in six years' time, five thousand businesses, including small enter-prises, have failed, each of them the victim of Krenter Werke. These businesses would no doubt still exist if all those machines had not been brought to Germany.

Stockmann wistfully recalls the old days. Four decades ago, he says, "Döbeln had thirty-five cigar factories. Young people got a job and learned the art of cigar making." The rise of the metal industry meant workers left the cigar factories because "metal" was better paid. But this could be reversed, he believes. With so many unemployed now, the city would do well to retrain them as cigar rollers. "Then Döbeln could again become the flourishing cigar town it once was." No one comments on Emil Stockmann's nostalgic musings. He then makes suggestions on how the DZW could increase its personnel numbers, and questions the owner about the machines and how they were paid for.

Isay Rottenberg will have none of it. He snaps back that Stockmann need not tell him how to run his business. "Herr Stockmann, that is no concern of yours. I don't ask, do I, what they cook for you at home?"

Shutting down the machines will only exacerbate unemployment, he argues.

> It is only in your fantasy that this will result in an increase in jobs. Say your suggestion were to be followed: the factory will go bankrupt and 670 people will be out of work. I need not sketch these unemployed folks' anger. [. . .] What is more important? That 670 more people have work, or that the 72,000 labourers in our sector each work a few minutes longer? I believe that the Reichs government is inclined toward the former.

These words are endorsed by nearly everyone present. Encouraged by this, Rottenberg adds, "Ruining a business simply because you feel like it, Mr.

Stockmann, is insane. It is nothing more than ill will." He then pulls out all the stops. As a foreigner he has done more for the city and the unemployed than the German Stockmann, who had had the chance to take over Krenter Werke, but had made "excessive" demands.

> When Krenter closed its doors two years ago, a friend came to me and kindled my interest in the firm. After extensive negotiations with federal tax officials, with the city, with the Americans, and so forth, I dared to take the step of establishing this new enterprise. It was a huge risk, one that no one else had the courage to undertake. I happen to know that the city also made Herr Stockmann an offer so the employees of Krenter Werke could get back to work. However, the conditions Herr Stockmann demanded of the city were excessive. I will not dredge them up again here. Another firm in Saxony wanted to assume operation of the factory, providing the city subsidize it to the tune of a million reichsmarks. I, on the other hand, did not ask for a single [mark of] subsidy from the city. While many were transferring their money out of the country, I brought my money from abroad to Germany and, slowly but surely, built up the company. I have done much. For two years I have provided approximately 670 people with work. That fact alone should evoke gratitude from anyone who cares about the unemployed. Until today, our company has not earned a pfennig [of profit]; on the contrary, we struggle to keep the factory running. This is not self-serving, but what you are doing, Herr Stockmann: that is self-serving. It is no more than a rival's jealousy. I am aware of a statement made by Herr Stockmann, in which he literally said: "I will not rest until that business has been destroyed."

Stokmann takes umbrage at this last statement and demands to know who told Rottenberg. But Saupe comes to Rottenberg's aid, recalling that the case against the DZW has been fought "by unfair means and by false assumptions." The regional Nazi leadership has had its fill of this business, Saupe says, and wants the dispute to be put to rest.

Assured of victory and buttressed by the comments of the others, Rottenberg asks for a guarantee of an end to the harassment and hostilities.

> I ask you now, once and for all, gentlemen, to put our company under your protection, in case tomorrow some other dissatisfied party comes along. Nearly all of those present here are tired of

having to continually attend to this issue in this way, and I myself am suffering from it. It is truly time for this nonsense to stop.

Just before that, Rottenberg poured out his heart in a monologue:

> Our firm has endured the most vicious of onslaughts. I do not believe it will keep up. However, I will certainly no longer defend our position but shall go on the offensive, for the situation is deteriorating. Lies and untruths are being used, and I can prove it. After the failed attempt to bring down the factory, I myself became the target. I was slandered to the Gestapo and other authorities. The public prosecutor in Freiberg debunked the case. This is how far some people are prepared to go. I am personally not a player in all this. Forget me, the Jew Rottenberg. When you obsess over me, you forget 670 of your own people. I can leave town tomorrow if I have to, but I do not think this is the answer. Look at the company itself. Is it not a shame to desire to bring down a business like this? If you truly wish to make good on the so often misused expression "society's interests go before self-interest" then you will be doing your own countrymen a great disservice if you force the factory to shut down its machines. I say this to you personally!

So our grandfather knew of Ernst Deter's complaint to the Gestapo! Apparently the Gestapo sent it on to the Justice Department, where the case was dismissed as irrelevant or lacking legal substance. How it all played out, or who came to his aid, we were unable to discover. Perhaps it was Mayor Denecke, who saw the whole affair as a spiteful trick played by a jealous business rival.

The complaint did not intimidate our grandfather; on the contrary, it only reinforced his belief that the Nazis needed him. People could gossip, insinuate, and inform on him all they liked, but it did not matter. He had protection.

He, a Jew, sat across the table from rivals and Nazi authorities and dared to upbraid them for not reckoning with their "own compatriots." You could hardly call it anything less than brazen or provocative—at home we'd have called it *chutzpah*. He is the only one in the room who says the word *Jew* out loud; the others would rather bite off their tongue than mention his "race" in his presence. At the same time he brings to light a taboo: that if it's to their benefit, even a diehard Nazi will co-operate with a Jew. And vice versa.

Winter relief

The first time we visited Döbeln, all we knew was that our grandfather ran a cigar factory and that he had been imprisoned and the business confiscated. Now we see how he sat down at the table with the Nazis and enlisted their aid in fending off his rivals.

We have kept contact with the historian Christian Kurzweg. One day he sent us an email with a report that the owner of the Deutsche Zigarren-Werke had donated to "winter relief" between November 1934 and March 1935. In other words, he had contributed to Hitler's fund for needy Germans. Kurzweg had found it in the magazine of *Sopade*, the exile organization of the German Social Democrats in Prague. According to the 1935 article, the factory did well after the Ministry of Economic Affairs had provided a letter of recommendation.

The article also reports the amount of 15,000 reichsmarks per month, which approximates the total salaries Rottenberg paid his employees in a week. So not just a symbolic sum, but a significant contribution to the Nazi regime's welfare program. Kurzweg warns us to take it with a grain of salt: "The reports from Germany are based on news that reached the exiled SPD organization in Prague. Not everything has to be entirely accurate, but it could be basically correct."

The following morning, I, Hella wake up with a stomachache. What can of worms have we opened? Do we want to know all this? Dark scenarios race through her mind.

Maybe it's not true. Kurzweg said it doesn't *have* to be. Can we leave this part out, or gloss it over as a minor detail? I find myself looking for a way to keep Granddad's—and our—name clean. As a journalist, I have always had a sharp eye for the facts. If I were to sweep things under the rug just because they happen to be personally inconvenient, then I'm not worth my salt as a journalist. May as well just drop the whole project. No, can't do that either—it would be the coward's way out.

I look up *Winterhilfe* in the *Lexicon Nationalsozialismus*: assistance to "truly needy fellow Germans." Further along it says: "Only racially worthy, genetically healthy families were supported by the National Socialist welfare system."

I confess to Sandra that same day that I'm upset and at a loss as to what to do. Sandra's response is cool and collected. Everything our grandfather did was a trade-off. "We'll get to the bottom of it," she says.

Fine, of course, that Sandra reacts like this. I calm down a bit and in rereading the winter relief piece I see that Granddad also is said to have hired political opponents of the Nazis, "Marxists." But a few days later, that feeling in the pit of my stomach returns when I go back through the

"Darstellung" in which he defends the factory, and see words and terms that cut me to the quick.

Do I want to expose my grandfather to the cold eyes of the outside world? Maybe those filthy Nazis pushed him into a corner, little by little. The "Darstellung" was written, after all, following the formal complaint against him. But how far did he go?

When we first went to Döbeln, I had installed an attractive, youthful picture of him on my cell phone as wallpaper. I have trouble looking at it now with pleasure or pride. But I don't remove it.

TOP: Isay Rottenberg, 1920s. BOTTOM: Isay (far left, back row) with his siblings and Abraham Ptasznik (seated, at left). Year unknown.

Isay (standing, with hat) with his sisters. Year unknown.

The Ptasznik Bros. firm at a trade show in Brussels, 1906. Seated at rear: Abraham Ptasznik.

Prosperous times, ca. 1927. From left to right: Lena, Edwin, unknown woman, unknown man, Alfred, Tini.

Abraham and Teofile Ptasznik's grandchildren, 1934. Top row, from left: Bob and Hans Franken, Alfred Rottenberg, Karel Citroen, Edwin Rottenberg. Front row, from left: Theo Franken, Lonny and Bea Ptasznik, Dé Granaat, Tini Rottenberg, Thea Citroen.

Teofile and Abraham Ptasznik, at home on the Hacquartstraat, Amsterdam, after the outbreak of war. On the buffet is a photograph of all the grandchildren.

TOP: The cigar factory in Döbeln, ca. 1931. CENTRE: The cigar factory in operation. BOTTOM: Döbeln train station.

TOP: Döbeln, city centre with city hall, 1933 or 1934. BOTTOM: Bulgaria advertisement in Dresden, 1932.

TOP (left) Deutsche Zigarren-Werke dossier from the municipal archives; (right) The Nazi banner hangs for the first time from Döbeln's city hall tower, 9 March 1933. Handwritten caption: "On the day of the national revolution." BOTTOM: Indian sticker album with Krenter logo.

Theodor Kunzemann

Hermann Groine

Rudolf Behr

Herbert Denecke

Frtiz Saupe   Otto Röher

The conference room in Döbeln city hall.

TOP: Antisemitic witch-hunt against Hugo Totschek in Der Stürmer. BOTTOM: Call to boycott Jewish businesses in the Döbeln Anzeiger, 31 March 1933.

TOP: Heimat festival in Döbeln, 1935. BOTTOM: The gymnastics club in the parade; NSDAP celebrates May Day in Döbeln on the square in front of city hall.

TOP: Max, Ruth, and Karl Glasberg with their aunt in Döbeln. BOTTOM: Kurt Arnhold, in a portrait by Otto Dix, 1927.

TOP: Johan Steenbergen and his wife Elisabeth Nussbaum at home in Dresden, 1930s (Steenbergen Foundation). BOTTOM: Isay Rottenberg on vacation with his childen, ca. 1936. In Germany? Standing, from left: Edwin, Alfred, unknown man; Seated: unknown man, Isay, unknown woman, Tini (Private collection of the Rottenberg and Jacobs families).

TOP AND CENTRE:
Lena and Isay in Vevey,
Switzerland, 1943. On
the mantlepiece are
photos of Abraham
and Teofile Ptasznik.
BOTTOM: Edwin and
Alfred Rottenberg as
officers with the British
Marines, London 1944.

TOP: (left) The cousins Karel Citroen, Alfred Rottenberg and Bob Franken, Perpignan 1942; (right) Isay in the drinking straw factory, 1959. BOTTOM: Rottenberg & Sons company outing, ca. 1950. From left to right: Alfred, Isay, Edwin.

TOP: Isay celebrates his seventieth birthday with the grandchildren, 1959. BOTTOM: Isay on his eightieth birthday with his grandchildren, 1969. Above, next to Isay: Hella and Sandra; middle row: Fedia, Sacha, Felix, Menno; bottom step: Michael.

10

THE **WORKERS REINED IN**

ON THE SCHIESSWIESE IS A SQUARE STAGE, ABOVE WHICH HANG three banners with swastikas. The photo in the *Döbelner Anzeiger* is just clear enough to make out the soldiers on and around the podium holding iron pikes bearing the Imperial Eagle and swastika. The Schiesswiese, the firing range that has long served the city's garrison, is now often put to use for Nazi mass rallies.

On Tuesday, 31 July 1934, the Schiesswiese is the venue for "the largest and most impressive mass rally Döbeln has ever seen." Some fifty thousand labourers from Döbeln and its surroundings throng—or, more likely, have been dragooned—to a public appearance by Robert Ley, chairman of the Deutsche Arbeitsfront. The Front has dissolved the former trade unions and now has installed its own representatives in enterprises to give the workers the impression of social solidarity and at the same time to keep an eye on their politics.

The middle pike sports the symbol of the Deutsche Arbeitsfront: a cog wheel with a swastika in the centre. Local Nazi bigwigs, with whom Isay Rottenberg has just met to discuss continued production and had shown around his factory, have positioned themselves alongside Ley. Among them is twenty-nine-year-old Rudolf Behr, the recently named NSDAP district leader. He is your prototype Nazi, with a military buzzcut and a brazen "I dare you" look. Next to him is his predecessor, Hermann Groine, who had been transferred three months earlier to a nearby town, and next to him, Mayor Herbert Denecke.

The Gestapo reports that the Deutsche Arbeitsfront is unpopular among the workers. There is dissent regarding membership fees. Workers even walk off, says the Gestapo, when one of Robert Ley's overblown speeches is read out at a factory.

So there's Ley, facing a crowd of workers who distrust and despise him. Ley was the one who dissolved their unions and took away their right to strike. Do they expect Ley, with his potbelly, his lust for alcohol, and his extravagant lifestyle, to stick up for them? Are they supposed to trust and obey the man who has wangled well-paid jobs for his Nazi cronies in the Arbeitsfront?

The next day the newspaper prints, more or less verbatim, Ley's entire speech, in which he makes clear his determination to rein in the workers. At first it has the tone of a church service. He recalls how profoundly Germany was humiliated by the Versailles "treaty of disgrace." Germans felt that the blood of their sons was spilled for nothing. But then, suddenly, someone dared to say, "*Jawohl*, I believe in Germany!" Ley: "It is an unimaginable miracle how this man arose from the *volk* and preached, and continued to preach, doggedly and determined: 'People, turn back, think and be wise!'" Everyday people, not career politicians, joined the movement, he tells his listeners. The National Socialists fight "for faith in Germany, in you!"

The salvation that Nazism promises to bring workers is not without pain. No one understands this better than Ley himself, he says—how painful it was for labourers to see their lovingly nurtured unions be dismantled a year earlier. His empathy is deep: "It was your second home because the nation had forsaken you. You felt betrayed and thought we had emerged as the puppets of capitalism. But we had no other choice, we could no longer tolerate this bastion of Marxism, we had to destroy it, so that you workers would be liberated."

He tells the crowd that the Deutsche Arbeitsfront, as an alternative for trade unions, builds a community of labourers, employees, and entrepreneurs; it promotes harmony instead of class struggle. Marxists—a blanket Nazi term for Communists and Social Democrats—yes, even Marxists are welcome. But (here Ley begins his attack) there is no place in Germany for those who turn their back on National Socialism. "The Führer sees everything as fostering [for the cause]. He proved as much recently when, in a deed never seen before in the history of the world, he had his close associates executed because they had betrayed him and the people."

A plainly worded message. Hitler's orders, just one month earlier, to send the SA leadership to the firing squad—known as the "Night of the

Long Knives" or the "Röhm Purge"—is still fresh in the common memory. It must have sent shivers up the spine of the listeners in the crowd. Cleverly, Ley turns the barrel of his gun slightly to one side: in the past, the authorities would nab the little guy and let the big fish go, but now "one forgives the little man, but destroys the big one if he is disloyal."

Ley ends his speech as he had begun it: on a pious note, with an ode to the Führer, whom the people love "as a child loves its mother." "Germany's strength lies not in cannon and machine guns, but in the sixty-five million hearts that overflow with faith and trust in the Führer Adolf Hitler. That is Germany's strength. Heil Hitler! Heil Deutschland!"

The group of seventeen

There are still Germans who, despite the intimidation, coercion, and terror still do not dance to the Nazis' tune. On 2 August 1934, on the death of the elderly president Hindenburg and two days after "Döbeln's largest-ever mass rally," Hitler takes over his function, combining the posts of president and chancellor. His title, from that moment on, is "Führer and Reichs Chancellor." A national referendum, held after the fact, confirms this final coup, giving complete control of the country to one single man. And yet, among the 17,000 votes cast in Döbeln (98.2 percent of the electorate), there are still 1,507 voters who dare vote against the proposal, and 361 who invalidate their ballots. It is no different in the rest of Germany: 10 percent say "no" to Hitler's power grab and 3 percent of the votes are voided.

No sooner had they assumed power in the first months of 1933 than the Nazis took aim at their opponents on the left. In Döbeln they arrested active Social Democrats and Communists, including former council members, and sent them to a hastily created internment camp twenty kilometres outside Döbeln. The camp, Hainichen, was a former sports complex and for three months served as an internment, interrogation, and torture centre for political arrestees from the Döbeln area. By the end of that period, some three hundred leftist opponents of the regime were imprisoned there. In June 1933 they were transferred to other internment camps in Saxony, to Colditz (later an Allied POW camp), and Sachsenburg. Among these were seventeen Communists from Döbeln accused of high treason.

The National Library in Leipzig, where we have requested archived newspaper and magazine articles, has a National Socialist data bank. When we enter the names of Döbeln Nazis, we don't get many hits, but the keyword *Döbeln* on its own provides more than forty. These are scanned copies of original documents from dozens of different German archives, and can be read directly on the computer monitor. Oddly enough, the trove also includes the verdict against Marinus van der Lubbe and his four codefendants in the case of the Reichstag fire of 27 February 1933. What does that have to do with Döbeln, we wonder.

The verdict is ninety-seven pages long, and the connection to Döbeln remains elusive, until we get to page 88. The city is one of seven German locations where Communists were suspected of planning an armed uprising. The Reichstag fire was, the Nazis believed, the signal to Communists nationwide to unleash a series of attacks and instigate a civil war. The Reichstag elections (went the theory), planned for 5 March, would be cancelled and the Nazis would be prevented from assuming power. Proof for this conspiracy came from statements by Communists arrested after the fire.

One of them, Franz Drechsel, was among the seventeen arrested Döbelners. The group had not even been formally charged yet, but Franz Drechsel's deposition would be presented as evidence in the Van der Lubbe case in September 1933. Even if one assumes that Van der Lubbe did set the Reichstag on fire on orders from the KPD (the Communist Party), the evidence is thin indeed. "The witness Drechsel discussed the issue of arms in regard to increasing political tensions on a directive from the local party leadership at the end of February 1933." This is all it says about the preparations in Döbeln for an "uprising" and civil war. Likewise, for the other six locations mentioned, the verdict hardly offers any concrete particulars.

Who were Franz Drechsel and his codefendants? In Döbeln itself no one knows anything about their background or their fate. Heimatfreund Jürgen Dettmer's meticulously assembled chronicle of Döbeln during the Nazi period, taken from the complete *Döbelner Anzeiger* archive, makes only two brief mentions of the seventeen Communists: when they were arrested in 1933, and when they heard the verdict in Berlin on 19 September 1934. The first four suspects were arrested in March 1933, the remaining thirteen in the ensuing months.

The Leipzig data bank provides us with far more information. The charges and verdict against the "Seventeen" survive. As minimal and, to some extent, biased as they are, the documents give an inkling of the anti-Nazi resistance in Döbeln, and the kind of people who participated in it.

Franz Drechsel was born in Döbeln and was forty years old at the time of his arrest. He had fought in World War I on the Eastern and the Western fronts. A former leatherworker, he later found odd jobs as a construction worker, but became unemployed in 1928. Thereafter he tried to earn a living as a market hawker. In 1929 he became a member of the KPD, and two years later he joined Kampfbund gegen den Faschismus. Founded after the prohibition of the paramilitary Rotfrontkämpferbund, this new organization was, in principle, unarmed, legal, and openly opposed to the

National Socialists, but it was no match for the Nazis and never managed to attract members from outside Communist circles.

The verdict also tells us that there were two active Kampfbund groups, each with between twenty and thirty members. They met once or twice a week at the party premises, where Franz Drechsel trained them in the struggle against political opponents. They practised fanning out in ranks, building blockades, taking cover, and hand-to-hand combat. Sure, the defendants say, it was called "military training" but it was hardly anything to speak of. One of them refers to it as "humbug."

The accused were all labourers, with the exception of the main defendant, Robert Wölfel, a former butcher who then owned his own transport firm. Many of them lost their jobs in the late 1920s as a result of the economic crash. Only then did they join the KPD and become active in the party and affiliated organizations. The men, says the verdict, discussed "acquiring materials one could use in the political struggle," such as "gunpowder, poison, explosives, and acid-filled light bulbs."

The case against the seventeen men was based on the discovery of an amount of potassium cyanide. Robert Wölfel, having been previously detained for minor misdemeanours, was arrested again in March 1933, not for political activities but for the theft of gasoline. In jail, Wölfel feared that if the police search his home, they would find the cyanide and he would be pinned as the mastermind behind any attacks. So he told the police of his own free will that he had cyanide in the house to eradicate mice and rats. So says the verdict, at least—there's no telling if a certain amount of physical coercion was necessary before Wölfel told them about the cyanide "of his own free will."

The house search turned up a metal sugar canister containing six "pieces of potassium cyanide, the size and shape of chicken's eggs." The poison was stolen, the defendants confessed, from the Köblerin silverware factory in the fall of 1932 by Kurt Birkner, who was employed there. Wölfel had asked him for the cyanide as a means of pest control in the party premises. Immediately following the Reichstag fire, Wölfel hid the poison at the home of a codefendant because he feared a house search. When it appeared the coast was clear, he took the canister back.

The prosecutor and the court do not believe for a minute that the poison was meant for "pest control." They assume the term is being used as a code word for the Nazis. The six egg-sized lumps of cyanide weigh 120 grams. Enough, says the Döbeln pharmacist Hardt, who has been brought in as an expert witness, to kill one hundred or two hundred people. These, in any case, are the figures the prosecutor cites in his charges. The verdict also draws on the testimony of the pharmacist, but then it says the poison was enough to kill at least four hundred people. The presence of the poison and their activities as Communists are, for the court, enough evidence of their murderous intentions.

However, the court admits, "it cannot be established whether there was a clear plan for the use of the poison." During his interrogation by the Döbeln police, Wölfel said that the poison was intended to liquidate the newly appointed Nazi Mayor Fritz Saupe, Police Commissioner Rönnecke, and others in the Döbeln police and Justice departments. Wölfel later rescinded this statement. A farmhand serving time told the court that just before the Reichstag elections on 5 March, he overheard a conversation of the Communists in a tavern they frequented, where they said it was easy to obtain potassium cyanide from the Köberlin silverware factory, and that certain persons, including Saupe, had already been targeted. He claimed a list of names was passed around.

The verdict mentions plans for poison attacks, but also for the theft of explosives from a quarry near Döbeln, the theft and sale of firearms, and the purchase of light bulbs that would be filled with acid and used as projectiles. None of these plans panned out, however. Reconnaissance of the quarry (by bicycle) was cancelled, six revolvers someone offered did not materialize, and the light bulbs and acid were never purchased.

Aside from the potassium cyanide, the police confiscated a stencil machine and a few handbills. On 1 March 1933 the group distributed a pamphlet denying that the Communists were behind the Reichstag fire. "The arsonist [Van der Lubbe] is not a Communist at all, as he claims, but rather a reprobate who had been bribed to carry out the orders of the ruling class." The Communists warn that the Reichstag fire will be used to exclude the KPD from the upcoming elections and call for "mass resistance to the plans of the bourgeoisie"—without, however, giving any specifics as to what kind of resistance they mean. A second handbill, circulated on 3 March, urges citizens to vote, and thus to defeat Hitler at the ballot box. "Workers! Give Hitler no respite. Hitler out! Vote KPD, List 3."

All things considered, the verdict does not give the impression that the Döbeln Communists were, as charged, on the verge of committing well-planned attacks or unleashing an armed uprising.

Perhaps the judges realized this, too. The sentences are mild, considering the defendants were found guilty of plotting high treason. They vary from one to three years, minus time already remanded in custody. Only the main defendant, Robert Wölfel, receives a harsh sentence: ten years in prison, plus ten years' parole. The court labels Wölfel a radical Communist who believes the KPD can achieve power only by force, and, with eighteen previous arrests, an incorrigible criminal. Wölfel's record shows that he *once* (twenty-three years prior) committed robbery and was sentenced to five years in prison. From 1920 onward he was repeatedly arrested for slander or political acts such as pasting placards, for which he was given a fine or spent a few days in jail. Incorrigible, certainly. But a criminal?

One defendant was acquitted and the case against one other was thrown out. In the context of the politicized judiciary of the Nazi state, this seems to be a remnant of legal prudence. Likewise, in the Reichstag fire case, which was intended as a deterrent show trial, the judges acquitted three of the four main defendants due to insufficient evidence, and convicted only Marinus van der Lubbe. Hitler was highly displeased with this verdict and established a "people's court" for political opponents, so as to avoid any future judicial surprises.

The Döbeln defendant who was acquitted was Erich Bökelmann, who, as leader of the Communist rifle club, had been accused of having organized illegal target practice. The court was convinced that the training served "treasonous aims," but since Bökelmann claimed to have obtained permission for the exercise from the police, and this was not disproved, they had no choice but to acquit him.

Yet more remarkable is the dismissal of Kurt Birkner's case. He was the one who had stolen the potassium cyanide from the silverware factory on Wölfel's orders. According to the court, Birkner knew full well what Wölfel planned to do with the cyanide. But because his crime had been committed before 1 December 1932, he fell under the amnesty law passed on 20 December of that year.

Amnesty law? Apparently, this law was passed in the last days of the Weimar Republic. At the end of 1932, when the country appeared to be slipping into civil war, the KPD, SPD, and NSDAP alike were out to protect their followers and combatants against prosecution or punishment for political activities or violence. After much palaver over who would fall under the amnesty, they submitted a joint proposal, which was approved. One would think that once the Nazis came to power, they would simply ignore it. But they didn't, and the law was still being applied in 1933 and 1934. And one man who benefited from this was the Döbeln cyanide thief, Kurt Birkner.

A measly pension, finally

The Nazis were not known to keep promises made to their opponents, or for clemency in any form. Ex-mayor Theodor Kunzemann found this out first-hand after he was removed from his post on 9 March 1933. The man who took his place, Lieutenant Commander Saupe, did not let any warm feelings about their mutual past get in the way.

Saupe told Kunzemann that he will be paid his salary for the months of April, May, and June, but thereafter won't receive another pfennig. Kunzemann, then fifty-eight years old, was well aware that with his politically sullied background, he would never get another job. He had started out as a machinist, followed by a job at the metalworkers' union. From 1920 onward he was employed by the city of Döbeln, first as a salaried alderman and later, from 1927, as mayor.

We read in his personnel dossier how he attempted to plead his case, politely at first, but then with growing desperation. In a first handwritten epistle (he no longer has a secretary), he points out that he was not fired on 9 March, but was put on leave and that formal dismissal proceedings were never carried out.

Saupe ignored this and decided that another rule applies to Kunzemann, namely that according to his dossier, Kunzemann had become a civil servant without "the customary training required for such a career, nor any other endorsement of his aptitude."

Kunzemann grasped for arguments that might strike a sympathetic chord with the Nazis: he was never a Communist, he had fought in the war of 1914–18, he acted apolitically as alderman and mayor, and he had an excellent rapport with the army garrison. It was all in vain. By the fall of 1933, his situation had deteriorated to the point that he asked the city for welfare assistance. The mayor of the municipality where Kunzemann lives confirmed in a letter to Döbeln that Kunzemann was unemployed. He spent all day tilling his garden, living a reclusive life, and did not go out to eat or drink. "He appears to be in dire financial straits," the letter superfluously concludes.

The day before Christmas 1933, Saupe's successor, Herbert Denecke, responded to the pleas. His tone is less vengeful, but alas, he writes, a pension is out of the question. But as a gesture of support, Kunzemann was sent a one-off sum of 300 reichsmarks, a third of his former monthly salary.

The dossier contains a lengthy correspondence in which Kunzemann tried—again in vain—to claim insurance money and workman's disability compensation. An in-law of Kunzemann, contributing to the appeal, quoted Hitler himself, who, after all, had proclaimed that "no one shall suffer hunger or cold." Even this was not enough to mollify the authorities. Poor Kunzemann persisted in petitioning his right to a pension until well into 1937. NSDAP district leader Rudolf Behr, the man with the buzzcut, writes curtly: "Assistance for him cannot count on *my* approval." Then there are four years with no contact.

But suddenly, on 19 December 1941, Denecke's successor writes:

Most Honorable Herr Kunzemann. I was deeply grieved to learn that your dear son Hans, in the struggle for Germany's freedom, has exhibited his loyalty to the Führer, the fatherland, and his native soil with a hero's death, sacrificing his life for all of us. I have the deepest desire to relieve you, in your profound grief, of some of your financial worries.

Starting in January 1942, Kunzemann would receive a measly pension of 200 reichsmarks per month. As it was Christmas, he was granted an extra 250 marks, for which the mayor, quite full of himself on his big-heartedness, took personal credit.

His son's death in Russia meant Kunzemann was able to eke out an existence for the next three years. He died, according to the family's death announcement, after a long period of physical hardship.

11

SWORD AND LIGHTNING

HAVING FORESTALLED HIS RIVALS, ISAY ROTTENBERG CAN ALLOW his cigar factory to operate relatively unhindered. But it was still not easy. As the Ministry of Finance had predicted, a maximum monthly production of five million cigars is not enough to make a profit. Rottenberg, trying to economize on fixed costs, asks the city authorities to lower the rent. The mayor approves the request in January 1935, granting the DZW a 25 percent rent reduction, equalling 500 reichsmarks per month, even retroactively to November 1933.

Rottenberg also achieves a small victory in the legal battle for the name Deutsche Zigarren-Werke. In Berlin, the Chamber of Commerce determines that there can be no objection to the name. It is a large-scale enterprise (Werke = Works) with more than six hundred employees and sales points in Berlin, Essen, Hamburg, Leipzig, and Dresden, as well as export to Norway and the Dutch West Indies. No verdict is issued on the use of *Deutsche*.

With this decision in hand, Rottenberg's lawyer Arndt Oehmichen writes to the Trade Association in Chemnitz, asking it to withdraw its challenge to the firm's name. The jobs of "hundreds of compatriots" (he uses the nationalistic term *Volksgenossen*, common parlance within the Nazi Party to denote *blood brothers*) will be endangered if the name has to be changed, he claims with a fair amount of exaggeration. He ends his letter with "Heil Hitler."

Oehmichen's correspondence shows that he was unreservedly assiduous in his work on behalf of the Deutsche Zigarren-Werke. He is always present at difficult meetings, and he goes along to the customs office and the ministries in Dresden and Berlin. He does his best for Rottenberg, and Rottenberg trusts him in return. While Oehmichen has no qualms about closing his correspondence with "Heil Hitler," this does not necessarily say anything about his real political persuasion. He likewise has no issues with representing a Jewish businessman, so it is perhaps wise to make an overt show of loyalty to the Nazis.

We have a hunch as to why our grandfather chose him as counsel when we come across earlier invoices from Oehmichen to the city. They are declarations for advising the curator of the bankrupt Krenter Werke. Oehmichen was thus already in good standing with the municipal authorities. Then he's just the man, Isay Rottenberg must have thought, to negotiate with the city on his behalf.

Months later, though, we read in a dossier quoting our grandfather that Oehmichen was a member of the Nazi Party. Stung by this revelation, Hella looks for mitigating circumstances. In 1932, when Granddad hired him, Oehmichen could not yet have been a member—this was surely only in 1934 or 1935, when they had already established an excellent working relationship and Rottenberg could not do without him. Sandra, as always, takes a different, distanced, approach. Half jokingly, she replies to Hella, "Granddad must have thought that was mighty handy, having a Nazi lawyer to fight for him."

Brownshirts

There is yet another shock in store for us. The archives of the East German Ministry of State Security for Nazi-era Saxony are located in Dresden. They also contain information about individuals. We are required to ask permission to see these documents. The Oehmichen dossier contains a decision taken by the "denazification commission" in Döbeln, dated 20 April 1948. In the questionnaire, which he completed himself, Oehmichen confirms having joined the NSDAP on 1 May 1933. He was then twenty-nine years old, and a first-year lawyer. It appears he also became an SA'er in 1933, complete—it's stated explicitly as incriminating evidence—with uniform. The document specifies his work for the SA: he was the legal adviser for Standarte 139, the SA regiment that was garrisoned in Döbeln and which marched through the city to the singing of the *Horst Wessel Song*:

"Die Fahnehoch!, die Reihen fest geschlossen! SA marchiert, mit ruhig festem Schritt."* Surely Isay Rottenberg knew that Oehmichen belonged to the SA. He must have seen Oehmichen—walked or sat next to him, even—in his brown suit, boots, and swastika armband.

"Dr. Oehmichen actively worked for, strengthened, and abetted the National Socialist reign of terror," reads the commission's conclusion. As punishment, he may no longer have a job in which he can hire or fire people or determine their conditions of employment. It's mild, as punishments go.

The men our grandfather dealt with varied greatly, and their ideas and behaviour did not neatly line up. Denecke wears an SA uniform, but in practice seems to be a run-of-the-mill civilian administrator who does not shy away from defending a Jewish businessman against his German competitors. Oehmichen is legal adviser to a Jew and likewise wears a brown uniform. Saupe is a bastard, but he stands up for our grandfather. The whole thing surprises us. Read all you like about the Nazis, but you still have no real idea of the day-to-day practices in a typical small city. Not that the Nazis are suddenly better than we thought, but what we see are pragmatic city managers for whom economic prosperity takes precedence over political dogma.

We also get to know our grandfather as a man who is able to go with the flow. He cannot be accused of harbouring Nazi sympathies, but he does sit down with them at the negotiating table, and contributes to German winter relief. That winter relief is still a sore spot for Hella. In the Netherlands, anyone who gave to the winter relief during the occupation was a collaborator. "Nog geen knoop van mijn gulp voor de Winterhulp," went the slogan: "Not a penny for winter relief." Isay Rottenberg was undoubtedly forced to contribute from November 1934 to March 1935—or at the very least, there would be consequences if he refused. It was pay, or lose the factory. Or was it? Was he so obsessed with that damned cigar factory that he would willingly donate money to appease the Nazis? I read Avraham Barkai's book *From Boycott to Annihilation*, which reconstructs the Aryanization of Jewish businesses from 1933 onward. On page 95 there is a passage that makes my heart leap. Until the winter of 1935, Barkai writes, Jews participated in the German winter relief as donors *and* as recipients. Only after the introduction of the Nuremberg race laws were the Jews excluded.

Speaking of relief! Other Jews also donated to winter aid, too, and the fund did not benefit only pure Aryans. Rescued by one little sentence in

---

* "Raise the flag! The ranks tightly closed! The SA marches with calm, steady step."

a book. I had removed Granddad's picture from my phone. I don't put it back because I'm still not sure what else will turn up. But at least I can now think of him again without mixed feelings.

Döbeln's municipal archives do not say much about the DZW in 1935. Things seem to run more or less smoothly. In June there are a few documents about a foreign exchange inspection—had the DZW crossed any lines there?—but otherwise no correspondence, memos, or meetings, as in the previous year. In September there is a letter from the factory to the city authorities with the dry remark that a new director had been found: a man "well known in our sector," Fritz Dannemann.

At that moment, Isay Rottenberg is in jail. Seven nerve-racking months had preceded his arrest.

Abducted by the Deutsche Bank

On 14 January 1935, a representative of the Deutsche Bank and two other men walked into Isay Rottenberg's office. What happened then we can almost hear our grandfather tell, although none of his letters from that time survive. His account of the incident is found in the notes taken by the Dutch consul in Dresden, Johan Steenbergen, after he visited Isay Rottenberg in jail in Dresden on 10 October of that year.

Rottenberg told him, writes Steenbergen, that one Dr. Veith, from the Deutsche Bank's legal department, and two private detectives appeared in his office and threatened to have him put in provisional detention. "Rottenberg would only talk to them if his lawyer Oehmichen was present," Steenbergen writes. He continues:

> Oehmichen, who is a member of the NSDAP, has always been the DZW's and Rottenberg's legal adviser and has always represented his interests with the utmost integrity. Rottenberg praised him for his propriety. Dr. Oehmichen protested against the outrageous behaviour of the Deutsche Bank, after which Veith took him aside and, appealing to his National Socialist sympathies, made it clear that he must not protect that Jew. The talks lasted the entire day. At the end, Rottenberg was dragged to Dresden and was detained in the Bristol Hotel, with round-the-clock surveillance. Under pressure of the circumstances and the threat of being held on remand, Rottenberg agreed to relinquish his shares of the DZW to the Deutsche Bank as collateral, but under the explicit condition that no personnel changes would be carried out and that he would remain director of the DZW.

When we began our research, our first line of reasoning was that foreign affairs must have a dossier on our grandfather's detention. On the cassette tape recording of her speech at the funeral of Sandra's father Edwin, our Aunt Tini talks about the Dutch consul Steenbergen's commitment to helping her father. Sandra knew an ex-diplomat who was willing to help us and ask around. But months later, nothing yet had surfaced.

A foreign affairs staff member gave us scant hope. He wrote: "There is nothing, in any case, in the inventory of the pre-war department archives. For any other traces [of information], if they exist, you would need to use the old, original archival inventories, quite a complicated job for someone inexperienced with the pre-war administrative system." He promised to give the National Archives a try. "That way I can at least see if there were any documents at all pertaining to your grandfather and his arrest. But do keep in mind that even if there were such documents, there is no guarantee we will actually see them. So much in the pre-war foreign affairs archive was destroyed willy-nilly, certainly around the time of the German invasion of 1940. And the Germans were not idle during the occupation, either."

A few days before leaving for our first visit to Döbeln, we went to the National Archive ourselves, as the matter was nagging us and we wanted to see first-hand if there was really no dossier. The inventory numbers we had requested indeed contained nothing relevant to our grandfather. But we didn't give up easily, and on the way out we double-checked the archive index. We requested permission to see the last few boxes—the very last ones—pertinent to Dutch citizens detained abroad. Ten minutes later, the folder containing the entire diplomatic correspondence regarding our grandfather's detention was ours, and that same afternoon we received an email from a staff member at Foreign Affairs with photos of the documents. Who says coincidence doesn't exist?

Raid

Thanks to the imprisonment dossier in the National Archives and the material about the Deutsche Bank in the Dresden state archives, we are able to get a picture of the raid and takeover of the cigar factory, and of the intrigues that preceded them.

After being taken from Döbeln to Dresden and held at Hotel Bristol, Isay Rottenberg is made to surrender his passport. He is forbidden to leave the city and therefore asks his legal adviser Oehmichen to oversee the payment of the factory workers' salaries. Then he names the DZW manager, the engineer Georg Berns, whom he considers "stalwart and competent," as codirector.

We find evidence of his amicable relationship with Berns, surprisingly, in Amsterdam. In one of Aunt Tini's photo albums we come across the birth announcement of Sylvia Margret Berns, 17 March 1935, with an address in Döbeln. The card's text is in English (Berns's wife was not German). This card is the only bit of correspondence between Döbeln and Amsterdam in the family's possession, and the only confirmation that Isay Rottenberg had anything at all to do with Döbeln.

Consul Steenbergen's notes make it sound like Rottenberg felt that, under the circumstances, it would be wise to have a codirector. He seems to still have things under control, and appoints Berns of his own free will, although he was probably too proud to admit he had no choice. Other documents show that the Deutsche Bank was already trying to sideline him.

The Deutsche Bank wanted Rottenberg remanded in custody that very day, 14 January, claiming the firm still had a large outstanding debt with the bank from the Krenter period. Rottenberg was accused of having committed bankruptcy fraud when he took over the factory, in order to help Krenter wriggle out of his debts. Veith threateningly produces a court request to place Rottenberg in preventive detention.

At the very back of the prison dossier we find the agreement reached after a full day of negotiation and under the threat of imprisonment. The document is signed by Isay Rottenberg, his lawyer Oehmichen, Veith, one Franz Barczel (one of the two detectives?), and the Dresden-based notary Hans Schubert, who had come to Döbeln for this meeting. It is clear from the text how thoroughly the case had been prepared beforehand.

Rottenberg can remain free if he or the firm pays 60,000 reichsmarks as bail, and additionally relinquish his share in the company to Veith as well as his voting rights. These will be restored only if the case is resolved in his favour. Rottenberg is able to turn over ten out of the one hundred stock certificates, as Vincenz Silvan, the tobacco buyer who had fled Germany, had brought the remaining ninety somewhere abroad for safekeeping. The agreement stipulates that Silvan must deliver these ninety shares post-haste to Berlin. Rottenberg must from now on share authority with Berns, or, should he leave the company, with someone else appointed by the Deutsche Bank. Of course: Berns had been installed by none other than Veith himself. Trust is one thing, Veith must have thought, but total control is better: alongside the shares and Berns, the bank cements its control of the factory by appointing its own accountant, "who has the right to enter the factory premises at any time, and to have access to the bookkeeping and other documents." The only condition that Isay Rottenberg succeeds in procuring is that there will be no personnel changes without his say-so. But even then, the promise has more holes than Swiss cheese.

Not two weeks later, the Deutsche Bank has possession of the deed. A notary in Berlin, one Dr. Konrad von Kries, hurries to the bank's main office in Berlin. Here he meets Hans-Joachim Veith, who lays all one hundred DZW shares (valued at 100,000 reichsmarks in total) on the table, at which the notary pronounces the Deutsche Bank in Berlin the sole owner of the factory. On the deed we see the Prussian herald: a menacing eagle clasping a sword in its right claw and two lightning bolts in its left. Centred on its breast is a swastika, and above, a ribbon with the text "God with us." Sword and lightning: Rottenberg is warned, but he refuses to see the writing on the wall.

Intrigues

How did Isay Rottenberg end up in this predicament? The simple answer is this: it was Germany in 1935, what else? It has been two years since the Nazis took power. How likely is it that a Russian Jew with a Dutch passport could operate a factory in Germany and be aided by the Nazis in his struggle against the competition? It had to go wrong eventually. And that moment is now.

Although this is broadly correct, we discovered that the whole business was more complex, and dirtier. Yes, the Deutsche Bank wanted to grab the factory, but Isidor Kronstein, too—Salomon Krenter's former adviser— also played a shady role. And most probably Krenter as well.

The moment Isay Rottenberg was jailed in Dresden, his wife Lena wrote to Steenbergen, sharing what she knew. First, she praises the factory as an enviable enterprise. "In Amsterdam, where my husband bought large quantities of tobacco, the factory enjoyed a generous credit limit and the DZW had a reputation within the tobacco branch as well run and one that could serve as an example not only for Germany, but for other countries as well."

She points to "a certain Dr. Kronstein" as the man who gave the Deutsche Bank the idea to snatch the factory. At the beginning of 1935 he "managed to convince the bank to take him up on a proposition, namely, to begin a civil lawsuit against the DZW with the argument that it was nothing more than an extension of Krenter Werke, so that the DZW's shares would belong to Krenter's creditors." The Deutsche Bank, she adds for clarification, was Krenter's chief creditor. Meanwhile it is known, she writes, that Kronstein would receive 45 percent of the net winnings of a successful lawsuit.

A month later, in their discussion in the Dresden jail, Isay Rottenberg fills Steenbergen in on Salomon Krenter's role in the affair. Rottenberg is not at all impressed by Krenter's talents as a businessman. Krenter was reckless—he calls him a "hasardeur"—who spent his money on advertising, directors, and too many employees. "Through hard work and frugality," he, Rottenberg, succeeded in turning the DZW around. When Krenter, whose mismanagement had driven the firm to failure, saw that the factory was up and running again, he and Kronstein tried to lay claim to a portion of the profits. "They're both swindlers" is Rottenberg's conclusion. "Kronstein managed to draw the Deutsche Bank into pursuing a civil lawsuit against him [Rottenberg], accusing him of being an accomplice to Krenter's bankruptcy fraud." Krenter and Kronstein were planning to split the booty. Krenter himself had fled the country, and was now apparently in Yugoslavia.

The Foreign Affairs dossier sheds some light on Rottenberg's and Krenter's business relationship. Isay Rottenberg had insufficient funds on hand in 1932 for the purchase of the cigar factory, he tells Steenbergen. Krenter was keen for him to take it over and offered to help him with the financing. Rottenberg borrowed 4,500 reichsmarks from Vincenz Silvan and 8,000 reichsmarks from one Mr. Lewin, the owner of the Bergmann Zigarrettenfabriken in Dresden. Via Krenter, Rottenberg borrowed 42,000 reichsmarks—his largest loan—from Krenter's business relation Salim Nouri, a tobacco dealer in Bulgaria. With this loan, Rottenberg could buy a shipment of cigars that German customs had confiscated because Krenter had outstanding tax debts. He then sold the cigars at a hefty markup, and used the profits to buy the Krenter Werke, set up the Deutsche Zigarren-Werke, and kick-start the factory.

Kronstein and the Deutsche Bank claim that the money Krenter had lent Rottenberg was not Nouri's, but had been drawn from his own nearly or already bankrupt business. Krenter therefore criminally defrauded his creditors. They imply that Rottenberg and Krenter connived to skirt around the debt to allow the factory to continue operating, making Rottenberg an accessory to fraud.

We cannot establish exactly how the factory was financed. It's clear that our grandfather did not have sufficient capital himself, so he managed to scrape funds together with loans from here and there, then bought that impounded shipment of Krenter cigars and resold it at a large profit in order to pay off, partly or in full, the original loans. A risky manoeuvre—especially that loan via Krenter—but at that moment Rottenberg had no reason to distrust him. He was so eager to get his hands on the factory that he was willing to take a calculated risk, which, after all, is part of being an entrepreneur.

Isay Rottenberg spends every moment trying to clear his name ever since Hans-Joachim Veith set foot in his Döbeln office. He is free to come and go, but the Deutsche Bank's civil lawsuit against him has been set into motion, and he has to ready himself for that. Knowing him, he'll have not wasted a moment and went straight to work drawing up a plan, assembling the facts, studying the legal aspects, and lining up witnesses.

And this debt case is not the only matter demanding his attention. Some time later he is confronted with the Saxony Ministry of Finance's foreign currency investigation. The case had been brought by the DZW's rivals, who had been thwarted in their efforts to force the factory to switch to handwork, and were now looking for another way to undermine it. They once again brought their baseless suspicions to the authorities. "The competition continually reminds us," writes the Döbeln branch of the Reichsbank to the Saxony Ministry of Finances, "that the financial workings of the Deutsche Zigarren-Werke are, for an outsider, completely opaque." They claim Rottenberg transfers his salary to Vincenz Silvan in the Netherlands, breaking the foreign currency laws.

Restrictions on foreign assets had been in place in Germany for many years. Anyone who receives foreign currency, through export or earnings abroad, must put that money into a separate account. And anyone who needs foreign currency, whether for payment or import, must ask permission for it.

In April 1935, inspectors show up at the factory to inspect the bookkeeping. And indeed, they find that Rottenberg had transferred money to Silvan. Rottenberg is suspected of also making money transfers to his father-in-law, Abraham Ptasznik.

Rottenberg is taking some hard knocks. The bank has grabbed his factory, in any case until the court decides in his favour. Strangers from the tax office and the Deutsche Bank are poking around in his books in search of irregularities or criminal offences.

Rottenberg wants to file a complaint against Veith's actions, but cannot get through to his superiors. Veith and Kronstein form a tight duo—every time Rottenberg appears before Veith in Berlin, Kronstein is there, too.

A ray of sunshine

There is one small ray of sunshine: the name Deutsche Zigarren-Werke has been approved. Three years after the complaint had been first introduced, the Döbeln court dismisses the Chemnitz Trade Chamber's objection to the name. The court devotes many pages of its verdict just to that *Deutsche*, replete with recent judicial rulings over who may call themselves German. When the firm's name was registered in 1932, the term *deutsch* was in general hardly more than a decorative filler, or an indication for foreign buyers that the company was located in Germany. After the national awakening, though, *deutsch* took on a loftier connotation, and it is therefore correct, says the court, that its use should now be held to higher standards than previously. But the original registration of the DZW was in no way intentionally misleading, the court finds.

More importantly, even though the owner of the Deutsche Zigarren-Werke was a foreigner and a non-Aryan, recent internal changes give the firm an unmistakable German character. The Döbeln engineer Georg Berns has been given a management post, and the "non-Aryan director Rottenberg may no longer represent the firm on his own." Moreover, the challenge to Rottenberg's sole ownership is by now a moot point: the Deutsche Bank in Berlin, rather, is now the owner. *Vielmehr* (rather) is the word the court uses, with a keen sense of subtlety: it is not yet *entirely* certain that the bank is the full owner of the DZW.

Kronstein and Rottenberg both try to find witnesses who can support their version of the factory's purchase. One such cross-examination, carried out on 7 August, is in Rottenberg's favour, giving him reason for optimism, as our grandmother writes to Steenbergen:

> Soon the case began to tip in my husband's favour, and the judge
> informed the opposing party that its evidence did not hold water,
> nor was there any indication that their claim to the shares was
> justified. The testimony of the main witnesses was then scheduled
> for 17 August, after which my husband could surely count on a
> favourable verdict.

Isay Rottenberg assumes he'll soon be back in control of the factory. This might be Germany, where anti-Semitism has been elevated to state ideology, but he must have regarded that as irrelevant to this matter. It is a dispute with two (Jewish, as it happens) swindlers, who have turned to the Deutsche Bank, like their big brother. Surely the court won't ignore the convincing testimony?

Afterwards, Arthur Theermann, Rottenberg's accountant, told consul Steenbergen that five days before the arrest, he travelled from Dresden to Döbeln with Rottenberg and that the latter was looking forward to the trial.

But it would not get that far. On Tuesday, 13 August 1935, four days before the key witnesses would be heard, the police arrest our grandfather. He is sick in bed that morning in the Westminster Hotel in Dresden. He hA a fever, but they take him anyway. Soon thereafter he is locked up in a cell in Dresden's infamous prison on the Münchner Platz.

That same day, Veith calls a special meeting of the shareholders of the Deutsche Zigarren-Werke, and, on behalf of the new owner, the Deutsche Bank, chairs the meeting. There are four points on the agenda: (1) remove Isay Rottenberg as director; (2) replace the three governors; (3) immediately annul the contract with the tobacco dealer Vincenz Silvan; and (4) instigate a financial investigation into the founding and management of the firm under Isay Rottenberg. The agenda is unanimously approved. Not surprising, because any potential opposition has been knocked out.

The Aryanization of the Deutsche Zigarren-Werke had been thoroughly prepared.

12
MÜNCHNER PLATZ

AUNT TINI WAS TWELVE YEARS OLD IN 1935. HER FATHER'S DIS-
appearance must have been quite traumatic, and even sixty years later, at
her brother Edwin's funeral in 1997, her voice trembled when she recalled
the incident. "Father had suddenly vanished, and we didn't know where to,
why, or how." Soon after reading the Claims Conference announcement
we listen again to the cassette tape of her speech, and in it we hear names
and places that will help put us on the right track, including that of the
consul who had gone out on a limb for our grandfather.

"Foreign Affairs was called in," Aunt Tini said, "and they instructed
consul Steenbergen in Dresden to look into the matter of the Dutch
national Isay Rottenberg. After some time, I can't remember how long
exactly, they found him in a dank jail cell in Dresden, deathly ill with kid-
ney stones and without medical assistance."

In Tini's recollection, the family waited weeks, even months, in uncertainty as to Isay's fate. But when we finally get our hands on the Foreign
Affairs dossier, we realize this can't be right. The first document is a letter
from our other great-grandfather, Abraham Ptasznik. It's a shock. The only
letter from him we had ever seen was a farewell postcard he threw out of
the train in 1943 as he and our great-grandmother, both in their eighties,
were deported from the Dutch transit camp Westerbork to the Sobibor
death camp.

The letter is addressed to the Foreign Office in The Hague and is dated 18 August 1935, five days after Isay's arrest. The letter is neatly typed and in formal Dutch.

> Gentlemen:
> This past Thursday I received word from a third party in Berlin that my son-in-law Isay Rottenberg, a Dutch subject, was, on the 13th of this month, unexpectedly placed under arrest in Döbeln, Saxony and was brought to a penitentiary on the Münchnerstrasse in Dresden.

Aside from two minor points—Isay was arrested in Dresden and brought to the Münchner Platz—the information is correct.

Ptasznik writes that Rottenberg has been commercial director of the Deutsche Zigarren-Werke since 1932 and that "approximately seven hundred workers are employed there." He emphasizes that neither Rottenberg nor his family had any foreboding of the arrest. "Despite the anti-Jewish government that came to power in Germany in 1933, Rottenberg, himself a Jew, has always maintained good relations with his personnel and the local authorities."

The family in Amsterdam knows that Isay is ill because Ptasznik insists that the Dutch consul visit him personally in jail to check on his health. He asks that "immediate" diplomatic measures be taken "because delay could bring irreparable suffering to the victim's family."

Ptasznik tries to keep the bad news from his daughter Lena, fearing she won't be able to handle it. "For the time being, these events are, for health reasons, being withheld from Mrs. Rottenberg; I therefore ask you to communicate only with me in regard to this matter." This could be why Tini had no information as to Isay's whereabouts. It couldn't have been for too long, though, because on 2 September, the diamond merchant and member of the Provincial Council, Abraham Asscher, whom the family approached for help, requests an audience with the secretary general of the Department of Foreign Affairs on behalf of Lena Rottenberg and her brother, Jos Ptasznik. But perhaps Lena kept news of Isay's detention from her children. Secrecy and tight-lippedness were the default mode of the Rottenberg family.

The Ptaszniks also take further measures. They hire lawyers in Dresden and Amsterdam, and they waste no time in collecting testimonials meant to convince the Nazis that Isay Rottenberg is not some louche Polish or Russian Jew, but a respectable, upstanding Dutch citizen who has never put a foot wrong and is respected by his business relations. Of course, it is less about the facts—the Nazis are convinced he is a con man, and no testimonial will change this stance—than imply that Isay Rottenberg has friends in high places in the Netherlands, and that his arrest will damage Dutch-German relations.

By late August, nine testimonials from Amsterdam authorities arrived in Dresden, including those from the chief of police, the public prosecutor, an alderman, and the directors of the Market Sector and the Commodity Inspection Services. This was followed by a petition arguing for Rottenberg's release, signed by the prominent Social Democrat and founder of the labour movement, Henri Polak, then a national senator, as well as several other members of parliament and a number of well-known university professors. Other influential Dutch figures who signed this petition were Abraham Asscher and Professor David Cohen, leaders of the Amsterdam Jewish community and (later) chairmen of the infamous Jewish Council during the occupation. The group writes: "It is the conviction of the undersigned, who know Mr. Rottenberg as not only an able businessman but also an honest and righteous man, that Mr. Rottenberg is not guilty of any behaviour that could justify the actions of the German authorities."

Our notion that the Ptaszniks and the Rottenbergs inhabited an island of East-European émigrés is apparently mistaken. Not only do they speak excellent Dutch and send their children to decent schools, but to our surprise, they appear be impressively well connected.

Honey and vinegar

The Münchner Platz prison still stands today. It is a huge, gloomy fortress with a central tower, behind which is a complex that once housed not only the jail but the offices and courtrooms belonging to the Saxon Royal Regional Court and, during the Nazi period, an "extraordinary court." Nowadays it is home to Dresden Technical University. Students chat cheerfully as they tread the broad staircase, but the building's dark history has not been glossed over. On the ground floor, a museum memorializes those imprisoned, interrogated, and executed here. Behind it, separate from the main building, is the prison, built in the form of a cross. In the courtyard is a monument, a sculpture depicting a small group of men and women. They exude resistance, desperation, comfort, and powerlessness.* It is a morbid spot. During the Third Reich the Münchner Platz was one of the places where executions were carried out. The verdict was pronounced in the courthouse, the guillotine stood ready in the courtyard. The spot

---

* See https://www.tracesofwar.com/sights/5155/Memorial-M%C3%BCnchner -Platz.htm.

where it stood is marked. After 1945, the guillotine remained operational, this time in the service of the East German regime. The blade fell for the last time in 1956. In total, some thirteen hundred prisoners were decapitated here.

From the moment he is aware of the arrest, Johan Steenbergen is deeply involved in the Rottenberg case. He visits Isay Rottenberg in his cell, takes meticulous notes of their conversations, and is tireless in his efforts to get Rottenberg released. During his first visit, the detainee complains "bitterly" about the prison doctor, but he refuses to file a complaint, nor does he wish to be transferred to the infirmary. He requests a softer bed and a daily bath. A week later, when nothing has improved, the consul approaches the prison doctor himself, who says that Rottenberg is putting on a show and is "oversensitive." The consul suggests that the extra care be paid for by Rottenberg's Dutch friends, but the doctor is implacable; he cannot give preference to foreigners.

Then Steenbergen applies the carrot-and-stick approach. "You know," he begins, "I recently spoke to Governor Mutschmann, the highest official in Saxony. He agreed with me that economic relations with the Netherlands were of the utmost importance. Well," Steenbergen warns him, "then it wouldn't do to 'muddy' the relationship with the Netherlands," alluding to the Rottenberg case. "Folks in Holland think that Herr Rottenberg is being badly treated," he says to the doctor, "and I would be happy to dispute that if you will agree [to the requests]." He, Steenbergen, schmoozes that the treatment in German prisons is "exemplary" and would very much like to convince the others of this. It would make a good impression indeed if Rottenberg's requests were granted. The doctor can't acquiesce fast enough. That same day, Isay Rottenberg is given a softer mattress and a tub to bathe in. And all of this is duly notated by Johan Steenbergen.

Steenbergen writes to the Dutch embassy in Berlin that he is unable to comment on the complicated matter for which Rottenberg has been detained. The testimonials are impressive, but he prefers to consult a more neutral person before making any judgment. He therefore contacts Arthur Theermann, the DZW accountant, who was not named as a character witness by either Rottenberg or his family.

Theermann praises Rottenberg to the skies. The DZW credits its success to his "fine mercantile instinct and industriousness." Rottenberg has run the business in the most advantageous way possible, Theermann says, followed by the dubious compliment that even "party people speak highly of him." Theermann, himself an NSDAP member, goes as far as to criticize the judicial orders, and was surprised at Rottenberg's sudden arrest based on statements by "an untrustworthy man."

Isay Rottenberg is forbidden to discuss his criminal case with outside parties. He may therefore give only the consul information about the civil case. But he does tell Steenbergen that his arrest was based on a statement made under oath by Dr. I. Kronstein, who had drawn up a memorandum for the Deutsche Bank. Salomon Krenter is said to have travelled specially to Vienna in order to file an incriminating deposition against Rottenberg. But in his declaration regarding the bankruptcy fraud, says Rottenberg, Krenter also incriminated himself, and he intends to petition the court for Krenter's extradition.

He just manages to tell Steenbergen that the Deutsche Bank had named one of their own representatives as a governor of the cigar factory, and that all Jewish personnel, including himself, have been fired. Then the prosecutor's secretary, also present, orders him to desist.

Aryanization

While the civil and criminal cases focus on a business dispute between the cigar factory's previous and present owners, the Deutsche Bank gets the loot and Aryanizes the company at the same time. Steenbergen, too, becomes more and more convinced of this, writing:

> This move by the Deutsche Bank, which has already installed
> new management and a new board of directors, is premature at
> the very least, and in my opinion even reckless and dangerous.
> There is a danger that capital, perhaps Dutch capital, or at least
> that of a Dutch citizen living in Germany, will be lost. The fact
> that these measures are supported by Rottenberg's detention
> sheds a suspicious light on the proceedings until now and raises
> the fear that there is the desire to remove a Dutch non-Aryan
> from the leadership of a large enterprise.

Legal measures to confiscate Jewish businesses were only introduced in Germany on 12 November 1938, two days after Kristallnacht. But by that time, between 70 and 80 percent of Jewish businesses were no longer in Jewish hands, says Avraham Barkai in *From Boycott to Annihilation*. The Aryanization laws were simply the final step in a long-term plan to economically exclude Jews and rob them of their livelihood.

This began in 1933 with the boycott of Jewish businesses on Saturday, 1 April. It had, as we saw, scant effect. Despite the hate campaign, regular citizens did not shun Jewish businesses or shops in any significant numbers.

Döbeln was no exception. Governmental organizations, including municipalities, had been prohibited two weeks earlier from placing orders at Jewish businesses. Civil servants were "strongly discouraged" from buying from Jews. In Döbeln this took place on 13 March, simultaneously with the decree for governmental services.

The first victims of the new regime were Jewish civil servants, who by law were fired in April 1933. Soon thereafter, the Nazi trade union NSBO pressured businesses to dismiss their Jewish employees. Jewish organizations and employers took the matter to court—in vain. Even the larger Jewish concerns were often forced to give in to the NSBO's demands. The Deutsche Zigarren-Werke managed to dodge the bullet. We don't know how many Jewish employees worked there. Rottenberg's tobacco buyer Vincenz Silvan was one, but surely there were more, until the factory was confiscated and Rottenberg himself was fired. Then the rest were thrown out, too.

For a long time, the perception persisted that between 1934 and 1938, the Nazis allowed the economic importance of Jewish businesses to prevail over their anti-Semitic ideology. But even during those years there was systematic Aryanization. Businesses were slapped with civil or criminal lawsuits. Jewish owners often received assistance from their non-Jewish colleagues in the sector to circumvent the Nazi roadblocks. Sometimes this assistance was genuine, sometimes it was simply a way of getting a foot in the door and becoming a partner. In any case, Jewish businessmen rarely managed to evade the clutches of the tax, foreign currency, or judicial authorities. During the next phase it became clear that even the non-Jewish partner was unable to help, which usually led to a buyout as the only solution.

When the government wasn't making things difficult for Jewish-owned businesses, it was the commercial sector and the banks. Business associations blackballed Jewish firms or rallied against them. Banks revoked loans and mortgages for the paltriest of reasons. The method did not matter, the bottom line was the same. Driven into dire financial straits, the owners had no choice but to sell out for peanuts.

According to Barkai's count, Germany in 1932 was home to more than 100,000 Jewish companies and small businesses: 55,000 shops, 8,000 wholesale or export companies, 8,000 factories, 9,000 craftsmen, 12,000 assorted professionals, and 10,000 other firms. By 1935, 20 to 25 percent of these were already liquidated or in Aryan hands. One-quarter of the Jewish population was, by that time, reduced to poverty and dependent on social welfare.

In general, larger firms held out the longest because they provided work, brought in foreign capital, and were useful to Germany's image abroad. The Deutsche Zigarren-Werke fell into this category. As a foreigner, Isay Rottenberg was not officially a target of anti-Jewish measures, but the DZW had nevertheless been on the boycott list of Jewish businesses on 1 April 1932, and the SA had raided the DZW offices. From the very start, his competitors in the cigar sector used his Jewishness against him. In her letter to Steenbergen after Isay's arrest, our grandmother writes that the cigar manufacturers "never missed a chance, through advertisements and articles in magazines, and by way of flyers, to remind the cigar branch that the Deutsche Zigarren-Werke was a Jewish concern."

That the DZW was confiscated relatively early on was probably a matter of "opportunity knocking." Isidor Kronstein, as a partner-in-crime of Salomon Krenter, set the whole process in motion. And from what Steenbergen notated during his conversations with our grandfather, it is clear that the raid on the DZW took place with the approval of the top echelons of the Deutsche Bank.

Enlisting the help of his own banker in Dresden, Kurt Arnhold, Rottenberg tried, months before his arrest, to set up a meeting in Berlin with the management of the Deutsche Bank. He failed to get a foot in the door, all the while getting referred back to Veith, the man Kronstein had brought in to wrest Rottenberg's factory shares from him.

It appears that Isay Rottenberg does not believe that such a solid institution would allow itself to be bamboozled. It must have been the work of a subordinate trying to make his way up the ladder, he'll have thought. Once the directors get wind of it, then ... It must have been a rude awakening, there in that prison cell.

Unexpected insight

In the course of researching this history, the recurring question was: Why did our grandfather stay in Germany after Hitler came to power? Was he stubborn, overconfident? Was it purely a business decision? Or were we, blinded by 20/20 hindsight, missing the point?

Coincidentally, much is known about the Jewish banking family Arnhold, the Dresden firm that served Krenter and subsequently the DZW. Although the Arnholds' position as German Jews differed from that of Isay Rottenberg, we are struck by the similarities. The story of the Arnhold family (which we only stumbled upon late in our research) makes us think we may have been examining our grandfather through the wrong glasses.

The Arnholds were a privileged family. Their bank, founded in 1864, stayed afloat during the turbulent Weimar Republic and in the early 1930s was one of Germany's most respected private banks. The founder, Georg

Arnhold, had four sons named—indicative of the level of assimilation of German Jews—Adolf, Heinrich, Kurt, and Hans. Kurt had fought in World War I and was awarded an Iron Cross for bravery.

Unlike many others who climbed the German social ladder, the Arnholds did not have themselves baptized. They were no longer religious, but they were active as wealthy patrons and held important posts within the Jewish community. For German society at large, they supported sports, science, and culture. Dresden's new outdoor swimming pool, for instance, was named after Georg Arnhold in 1926, when the future was still rosy. They considered themselves Germans *and* Jews, and they saw no contradiction in this.

They were not, however, blind to rising anti-Semitism. Adolf was on the board of the Association Against Antisemitism, and Heinrich wrote an essay entitled "The Jewish Question."

They were shocked by Hitler's takeover and the boycott of Jewish businesses on 1 April 1933, but when the Nazi leadership, fearing damage to Germany's diplomatic image and economic relations abroad, reined in the National Socialist revolution, the Arnholds reassured themselves that it would go no further.

Reality was harsher. Intimidation of the bank began as early as 1933. The Saxony governor Mutschmann, a virulent anti-Semite, set his sights on the Arnhold Bros. Bank. He let them know, through the grapevine, that he would personally like to see them leave Germany. At the end of 1933, Adolf Arnhold, the eldest brother, stepped down as director and was replaced by an Aryan banker, ostensibly to protect the bank. That aim failed, however, for a few months later the Justice Department accused the Arnhold brothers that five years earlier they had falsified the accounts of Sachsenwerk, a large transformer factory, just before it was to be taken over by AEG. AEG therefore had supposedly invested in a bankrupt company. Heinrich Arnhold was grilled for a solid day, and his brothers Adolf and Kurt were also interrogated for hours on end.

The historian Simone Lässig was allowed to peruse the memoires and diaries of the family, and is thus aware of their reaction. Heinrich, trained as a lawyer, was shocked by the false accusations but looked forward to the trial, where he would set things right and restore the bank's good name. He was still thinking in terms of a country governed by the rule of law; his faith in honest German civil servants was still intact. Lässig remarks that Heinrich Arnhold was in no way an exception. German Jews had not forgotten that it was the enlightened civil servants who had spurred their emancipation at the end of the nineteenth century. The Arnholds simply could not believe that the superior Prussian legal system had, nearly overnight, become Hitler's personal instrument of power.

The case against the Arnhold Bros. was deferred, but it hung over them like Damocles's sword and damaged the bank's name. Thirty German businesses immediately expelled the bankers from their board of governors. They were spared neither insult nor humiliation. In the summer of 1935, signs saying "Forbidden for Jews" appeared in Dresden's public spaces, including swimming pools. Kurt Arnhold wrote to the city authorities, kindly requesting that his father's name no longer be used for the outdoor pool, now that its original purpose—"the well-being of Dresden's youth and society as a whole"—was no longer certain. Two days later, the swimming pool was renamed.

Meanwhile, a new case into a trivial issue was opened. The bank was accused of breaking foreign exchange laws in a transaction with a Bulgarian tobacco dealer. It concerned the sum of 9,000 reichsmarks, a negligible amount when you consider that bank's turnover was in the millions. But a conviction could result in the bank losing its foreign exchange authorization, making it an easy target for a non-Jewish and legally unsullied competitor.

The strain was too much for Heinrich Arnhold. In October 1935, at the age of fifty, he died of a stroke. The Dresdner Bank wasted no time in making an offer on the bank. The Arnholds were unable to resist the pressure any longer and sold their main branch in Dresden. But still they did not give up on Germany, holding onto their Berlin branch. There, they were safely out of Mutschmann's reach, and moreover they were close to Hjalmar Schacht, president of the Reichsbank and Hitler's key economic adviser. Schacht had a reputation for professionalism and leaving ideology to others. The Arnholds knew him personally—he even used to visit them at home—and in German-Jewish circles he was said to have a "protective hand."

Until 1936, the subject of emigration was hardly discussed in the Arnhold family. In Brazil in 1940, Adolf Arnhold looked back on that time. "Reading Hitler's book should have taught and showed me what was in store for the Jews. But on the other hand, we still enjoyed a privileged position, and of the National Socialist agenda's many goals, hardly a single one had been realized."

Heinrich's death, writes Simone Lässig, illustrates this paradox. Countless non-Jewish colleagues, friends, and acquaintances expressed their condolences and praised the eminent banker in glowing obituaries—while carefully avoiding any mention of his being a Jew.

The Arnholds believed, or hoped against their better judgment, that Nazism was no more than a passing phase, a raging river that would one day dry up, revealing their beloved and trusted German society.

Just to be on the safe side, the Arnholds sent their children abroad to study, but they stayed behind, first to rescue their Berlin branch and later, when they were forced to give it up anyway, to at least try to get a reasonable price for it. During the negotiations—along came the Dresdner Bank, once again—Kurt Arnhold was arrested. He was released on bail and fled that very same day, without a passport, to the Netherlands. After arriving at the Park Hotel in Amsterdam, he recorded the details of his escape on hotel stationery. "What we used to call 'the luck of the Arnholds' abandoned me for a year, but during this escapade [his escape] my luck returned in spades: it was clear to us that this was a matter of our freedom and our life." Kurt Arnhold penned these words at the end of November 1938, after Kristallnacht, when even he had to acknowledge that Germany was no longer a place for Jews.

Isay Rottenberg might have been a Russian Jew, officially residing in the Netherlands, but his outlook and mentality feel a whole lot like the Arnholds', assimilated German Jews. The language spoken at home was not Yiddish, not Polish, not Russian, but German, as we discovered when researching his past. As a young man he had traded the anti-Semitic Russian Empire for Berlin, where he could spread his wings and evolve as a businessman. In Berlin he went to the theatre and he devoured German literature. He thrived on the culture, the courtesy, and the *tüchtig* (diligent) work ethic. Before starting a family in Amsterdam in 1918, he had lived in Berlin for some ten years. If his wife had agreed, he might have preferred to stay there. He thought he knew Germany through and through. When he returned there in 1932 as a factory owner, it was a "homecoming." If we arrange the puzzle pieces that way, it all fits together better.

Like the Arnholds, Isay Rottenberg was convinced that in Germany, if you were accused of something, the law would let you set things right. Did he still believe that when the powerful Deutsche Bank had him arrested, stole his factory, fired him, and opened a second fraud case against him?

Word of honour

Isay Rottenberg is interrogated daily in the Münchner Platz prison. He has the occasional visitor: his German lawyer, or the Dutch consul Steenbergen. His Dutch lawyer, E. de Vlugt, also comes to Dresden. The consul sees that Rottenberg is in a tight spot, being a Jew, but he hopes for an "unbiased solution," seeing as "this non-Aryan is a Dutchman."

At the end of September, Steenbergen submits a request for Rottenberg's release. He approaches the court directly, deliberately avoiding the political detour via the Saxony state chancellery, because "Governor Mutschmann has a very unfavourable view of non-Aryans."

Bail is set at 75,000 reichsmarks—equivalent to more than $600,000 Canadian in terms of today's purchasing power. It is an amount the family can't possibly scrape together. Father-in-law Ptasznik is able to offer a bank guarantee of 15,000 reichsmarks maximum. Isay Rottenberg himself has money in Germany in addition to the DZW (as we read in the prison dossier), but this, too, has meanwhile been confiscated by the Deutsche Bank.

Steenbergen is tireless in his efforts to get Rottenberg freed from jail. Not only does he register a complaint protesting the exorbitant bail, but he pleads Rottenberg's case directly with the president of the court, Dr. Franke. His tactic, which had served him well earlier with the prison doctor, is the combination of flattery and the spectre of Germany's damaged reputation. He will try to keep the arrest under wraps, he tells Franke, but it's quite likely that the Dutch press will get wind of it. But his attempts to talk down the bail do not seem to work. Then the consul suggests trusting Rottenberg at his word that he will not flee Germany, and if he does, he will forfeit his holdings in Germany entirely, which will then be given to charity. Steenbergen even suggests "winter relief" as beneficiary.

A few days later, his appeal is rejected. The court acknowledges that the incriminating testimony of two witnesses, Kronstein and Krenter, might not be entirely trustworthy. Krenter's lack of scruples is well known, writes the court's president, and he can quite rightly be presumed guilty of bankruptcy fraud, but that Rottenberg's guilt as an accessory, taking into account other witnesses, is therefore also likely.

Steenbergen has no choice but to write to the embassy in Berlin on 22 November: "The Rottenberg case is now at a stage where the consulate is unable to do much more." Steenbergen clearly commiserates with our grandfather. He cannot judge whether a punishable act has been committed, but if it is true what "prominent Amsterdam citizens who are well acquainted with Rottenberg" write, then he is in no way a criminal. If he is proved innocent in the end, "then the extremely detrimental consequences of his remand will be felt, seeing as the factory that Rottenberg has nurtured with such dedication has been left to fend for itself."

Steenbergen was a name that our aunt, some sixty years later, still had at the ready for her speech at Edwin's funeral. So he must have been talked about at home. We imagine that Steenbergen and our grandfather hit it off. They had a lot in common: they were both industrialists and about the same age. Johan Steenbergen was an enterprising man. He grew up in Meppel, in the northeast of the Netherlands, above his father's fabric store. His mother was German. His father died young, and Johan had to take over the business.

He was, however, more interested in photography. At the age of eighteen, he supplemented his work at the shop with his own business in photographic products and chemicals. His guardian sent him to Dresden to learn to be a tailor. Instead, Johan studied photography, received a patent at age twenty-four, and in 1912 set up the Ihagee Kamerawerke in Dresden, which grew into a flourishing company. Ihagee manufactured countless models of camera and exported them worldwide. His breakthrough came in the 1930s, with the invention of the first single-lens reflex camera for 127 roll film, the Exacta. To this day, camera enthusiasts are full of excited stories about the Exacta's compact design and fine mechanism.

Steenbergen manoeuvred his company through World War I, postwar hyperinflation, and the Depression. He clung to the firm even when the Nazis came to power. In his biography is a group photo of Ihagee personnel, with Steenbergen in the centre, in the factory's courtyard. The group poses in front of a life-size portrait of Hitler in uniform, a swastika, and a pair of loudspeakers. The photo, while undated, carries the embarrassed caption, "A sign of the times."

In 1929 the Dutch embassy in Berlin invited Steenbergen to become honorary consul in Dresden. He hesitated, for he had his hands full with his factory, but the status and honour of such a function was too good to pass up, and would open doors to higher echelons, suggests his biographer Halbertsma.

Steenbergen was a bachelor until 1931, when he married Elisabeth Nussbaum, a Jewish woman his age, originally from San Francisco but raised in Bonn. She moved in with him in Dresden. Through her, he saw German anti-Semitism first-hand, and undoubtedly identified with Jews like Isay Rottenberg. His biographer relates that he became ever more reluctant to leave Elisabeth at home alone. As a form of protection, he always carried with him a personal invitation he had once received from a high-placed Nazi. According to the Steenbergen family's stories, it was a letter from SS chief Heinrich Himmler.

In the middle of the war, when he and his wife had already left Germany for America, Steenbergen looked back on his years in Nazi Germany. Without mentioning his name specifically, he referred to his involvement with our grandfather and another Jewish Dutchman, who did not survive. He writes:

> This same empire pretended to be one with high morals, when
> prior to the war it arrested two Jewish countrymen for whom

I had the highest regard and who, as factory directors, lived in
the consulate's region, under the pretense of financial irregularities and fraudulent bankruptcy, and eventually expelled them
from Germany. One of them will no longer receive justice once
the Nazis are called to account, as he was murdered in the
Mauthausen death camp.

Back to 1935 and Steenbergen's attempts to get Isay Rottenberg freed from
remand. The consul continues to parry the German authorities with the
potential fallout from negative publicity caused by the Rottenberg case. In
his letters to his superiors in Berlin and The Hague, however, he strongly
advises against alerting the media. By December 1935, our grandmother's
patience had worn out, and announces her desire to call in the press.
Steenbergen objects strenuously:

> In my opinion, it would be a bad idea to bring the case into
> the public eye as long as no decisions have been taken. The
> Consulate, of course, cannot participate in public statements for
> which there is no positive evidence, and could possibly only result
> in negatively influencing public opinion, to the detriment of
> Dutch-German trade.

On 1 February 1936, Steenbergen suddenly reports that Rottenberg has
been freed from custody and may return home for a few weeks. He must
report back in Dresden on 27 February. It is not clear from the documents
on what grounds our grandfather was allowed to leave prison and even
travel to Amsterdam. Have new witnesses been interviewed? Are the
authorities looking for a way out of the case?

Isay Rottenberg is elated to be free, as we read in a letter from him
dated 21 February to the secretary-general of the Ministry of Foreign
Affairs:

> Undoubtedly thanks in part to your intervention, the German
> authorities have given me leave, pending further investigation
> to the legal case against me, to pay a brief visit to my family in
> Amsterdam. I am obliged to offer you my sincerest thanks for
> your efforts on my behalf, both from you personally and from
> your department. I struggle to find the words to express my grati-
> tude for the personal and heartfelt dedication extended me by
> Mr. Steenbergen. His robust and warm support have enabled me
> to withstand these sombre times.

Once Isay Rottenberg was reunited with his family and recovered from his hardships, Steenbergen weighs up the options. He suggests to the ministry that it might be handy for the court if Rottenberg did not keep his promise to return to Germany "because then this thorny legal matter would be rendered moot." Although the charges have not been proven at all, Steenbergen writes, the portents are not favourable. "Mr. Rottenberg's position is, in my opinion, a difficult one because in light of the present circumstances of racial laws, he is seen, as a non-Aryan, *a priori* as inferior and untrustworthy." His advice is to leave it to Van de Vlucht, Rottenberg's Dutch lawyer, to examine the case further.

Our grandfather ignores Steenbergen's advice. He knows he is in the right, and will prove it. He reports to Dresden promptly on 27 February.

13

UNDAUNTABLE

ONE EVENING WE'RE AT OUR COUSIN SACHA'S, WATCHING HIS MOTHer's (our Aunt Tini's) recollections recorded for Steven Spielberg's *Visual History Archive*, which includes testimony from some fifty-five thousand Holocaust survivors. The recording dates from 1996 or 1997, when Tini was seventy-three and still a beauty. She considers her thoughts carefully and gives articulate, well-formulated answers. Aside from being comfortingly familiar—the sound of her voice, her intonation, her gestures—it is very moving because she offers a lively, detailed account of the family before the war, something we almost never heard about from our fathers, and over which Granddad, too, kept mum.

Meanwhile we know much more about our grandfather and his history. The foreigner's registration, ID cards, marriage certificate, and Chamber of Commerce documents provide us with dates and facts we were never able to piece together. He emerges from the Döbeln municipal archive and the imprisonment dossier as an unfamiliar figure to us, his grandchildren.

Aunt Tini's words fill in the story. Sometimes she gets dates and the order of things mixed up, so we're not sure how accurate her memory is. But much of what she says is an eye-opener because no one had ever mentioned it before.

According to Tini, her mother decided to move to the Noorder Amstellaan (now the Churchill-laan) in 1935, when Isay was imprisoned, uncertain whether he would ever be set free and whether she could keep the large house on the Valeriusplein. Lena did so without consulting Isay, and he was angry about it. The year she gives is incorrect: according to the Amsterdam municipal archives, they moved in June 1934, when our grandfather was still free and was in no danger of being arrested.

So why did they move from their own five-storey brownstone to a modest rental? Did the DZW bring in too little money? Were there debts? Or was Isay unable, due to the German foreign currency laws, to send enough money home?

Tini's account does not answer this particular question, but it does shed light on Isay's original plans. When he took over the factory in Döbeln, he wanted his family to move to Germany with him. "Nothing doing," our grandmother said, according to Tini. "We're Dutch Jews!" And she was right, considering the circumstances in Germany in 1932. It confirms yet again our idea that our grandfather felt at home in Germany, more so than in the Netherlands, and that his fervent hope that his German enterprise would succeed blinded him to the political reality.

Isay acceded to Lena's refusal and commuted between Döbeln and Amsterdam—that is, he was occasionally home with the family. The uncertainty of his venture was too much for Lena, and led her to downsize.

As we have said, we children knew almost nothing about our grandfather's time in Germany. But one story did get told during Hella's youth: that her father Alfred, the eldest of the three children, was taken out of school just as he was about to finish gymnasium. Alfred himself never talked about it: the story always came from Hella's mother. "Granddad was in prison in Germany. Alfred had to get a job. He went to work at the Bijenkorf department store for twenty-five guilders a month!" There was always a tone of indignation. The family, she said, had enough money to help out, but no, Alfred had to drop out of school. Hella's mother, who met the Rottenbergs only after the war, was still miffed about it. Alfred never did get to do his final exams, nor did anything come of further study or enrolling in music conservatory to further develop his talent on the piano, because the war broke out a few years later.

The decision could have come from Abraham Ptasznik, who took family matters into his hands after Isay's arrest. "You're the eldest, we don't know what the future has in store, and you'll have to learn to support the family," we imagine him saying to Alfred.

Grandpa Ptasznik, Tini recalls, dropped by at the new address every week to give his daughter twenty-five guilders for household expenses (equivalent to about $400 Canadian today). "Every week!" cries Tini, horrified by the apparent humiliation to which her mother was subjected. "Couldn't he just bring around that money once a month?"

"In those days, in the Netherlands, having a family member in prison was something to be deeply ashamed of,"Tini says on the Spielberg video-tape. "A stain on the family . . . So you didn't mention it to anyone, at least we didn't."Theo Franken, their youngest cousin, has vivid memories of the secretive atmosphere within the Ptasznik family. Isay's being in jail was only whispered about. And then mostly in Polish, so that the grandchildren wouldn't understand. "They never talked about Uncle Szaja when the children were around,"Theo said. "I knew that something was up. But I also knew he hadn't been accused of robbery or murder." We imagine that on Friday evenings when, as always, the family came together to celebrate the Sabbath, they would share the latest news about family, business, culture, and politics. And, off in a corner, they would quietly, in Polish, discuss Isay.

Mayor Denecke fired

Isay Rottenberg uses the first two weeks of his newly gained freedom to suss things out. He spends about ten days with his family in Amsterdam before returning to Dresden. He no longer has any reason to be in Döbeln; even the factory is off limits.

The Döbeln municipal authorities and the NSDAP were aware of Rottenberg's arrest. Alderman Otto Röher had been allowed to read the Deutsche Bank's charges at the local party office. From it, he deduced that after Rottenberg took over the business, a dispute arose between Krenter and Rottenberg concerning the company's shares. The Jew Kronstein also played a role, he remarks. His notes exude outrage and contempt: not only Krenter, but Rottenberg, too, turned out to be a crook.

A message is sent post-haste from the Dresden court. Who among the civil servants or policemen in Döbeln would be prepared to testify in the Rottenberg case? Who knows the ins and outs of the takeover? Röher and the director of the municipal bank, Curt Reuther, volunteer. One name is missing from the correspondence—the man who had been actively involved in the fate of the DZW and had kept in constant contact with Isay Rottenberg: Mayor Herbert Denecke.

Denecke, we determine from the minutes of the city administration, has suddenly vanished. We are unable to reconstruct what exactly hap-pened. But it's clear Denecke and Rudolf Behr, the brazen Nazi Party boss in Döbeln, had a falling-out. A trace of it turns up in the Nazi data bank in Leipzig. Among the Döbeln hits is courtroom testimony by one Walter Haensch, who stood trial in 1946 in Nuremburg for war crimes committed in the Ukraine as the leader of an *SS-Einsatzgruppe*.

In his defence, Haensch told the Nuremburg court that he had always preferred to work in civilian positions. As proof he presents a brief stint in Döbeln, in 1935, when he worked for the city administration. He became embroiled in a conflict between Mayor Denecke and NSDAP leader Behr, and as a result was transferred, allegedly against his will, to the Sicherheitsdienst. If he had had his way, he'd have stayed in Döbeln and would never have ended up in the Ukraine as head of an SS unit.

The bottom line is that Behr emerged as the winner, and that the Nazis deemed Denecke to be insufficiently reliable to the party line. At this, the Döbeln city council dismissed him from his post. But Denecke's fate is a separate issue unrelated to Rottenberg.

Even if Denecke had remained firmly in the saddle, there was probably not much he could have done to sway the case. Defending a factory run by a Jew was one thing, but personally protecting a Jew in a lawsuit brought by the Deutsche Bank and public prosecutors was another story, and Denecke's influence did not reach that far.

Being ousted from his post in Döbeln (apparently already in April 1935) meant the end of Denecke's career as an administrator. In October of that year he received a warning from a Nazi Party tribunal, but was not expelled or otherwise punished. He remained a party member and was allowed to return to his former profession as criminal court judge. He even climbed the ladder to the point of being chosen, in 1940, to lead the regional court in Freiberg, which included a "special chamber" for pronouncing verdicts on political offences.

Der Jude Rottenberg

Once back in Dresden, Rottenberg calls on Steenbergen for assistance. Alongside the bankruptcy fraud lawsuit, he is also charged with a second offence, namely violating foreign exchange rules. According to the prosecutor, he was not allowed to pay the tobacco buyer Vincenz Silvan without special prior consent. Rottenberg's defence is that Silvan had not fled the country, but was abroad only temporarily and that the payment therefore, according to German law, must be regarded as a domestic transaction.

Steenbergen visits the prosecutor and discusses the case with him at length. He returns from the consultation under the impression that the case will fizzle out. The prosecutor admits that it is not such a serious matter and that he might only impose a fine. A few days later Steenbergen goes to the Saxony Ministry of Finance's foreign exchange office to work on the civil servant who brought the charges. He does not succeed, however, in convincing the man in question—who, Steenbergen emphasizes, received him wearing an SA uniform—to rescind the charges. But the consul does not give up and presents a written proposal for a settlement, and here he once again plays his trump card: the importance of the economic ties between Germany and the Netherlands. If the case is withdrawn or settled out of court, he writes, then there is less chance of it negatively influencing public opinion in the Netherlands.

His intervention works: A month later, on 28 April 1936, the case against Isay Rottenberg is dropped. All's well that ends well. Or is it?

Continued perusal of the documents shows that the foreign exchange case resurfaced. The same prosecutor who had closed down the case in April 1936 reopens it six months later, asking the judge conducting the preliminary research into the bankruptcy case to expand his investigation to include foreign exchange fraud. And because the two cases combined carry a higher penalty, he advises the court to remand Rottenberg into custody once again to prevent him from fleeing until his case comes to trial.

We do not know where Isay Rottenberg is at that moment. We do know that he still has not given up his quest to clear his name and call the Deutsche Bank to account. Steenbergen recalls that after being released from prison, Rottenberg was "very optimistic and confident that the case will be resolved in his favour."

Our grandfather bases that confidence on the fact that he was released from custody after being questioned almost daily for six months. He is innocent and they have no evidence to the contrary, he concludes, stubbornly clinging to the notion that the German judicial system still adheres to the rule of law and applies it assiduously. Is he ignoring reality? Germany passed the Nuremburg racial laws while he was in prison. Jews, from that moment on, are officially second-class citizens. Judges and prosecutors are by now thoroughly drenched in Nazi ideology. Of course Isay Rottenberg considers himself a Jew, but in Germany he seems to regard himself—legally, at least—more as a foreigner, a Dutch subject, with a passport that will offer him protection.

A conversation between Steenbergen and Illgen, the Dresden prosecutor, in May 1936 gives us an idea of how a German prosecutor sees Isay Rottenberg. Illgen is about sixty years old and wears an NSDAP lapel pin. His desk is piled with dossiers pertaining to the Deutsche Zigarren-Werke bankruptcy fraud. He considers it a tricky case, and is keen to hear Steenbergen's opinion of Rottenberg. This Rottenberg, isn't he simply a Pole who only just recently got Dutch citizenship? The fact that the Netherlands naturalized him, Steenbergen says, means he is clean. But even in Germany, counters Illgen, there was a time when citizenship could easily be bought.

On the Spielberg videotape Tini recounts how her father continued to pursue the case after his release, and when he was in Amsterdam was more a visitor than a resident. His sisters, who were very fond of him, would drop by and the whole family would gather around as he told them about his court cases. "For us children, that was *so* boring," she says. When he was there, the living room was thick with cigarette smoke, and there was always a bridge game going because of course he didn't have work in the Netherlands and had nothing else to do. The children couldn't stand all that smoking and bridge, and all three maintained a lifelong abhorrence of both. Tini recalls the words her father used when talking about his adventures in Germany: "Der Jude Rottenberg." And then he'd laugh. She thought it was horrible. Oppressive.

Resold

The civil and criminal lawsuits are still going on in January 1937, when the Deutsche Bank sells the DZW to the Lübbecke manufacturer August Blase. The price is 400,000 reichsmarks, four times what Rottenberg paid for it in 1932. For Blase, the DZW is an extremely attractive acquisition. He owns a cigar factory in Westphalia and more than fifty home-labour branches. In 1932 he employed nearly four thousand people, but the machine ban forced Blase to cease automated production and expand his workforce: in 1935 the firm employed some fifty-five hundred people, making him Germany's largest cigar producer. It was common knowledge within the sector that the Deutsche Zigarren-Werke was the only firm to survive the machine ban, and that the fully automatic American machines produced cigars at an unheard-of speed. Who wouldn't want to own a factory like that, the most modern in all of Germany?

It's not clear who took the initiative to sell the DZW. Generally, a German firm interested in acquiring a Jewish business would approach the bank, writes the economic historian Harold James in *The Deutsche Bank and the Nazi Economic War against the Jews*. The company in question would have already been in troubled waters as a result of credit issues or chicanery on the part of the authorities. If the owners did not make a snap decision or were disinclined to accept a low selling price, new accusations were fabricated. The German banks vied among themselves for the choicest pickings. Banks often held onto their shares for a while in the hope of turning a tidy profit, as the value of a firm would often increase after the Jewish owner was pushed out.

The DZW's sale contract includes the condition that the Deutsche Bank was not obliged to turn its shares over to Blase immediately, but rather only after the courts have determined the ownership of said shares. Both parties can nullify the contract should the court unexpectedly stand in the Deutsche Bank's way. So we conclude there is an ongoing lawsuit concerning the ownership of the shares, but the Deutsche Bank and Blase, unwilling to wait for the verdict, assume that the court will rubber-stamp the DZW's Aryanization—a legitimate assumption, all things considered.

The deal—its details are kept strictly confidential—is set in motion. The Deutsche Bank ousts the Arnhold Brothers, the DZW's house bank in Berlin, as well as the Dresdner Bank, which had taken over the Arnholds' main branch, making them, the Deutsche Bank, the cigar factory's sole creditor. The bank also stipulates in a secret clause that Blase is not to take his business to any other bank except the Döbeln municipal bank for small bridging loans only, and then only with permission from the Deutsche Bank.

A few weeks after signing the contract, August Blase puts his own people in charge of the factory, which is from that point a branch of Blase's imperium. The new director is Emil Leschinsky, formerly the boss of the home-labour branches in Westphalia. He was known and feared there for his precision and strictness. If cigar makers heard he was going to drop by, the story goes, they would disappear until he moved on to the next village.

Blase has paid for the buyout and, keeping in mind the annual share-holders' meeting in June, he is anxious to get his hands on his shares. So the Deutsche Bank must do something to placate him, and it puts aside a packet of 40 percent of the shares in a safe-deposit box. This is all Veith can do at the moment, he says in a letter to Blase. Then Veith refers to the conditions of the contract regarding the current lawsuit. But now the condition is more concrete: on 5 February 1937 the court ruled *against* the Deutsche Bank! We can hand over the shares, Veith writes, only when this provision is nullified.

Isay Rottenberg has apparently won a battle. Strident, stubborn, con-vinced he is in the right, and refusing to give in to the inevitable, he—a Jew in Nazi Germany—has thrown a wrench into the plans of the Deutsche Bank. We see his behaviour as reckless and maniacal. He has done time in jail, the fraud case against him is still pending, the foreign currency case has been reopened, he can be locked up again at any moment. And yet he still travels back and forth to Germany. He is there more often than safely in Amsterdam, and even dares to bring a lawsuit against a powerful adversary.

But for him, it must have looked otherwise. When he started out in Döbeln, he ignored his competitors' anti-Semitic slander; he stood up to the machine ban; he saw an official complaint by the Gestapo amount to nothing; he survived a smear campaign waged by the entire cigar sector;

he was arrested on false charges and then released. He has fended off all these attacks. He does not see himself as a vulnerable Jew: he can take them all on. Just try me, he thinks. And look: even the Deutsche Bank is not invincible.

We do not know the judge's exact verdict on 5 February 1937; only indirect snippets of information from the court cases survive. What we do know, from reading the correspondence between the bank and Blase, is that the court forced the Deutsche Bank to negotiate a settlement with Rottenberg.

What is also certain is that these negotiations led nowhere. Perhaps Isay Rottenberg smelled victory and refused their offer. Maybe he knew that the court case against him would peter out, or else he gambled it would. The foreign currency case was indeed dismissed at the end of November 1937 due to lack of evidence. It is not clear whether the other charges—the supposed bankruptcy fraud—were dropped at the same time or later, but in any event, the Deutsche Bank did not win the case.

After that, writes consul Steenbergen in May 1938, Rottenberg resumes his civil action against the Deutsche Bank, as he is free to do so now that the criminal suits have been dropped. Steenbergen's letter indicates that he even pressed multiple cases. The Saxony government, however, has had enough (or has been pressured by the Deutsche Bank), and on 17 May 1938 orders Isay Rottenberg's expulsion.

True to form, our grandfather does not take this lying down. He enters an appeal to the Dresden police commissioner: Saxony does not have the right to expel him, a Dutch citizen. Only the German Reich does, he insists. Legal matters require him to be in Dresden. And, finally, in black and white: he is suing both the Deutsche Bank *and* the Deutsche Zigarren-Werke.

There are no legal grounds, he says, on which to expel him from Dresden. "I am here to tend to my business, calmly and with respect for German law, and have to my knowledge never given cause to be regarded as an undesirable alien." Steenbergen sends another letter strongly objecting to Rottenberg's expulsion. Saxony does not budge. But then, thanks to intervention by the Dutch embassy in Berlin, the German Ministry of Foreign Affairs gives Rottenberg permission to be in Dresden whenever there is a hearing. He must continually reapply for permission, each time receiving a permit for just a few days.

The Dutch envoy in Berlin, Van Haersma de With, takes issue with the fact that Rottenberg, "who has committed no crime," may stay in Dresden only temporarily, as a kind of favour. He plans to tackle this issue, but first wants to know "whether, under the present circumstances, Mr. Rottenberg in fact desires to remain in Germany." His letter is dated 26 January 1939. It is the last-dated document in Isay Rottenberg's dossier in the Dutch Foreign Affairs archive. Preceding that is a memo from the German Auswärtiges Amt (Foreign Office) stating that Rottenberg has been granted permission to stay in Dresden for the period 6–11 November 1938.

We reread this, and sure enough, that is what is says. Between 6 and 11 November 1938. Then he was probably in Dresden on the night of 9 November—Kristallnacht.

14

AND THEN, WAR

IN DÖBELN, KRISTALLNACHT WAS HARDLY NECESSARY TO CHASE away the Jews. On 10 October 1938 the *Döbelner Anzeiger* ran an item headed "Döbeln Liberated from Jewish Businesses," reporting that the second and last Jewish-owned department store, the popular Wohlwert's, is now in Aryan hands. Nazi bigwigs, Mayor Walter Gottschalk (Denecke's successor), and the store's personnel celebrate the takeover. Nazi leader Behr looks back fondly on having issued the call, on 20 April, Hitler's birthday, to clear the city of Jews within six months. Now this "Jewish five-and-dime," Behr says, will be transformed into a shop embracing "good German spirit."

In his memoires, Helfrid Piper devotes a few passages to the reaction in Döbeln to Kristallnacht. On the morning of 10 November, he writes, a delivery truck from Leipzig arrived at his parents' shop. The driver was agitated, exclaiming, "In Leipzig they've set fire to shops and the synagogue. Have those apes gone mad?" Shortly thereafter, a truck arrived from Halle with the news that shop windows were smashed and the businesses ransacked. Everyone who heard this was upset, Piper recalls. "No one thought it was right—even our Döbeln NSDAP leader couldn't believe his ears." Piper calls Kristallnacht "simply a disgrace," followed by the dry comment that in Döbeln there had been "only two businesses where the glass in the doors had been smashed." Hardly worth being bothered about, he suggests, leaving out the simple fact that by then, nearly all of Döbeln's Jewish-owned businesses had been driven out.

Sophie Spitzer and Stephan Conrad from the Nazi history workgroup take us past the former mercery owned by the Heynemann family, who, after Kristallnacht, had no means to support themselves in Döbeln and thus left for Berlin, whence they were later deported; the Rosenthals' old house on the Ritterstrasse; Lachmann's department store; the home of the Jacobi family on the Breite Strasse.

Stopping at the small brass "stumbling stones" cemented into the pavement in front of these addresses, Conny and Sophie tell us about the individuals who lived there. Döbelners old enough to remember the 1930s recall their Jewish neighbours from school or work, as a doctor or shop-keeper, but for the generations that follow, it's not only a history they did not experience first-hand, but one that has been erased by modern times.

Many local gymnasium students, though, are aware of the city's history. Back when Judith Schilling, another active member of the workgroup, attended the school, its principal, Michael Höhme, offered an open course in Jewish history and culture. He does so every year. He and his son have researched the fate of the Glasberg family, who had three children at that very school, and created an exhibition about them. Specially for our visit, it was reinstalled in Döbeln's municipal museum. The story of the Glasbergs shows how impossible life had become for Döbeln's Jews, and how fanatical Nazis had instigated the persecution early on.

Max, Karl, and Ruth Glasberg were orphaned at a young age and were taken in by family who also lived in Döbeln. Their foster parents, David and Helene Gutherz, decided in 1936 to move to Berlin because of the increasing difficulties Helene, a gynecologist and pediatrician, experienced in her practice: patients who continued to visit her were gossiped about and threatened. Max Glasberg, the eldest son, moved to Berlin with them, but Karl and Ruth stayed behind in Döbeln with an aunt. They were both students at the local gymnasium and the family hoped they would be able to finish school. In 1938 a new principal arrived, an *Obersturmbannführer* with the SA who wore his brown uniform to school. He made Ruth and Karl sit separately in the classroom, so as not to "infect" their German classmates. In May 1938, the Jewish students were expelled from school altogether, six months before the Nazis put this into practice nationwide. So Karl and Ruth moved to Berlin.

One last visit to their aunt in Döbeln proved fatal to Max. A policeman recognized him, and had him put in jail. A week later, he was transferred to Leipzig, and from there, to Sachsenhausen concentration camp. The family received word of his death a few months later, in March 1940. Karl had returned to Berlin, where he was arrested; he was later murdered in

Auschwitz. Their foster parents, David and Helene Gutherz, were arrested and separated. Helene did not wait to see what was to come, and took a poison pill. David was murdered in Auschwitz. Only the youngest child, Ruth, survived the Nazis, having been smuggled to Sweden on "kinder-transport" in 1940.

Ruth returned to Döbeln in 1950. She was struck by how many people looked away and kept quiet when they recognized her. Fortunately, there were exceptions, like the acquaintances who returned her family photo albums. Not everyone participated in the Nazi purge of Jews, Ruth recalled when she visited Döbeln again in 1999. "Most people were indifferent or afraid. That's human nature, I can understand that. Even though there's always so much talk of solidarity, people generally think of themselves first."

The Döbeln chronicles assembled by Heimatfreund Jürgen Dettmer, based on the fully surviving newspaper articles of the day, allow us to watch Döbeln become swept up in pre-war fervour.

Kristallnacht is the signal for the *Döbelner Anzeiger* to pull out all the stops. Violent language dominates its headlines: "Jews Are Murderers!" "When the German *Volk* Strikes, It Strikes Hard." "Lice Are Lice, and Jews Are Jews."

After German troops invade Czechoslovakia in March 1939, the Obermarkt in front of city hall—already called "Hindenburgplatz" for six years now—is the stage for week after week of organized enthusiasm. Manifestations and parades, the voices of Hitler and Goebbels thunder-ing out of loudspeakers, Nazi leaders from Dresden and Berlin coming to Döbeln in person to whip up the locals as the war approaches.

The war starts on 1 September with the invasion of Poland, and the Döbeln regiment participates in the battle. Three weeks later the first Polish POWs arrive, a thousand of them, brought to the city in a special train. They are divided among the neighbouring villages and are put to work with the fall harvest.

Rudolf Behr keeps a close eye on the "purity" of the residents. A local girl was caught being photographed with a Polish prisoner of war, and the NSDAP leader saw to it that she was put outside city hall in the cold, her head shaved, to be mocked by the townsfolk.

Many years later, the girl's mother testifies in the case against Behr, who is accused of crimes against humanity. It was an act of vengeance, she says. He and a few men came into her tavern and demanded "decent food." She offered to make them soup with potatoes and eggs for free, but he turned it down. He wanted ham and sausages, also for free. She refused, and he stormed out, cursing. A few weeks later Behr had the woman and her daughter arrested, their heads shaved, and left them outside city hall in freezing-cold weather to be gawked at by townspeople. The crowd taunted them and pelted them with snowballs. After that, the mother and daughter were brought to Leipzig, acquitted by the judge, but then jailed by the Gestapo again. The daughter was sent to Ravensbrück concentration camp, where she was imprisoned for four months. The mother ended up in the hospital because of the physical abuse at the hands of the Gestapo.

At the beginning of 1940, hundreds of *Volksdeutsche* brought to Germany from Poland as part of the "Heim ins Reich" campaign are quartered in Döbeln. Their accommodation was so primitive, however, that dozens of small children died.

On 1 October 1940, Döbeln celebrates the return of its troops, who had been waging war throughout Europe for the past year. The shops close for the day in order to give the soldiers a heroes' welcome.

Döbeln receives word that Hermann Groine, the former NSDAP district leader, was killed shortly after the commencement of Operation Barbarossa, the surprise attack on the Soviet Union in June 1941. Partly thanks to him, our grandfather had been able to fend off the machine ban at the DZW because at the first meeting between Isay Rottenberg and his adversaries, it was Groine who had tipped the scales in Rottenberg's favour. Although Groine had been transferred to a neighbouring city in 1934, he was such an important figure to Döbelners that he was commemorated in a public memorial. He was the one, let us recall, who sealed the Nazi takeover in Döbeln by answering Mayor Kunzemann's question "Mr. Groine, do you intend to use force to prevent me from executing my function?" with "Yes."

Hermann Groine was forty-four years old.

Groine's successor, Rudolf Behr, is called up for military service in early 1942. Later that year he is injured and returns to Döbeln to recuperate. Aiming to boost morale, he addresses a full hall, enthusing about Germany's successes on the Eastern Front. "It all comes down to us!"

On 29 January 1943, Behr is the keynote speaker at an event celebrating the tenth anniversary of the Nazis' rise to power. Naturally, he pretends there is a lot to celebrate, but the underinformed populace has no clue how the war is actually progressing. A week after the festivities, the cinemas, theatres, restaurants, and cafés are closed. They remain so for days because there is nothing to celebrate now that the Sixth Army, surrounded after a months-long siege of Stalingrad, has capitulated. One hundred ten thousand German soldiers are sent to Russian prisoner of war camps. Only six thousand will return.

There are Döbelners, too, among the Stalingrad soldiers. The Wehrmacht opens an information desk at Bahnhofstrasse 11A, where family members can inquire as to the fate of their loved one. Mayor Gottschalk commemorates "the heroes of Stalingrad" at city hall.

From now on it's all hands on deck. Men from seventeen to sixty-five years old and women between eighteen and thirty-five must register at the Burgstrasse employment office to be assigned to work in the armaments industry. Businesses considered nonessential for daily necessities or weaponry lose their personnel and have to shut down. The atmosphere in Döbeln becomes increasingly grim. There is a nighttime curfew, and residents must camouflage their attic windows. The city hall tower acts as an air-raid signal: if the clock is dimly lit, then this means it is safe; if it goes dark, then people must take shelter. Gauleiter Mutschmann forbids American jazz or "suchlike so-called music incompatible with German cultural sensibilities."

Some businesses thrive in these times, distinguishing themselves as model Nazi enterprises. The Nazis have transformed industrial Saxony, "Germany's workplace," into an armaments factory. With its many metal-working factories and excellent transport links, Döbeln is among the first to contribute to weapons production. Nazi leaders visit factories there to determine each workplace's contribution. The Grossfuss company, for example, is assigned the task of improving the MG 34 machine gun. Engineers set to work, and the result is the MG 42, designed by the Döbeln engineer Werner Gruner. It became the fastest machine gun in World War II and is known as "Hitler's buzzsaw." This technical feat earns Gruner a reward from Mutschmann and spotlighted Grossfuss as a model company within the weapons industry.

Our grandfather's angry competitor Emil Stockmann receives a Nazi distinction as well. He got his revenge by taking over a cigar factory in Heidelberg from a Jewish owner as part of the sector's forced Aryanization, buying the factory for his son. But it wasn't for this that he was decorated: his factory in Döbeln was largely revamped for the production of army material.

At the beginning of 1944, Döbeln's official population includes, alongside 25,000 Germans, more than 1,300 forced labourers, all but 54 of them male. Conny and Sophie are convinced there must have been more. Their research shows 2,000 forced labourers working for some 143 businesses. "That's nearly 10 percent of the population," Conny says. During our walks through town, they point to various buildings. "There was a business with forced labourers on every street corner."

From the end of August 1944, life revolves entirely around the war. Concerts and theatrical performances are cancelled, education is restricted, the workweek is extended to sixty hours per week. The statue of Luther in Luther Square disappears, most likely melted down for the weapons industry.

Allied air strikes on 13 and 14 February 1945 leave Dresden in utter ruins. Döbeln is unharmed, but air-raid sirens go off every day. Two bombs hit houses in Döbeln on 17 March, but the damage is minimal and there are no casualties.

With the Allies approaching, the Nazis evacuate the concentration camps. "Death marches" of prisoners from Colditz and Buchenwald pass through Döbeln on their way to Freiberg and to Theresianstadt in Bohemia. Seven prisoners collapse from exhaustion in Döbeln and are shot on the spot.

On 1 May, flyers are handed out on Martin Mutschmannplatz with the message: "Adolf Hitler has died for Germany." The NSDAP building on the Bahnhofstrasse flies its flag at half-mast, but the barracks do not. Citizens hang black ribbons out of their windows. The Nazis start burning documents.

On 6 May, Soviet and American troops have approached to within a few kilometres of Döbeln on both sides. The Americans halt, the Red Army prepares to take Döbeln. Mayor Walter Gottschalk is desperate; he has received no instructions on whether to surrender or resist. He gets in his car and flees the city. The Red Army enters the city without firing a single shot.

To certify the takeover, the Russian commander goes to city hall, but finds it empty except for a single alderman, waiting on his own in room 7. It is none other than Otto Röher, the former deputy mayor who, together with Mayor Kunzemann, had brought the Deutsche Zigarren-Werke to Döbeln in the first place. He signs the surrender. He has a motto, "Always be indispensable," before the Nazis came to power, while they were in charge, and now that the Third Reich has collapsed. Röher accepts this responsibility, and is rewarded for it. For even though he was quick to join the Nazis in 1933, he is appointed to the first postwar "antifascist democratic" city administration as the alderman in charge of finances. As though the past twelve years never happened.

DZW *under new ownership*

The Deutsche Zigarren-Werke is able to continue operating smoothly after being expropriated in 1935. The conflict around mechanical production has been put to rest—not only because the Jewish owner, the foreigner, the troublemaker, has been ousted. It is also thanks to Germany's rearmament program, which eradicated unemployment, boosted the economy, and allowed consumers to enjoy their cigars once again. This rejuvenated market made it less of a struggle for smaller cigar manufacturers to survive.

The resistance to machine-made cigars has also waned. Cigar manufacturers start to show interest in the new production methods. At the end of 1935, the Reichsverband der Deutschen Zigarrenhersteller's newsletter includes a small announcement: interested parties are invited to apply for a trip to America to study modern cigar-making methods. The ship will leave from Hamburg, foreign currency restrictions will be lifted, and the low rate of exchange will keep the costs down. Interest is so great that not everyone can enrol, prompting the union to schedule a second one, and a third. The study trips are a rousing success.

The Deutsche Zigarren-Werke's new owner, the Deutsche Bank, appoints Fritz Dannemann from Dresden to the management, alongside engineer Georg Berns. We're surprised to encounter this name. Might he be a relative of the cigar multinational Dannemann that now owns the building and premises of our grandfather's former factory? Or is it just a coincidence?

Fritz Dannemann, incidentally, had but a brief stint as director. He was replaced in 1937 by Emil Leschinsky, August Blase's confidant sent to Döbeln immediately after Blase had bought the shares from the Deutsche Bank.

After the war, Leschinsky was called to account by a commission of the new, Communist management. The Deutsche Zigarren-Werke, after all, could easily have earned itself an award as a model Nazist business. Leschinsky, an NSDAP member since 1933, apparently held "company roll calls," marked by speeches with a National-Socialist tenor. The staff rooms would be decorated with banners and a portrait of the Führer. Prominent Nazis, including Gauleiter Mutschmann, were in attendance at factory celebrations. The company had a "work squad": uniformed employees who kept an eye on the political convictions of the personnel. There was also an active Nazi women's group. And collections were held regularly for National Socialist charities.

Another all-too-familiar name crops up: the industrialist and fervent Nazi Fritz Saupe. In 1939 he was made a governor of the Deutsche Zigarren-Werke, but gave up his post upon volunteering for the army in 1940. He survived the war, was jailed by the occupying Allied forces, and died shortly thereafter.

In the wake of Krenter's failed plans, the city, following the DZW's Aryanization, was still the owner of the facility and grounds. At the end of 1938, August Blase purchased the entire parcel for 250,000 reichsmarks, enough for the city to pay the bank approximately half the outstanding debts it had run up as guarantor. The rest had to be written off as a loss.

The maximum annual production quota of sixty-two million cigarettes still held. Shortly after the German invasion of Poland in 1939, Blase asked Berlin to raise it to ninety million. After the departure (read: mobilization) of workers from his factory in Lübbecke, he aimed to transfer production

from there to Döbeln. His request was denied. There was no legal mechanism to raise the quota, and doing so would disadvantage other factories,
which were also suffering from a shortage of employees due to the "extraordinary circumstances."

Beyond this, it appears that the Deutsche Zigarren-Werke does not
experience any particular setbacks because of the war. The factory receives
enough orders, in particular from the Wehrmacht. At the end of 1943, when
the flush of military success had turned into a desperate slog, the *Döbelner
Anzeiger* enthusiastically reported that "we still have the only fully automatic cigar factory in the Reich." The newspaper recalls:

> We can still clearly remember the storms that raged when the
> factory just started up. Our city achieved a sort of "notoriety,"
> at first however not in the most positive sense of the word. But
> in the meantime many of the prejudices against machine-made
> cigars have faded and the rest are also certain to disappear.

A single machine produces thirteen thousand cigars per day, while a
trained handworker can roll at most five hundred per day, the newspaper
writes, gushing with amazement at the wonders of modern technology. The
machines, moreover, are German-made: "they are by no means American
any longer." We are unable to ascertain whether this is fact or propaganda.
But the machines were brand-new in 1930 and would have lasted a good
twenty or twenty-five years. From the moment that Germany and America
were at war, in late 1941, spare parts would be hard to come by, but would
the DZW have replaced all its machines with German ones?

Two POWs and three Ukrainian forced labourers work at the DZW
during the war. In 1944, one production hall is refitted for the war industry,
making airplane parts. The number of labourers and other employees drops
to 360.

Shortly after the war, the occupying Soviet military administration issued
"Decree No. 124": the confiscation of property belonging to active Nazis
and Nazi organizations. Anyone wishing to hold on to his property had
to prove he had no Nazi affiliation. Director Leschinsky claimed that
August Blase was not an active Nazi and had no leadership role in the Nazi
regime's economic sector, nor was he a war criminal or otherwise culpable.
He had been a member of the NSDAP since 1937, but only "in name." So the

decision to confiscate the factory was quickly rescinded. For the moment, it could remain in Blase's possession as a branch of the main factory located in Lübbecke, in the British zone of Allied-occupied Germany.

Early in 1948 there was another, more detailed, ownership review. Leschinsky, still director, wrote down what he knew. The shares were owned by August Blase, who bought them in 1937 from the Deutsche Bank. This is correct. "As far as is known, the shares were in the possession of the Deutsche Bank since the factory's founding in 1932." This is incorrect. But Leschinsky either assumed the truth would not come out, or he actively saw to it that it did not. The company documents, he said, were "probably turned over to the Dresden court in 1935," and, well, they were burned in the bombardment.

The city administrators smelled a rat, but they were unable to lay their hands on proof of Aryanization. "It is not even possible to ascertain whether the former Jewish director or manager was a shareholder." At least, that is what the memo said. Of course there are plenty of Döbelners who knew how things stood. Otto Röher had a front-row seat for the entire show. He knew that the Deutsche Bank stole the company in 1935, after having accused Isay Rottenberg of fraud, and then two years later, sold it to Blase for 400,000 reichsmarks. Whatever the reason, the city authorities let the case go stale, and no one took any notice.

The Deutsche Zigarren-Werke remains in business, even retaining its name. In 1952 the East German government takes over the factory. Did they pay Blase for it? Probably not. The factory was merged with another nationalized cigar company in nearby Leisnig. In 1969 the two factories employ some seventeen-hundred people. Modernization in 1977 means they can lay off more than half their employees and at the same time produce 30 percent more cigars. The "Jagdkammer" brand from Döbeln is well-known throughout the GDR.

A few years after those costly investments, in 1981, the Döbeln candy factory takes over the buildings. Cigar production stops. Instead of smelling of tobacco, the production halls now smell of chocolate and sweets.

Almost immediately after the Wende in 1989, the Lübbecke-based Dannemann company, which took over the factory from Blase in 1980, makes a claim to the assets, buildings, and premises of the former Deutsche Zigarren-Werke. The investigation and decision are quick: the city is to return the Deutsche Zigarren-Werke to Dannemann. The state in which Dannemann finds the buildings can be seen on the photographs the company was so kind to send us. Since then, new fences have been installed, as well as the floodlights that illuminate the buildings at night. Otherwise, nothing seems to have been touched. The old machines stand shoved together collecting dust in the production rooms. Perhaps Dannemann dreamt of putting the buildings back to use, but a combination of laws and impracticalities stood in the way. "What would we do with those buildings if we ever got them back?" we joke as we stand in front of the abandoned factory.

Isay Rottenberg

After Kristallnacht, Isay Rottenberg finally abandoned the notion of travelling to Germany to pursue his court cases. From what Aunt Tini says on the Spielberg tape, our grandfather won his court cases and received financial compensation for the confiscated factory, but he couldn't get the money out of Germany. So the family went there, she said, and bought clothes and other items with it. She even says that the family went on vacation in Germany—Nazi Germany!—a few times.

She doesn't say exactly when that was, but that she does recall seeing the Hitler Youth march. We are stunned. Neither Hella's nor Sandra's father ever uttered a word about this. Did the brothers not go with them? Or were they too ashamed to mention it? They did tell us one memory from those days. They and their father hiked over the Tatra Mountains to Czechoslovakia, and they had a grand time. Hella remembers one of her father's prized souvenirs at home, a wooden hiking stick with small metal plaques hammered in from each cabin where they spent the night. The year, Sandra knows, was 1936.

In one of Tini's albums we come across a photo we had never seen before. A vacation snapshot in front of a waterfall. Granddad sits on a boulder looking puckish and holding a hiking stick. Judging from Alfred, Edwin, and Tini's ages, it must have been taken around 1936. Also in that photo is a man, a woman, and a boy we don't recognize. Is this one of those vacations in Nazi Germany?

Who knows? Maybe that picture was taken in Czechoslovakia, Austria, or Switzerland. Could be. But if we are to believe Tini, the family had no money to spend outside Germany and it's more likely we are looking at a genuine German waterfall. And that later, the Rottenbergs were so embarrassed by their outings to Nazi Germany that they never mentioned them.

One of Aunt Tini's comments sheds new light on a question that's been nagging us for months now. Why did our grandfather keep working in Germany after Hitler came to power? We examined every possible reason. Maybe he had sunk too much money into the factory and run up debts. Once the machine ban had been decreed, the factory would have depreciated in value. He had to revive it before selling. Or was he just too stubborn to give up? His fighting spirit had been triggered and he was not about to let them chase him away.

Aunt Tini said, "Father lost a lot of money in 1929. He had houses in Berlin, in Charlottenburg. All our money was in Germany." This remark, alongside a few sentences written by consul Steenbergen that we had previously overlooked, clarify the situation somewhat. In contesting Isay Rottenberg's expulsion from Saxony in May 1938, Steenbergen writes to the Dresden police commissioner that deportation "would be particularly harsh for Herr Rottenberg, because—and he is prepared to prove this—in 1929 he had invested his entire fortune in Germany against the then-exchange rate, and subsequently kept it here." Steenbergen explains that the Netherlands cannot "approve" of supporting Rottenberg, should he be expelled, while his funds are stuck in Germany. After all, Germany will not give him permission to sell his assets and transfer the money to the Netherlands.

As we understand it, our grandfather lost much of his capital in the 1929 crash. Some of it had been invested in real estate: we were able to trace one address in Berlin-Charlottenberg. So he had apparently already set his sights on Germany. In a way, it makes his decision to take over the cigar factory in 1932 seem more logical. And it makes it easier to understand his refusal to accept his losses and setbacks—Hitler, the machine ban, confiscation. Even if he had sold his factory and other property, the foreign currency restrictions would have prevented him from getting the money out of the country anyway. He was stuck.

He had no savings in the Netherlands, no income, and no job. From the moment of his arrest, his family in Amsterdam was being supported by his in-laws. The Dutch consul assumes that rent income from the house in Charlottenberg covered his travel expenses and accommodation in Germany. Without his factory, Rottenberg was wiped out.

Well-informed

There is another Rottenberg family testimony from the 1930s. Edwin, like Tini, was interviewed for the Spielberg project. His statements show that the family was not the least bit naive or ill-informed about National Socialism. According to Edwin, they were well informed about the events in Germany, and not only through the news media. German-Jewish refugees were frequent visitors to their home. Whether that was directly after the Nazi takeover or only after Kristallnacht, Edwin does not say. "Many of them were fantastic people, with sharp, analytical minds; intelligent and highly educated people who were unable to practise their professions. Lawyers, doctors, actors, writers. Those people were part of my parents' circle, and being around them was an incredibly enriching experience [. . .] My parents were very hospitable. And the folks who came to the house were very interesting."

To the interviewer's question about how vulnerable or anxious the family felt after the German occupation of the Netherlands, Edwin replies, "Yes, well . . . things were pretty bottled up." Talk about being bottled up: in that entire two-hour video interview, Edwin does not say a single word about his father living and working in Germany, doing time in a German prison, and experiencing Nazism first-hand.

So back to Aunt Tini, the only family member who mentioned Isay's German adventure. She recalls with admiration her father's actions in the period following Kristallnacht: "My father was a wonderful man. A fighter. Of course, he had many Jewish friends. In Germany, and in Prague. He smuggled some of them to Holland—either by train or by some other means. 'I've got them,' he'd say. He travelled with them from Germany or Czechoslovakia and made sure they got over the border." Tini recalls one couple whom he had brought by train from Prague. At the border, when the carriage in which they were sitting suddenly reversed direction, heading back to Germany, he jumped out, pressed 100 guilders into the Dutch station manager's hand, and said, 'I *must* get these people out.'" She continues: "Father felt invincible with his Dutch passport!"

After Kristallnacht, our grandfather tried to find his footing in Amsterdam. He had already started a new enterprise even before the German invasion. His business partner's name came up regularly and with a certain respect during our youth. It was an exotic name—Yohai—and was always followed by "a Turkish Jew." They had something to do with cigarettes and cigarette mouthpieces.

The occupation

As a child, I, Hella, always wondered why Granddad didn't emigrate to America with his family in time. He had spent time in a German jail, so you would think he knew what the Nazis had in store for the Jews. I never dared ask him. When I asked my father, my tone betrayed my incomprehension. How could he—how could you all—have been so stupid, so passive and unassertive?

On the other hand, our mothers, the daughters-in-law, spoke of the Rottenbergs with admiration. Sandra's mother never tired of saying, "The Rottenbergs never wore a yellow star." And Hella's mother stressed the fact that the Rottenbergs were a very, very rare exception: an Amsterdam Jewish family who was reunited safe and sound after the war.

A friend of the Rottenbergs was picked up during one of the first razzias in Amsterdam, in February 1941. A few months later, Edwin was sent to the southern province of Brabant for a short time, after Jewish youngsters in the neighbourhood were snatched from the street. In December 1941, two cousins, Karel Citroen and Bob Franken, decided to flee the country. "My father approved," Edwin says on the Spielberg tape. As that winter was so cold, Edwin himself put off leaving until the following March.

His father brought him to the train. Edwin recalls the farewell as "not too dramatic." He says that he intentionally repressed his emotions. "I didn't want that, not then, because it gets in the way of your determination. Emotions sap your energy and distract you from your goal." He had addresses of reliable business contacts of Isay's and of an old school friend where he could stop along the way. After Brussels he travelled to Lille and Paris, then further south, making his way over the Pyrenees via a smugglers' route. Near Barcelona he was detained by the Spanish Guardia Civil and held in the internment camp Miranda del Ebro, initially built to incarcerate the International Brigade, which had fought against Franco. He was released in the summer of 1943 and managed to get a place on a small airplane, which left from a Lisbon beach for England.

In early 1942 Alfred, then twenty-four years old, closed the door to the flat on the Noorder Amstellaan behind him. At his father's request, he kept a diary, beginning with "the day I left my parents' home for the first time in my life." He did not tell his mother or sister Tini that he was going to join Edwin. He said goodbye to his father at the factory, where together they had packed his bag. "It was gut-wrenching," Alfred writes, "to see him wave me off."

In July 1942, two more cousins, Hans and Theo Franken, also left with the goal of reaching Switzerland.

Alfred travelled through Brussels to France, where he was arrested and put in jail. He managed to escape and reached a refuge for Dutch "Engelandvaarders" in the Pyrenees. After a three-month wait, he was able to cross the mountains by foot into Spain. Once in Madrid, he attempted in vain to get his brother Edwin released from the Spanish camp. In the end, Alfred travelled to London via Curaçao and Canada, arriving in April 1943, nearly a year after fleeing the Netherlands. After a thorough interrogation by British intelligence to confirm that he was politically reliable, Alfred was assigned to the Marines as a decoder and interpreter on board a destroyer.

Edwin reached London in September 1943 and reported to the Dutch Marines. Like Alfred, he was detached as a decoder on British warships. Their knowledge of languages, especially German, was useful to the British in eavesdropping on the enemy U-boats in the vicinity. In addition to Alfred and Edwin, their cousins Karel and Bob, after a short spell in Switzerland, arrived safely in England and were assigned to the British marines. Hans joined the Italian partisans. Only Theo, the youngest, remained in Switzerland. Edwin was occasionally on duty with Karel and Bob, and when they were on leave, the brothers and cousins sometimes met up in London.

The brothers Hans, Theo, and Bob Franken managed to escape from Holland, but their parents were unable to follow them. Theo described the tragedy: "Bob wrote to my parents from Switzerland on 3 or 4 August 1942 in a sort of secret code we had, to tell them we were safe. The plan was for them to follow the same route on 10 August. But just one day earlier, on the ninth, all the Jews on their street were taken away. So they never made it."

Isay finally flees, too

Thanks to Tini's Spielberg videotape and our talks with Theo, the story of Isay, Lena, and Tini's flight finally starts to make sense. The children and grandchildren of the elder Ptaszniks must have discussed leaving the country and the various possible routes, and each made his or her own decision. We had always been convinced that Isay planned to leave Holland as soon as possible after Edwin and Alfred left. But now, with a better overview of the events, we are less sure of that. We now know that he fled in a panic, without thorough preparation.

Sometime in July 1942, Isay suddenly decided that they had to get out. Tini had been arrested, but was then released after a few days. When she arrived back home, understandably distraught, Isay and Lena realized it was too dangerous to stay put any longer. They moved to the factory on the Oudezijds Achterburgwal in the city centre, and from there Isay arranged their escape. The family was brought to Brabant in the back of a delivery truck. During a cursory inspection along the way, they were not discovered among the goods. They stayed with a farming family for a day or two—acquaintances of Lena's where she went to pick mushrooms every year—and planned the next step of their journey. Hidden under the tarpaulin of a tractor-trailer, they made their way to the border. Isay thought he had arranged reliable smugglers, but they turned out to be profiteers and he had to pay them double. While crossing a cornfield on foot, they suddenly came face to face with a Dutch border patrolman. "What are you doing here?" the man demanded. Isay was dumbstruck, but Tini put all her charm into the situation, and the man let them pass. By bicycle and via a number of intermediary stops, they reached Antwerp.

According to Tini, her father, whom she had always known to be tough and decisive, was desperate and in tears. Lena stepped in and said sternly, "Szaja, be strong!"

In Brussels they waited a few weeks for false documents. They were to travel with a group of refugees. Isay didn't trust it, but in the end they left: first by train via Nancy to Belfort, and then by bus to the Swiss frontier, where they had to sneak over the border. They got lost; it was three harrowing days before they reached Switzerland.

Once in Switzerland, Isay was immediately put into jail. Thanks to a distant in-law in New York who agreed to the financial guarantee demanded by the Swiss government, they were allowed to stay.

At first they lived in a refugee camp. Later, they had their own apartment near Vevey, on Lake Geneva. There are a few surviving photographs from their wartime stay in Switzerland. On one of them, our grandparents are sitting at the table; behind them is a large wall map of Europe and North Africa. They followed the progress of the war, pinning thumbtacks to the map. Another photo shows Isay intently listening to the radio, his back to Lena and Tini.

Our grandfather was not one to sit around and wait for something to happen. He made himself useful by helping other Jewish refugees, and was already making plans in his mind for when the war was over. From a distance he kept tabs on the business Yohai & Co. that he left behind in Amsterdam, hoping to prevent the business from being stolen or taken over. Through an acquaintance he tried to arrange the "quasi-Aryanization" of the business. In a letter to Edwin in which he shares his thoughts on this matter, he refers in an aside to his experience with the Deutsche Zigarren-Werke. "I purposely did not leave behind any provisions for a proxy because it could then—you know this from the DZW—open the door to 'legal' robbery. So now I refuse to put my signature on anything."

Isay assumes that after the war, his sons will come work for him in either the tobacco business or, if it no longer exists, whatever new enterprise he sets up. In a letter dated 23 February 1943 he encourages Edwin to put his time in the camp to good use by learning Spanish.

> From your last letter I take it your French has improved greatly;
> I would much like for you to also perfect your Spanish, because
> later I want to "exploit" you, with your languages, for the export
> of our products, which will have a large overseas market. I am
> determined to do this and am convinced we will enjoy great suc-
> cess in our work.

In that same letter, he expounds on his vision of the postwar economy. He lambasts the radical ideas and newfangled approaches that Edwin, inspired by his contact with the International Brigade, might have suggested to his father. "Horsefeathers," is Isay's answer.

> Plantwirtschaft, Grossraumwirtschaft, freie Wirtschaft, etc. etc.—these are nothing but words. [. . .] the notion that society will experience an overwhelming transformation is, in my opin- ion, utopian. The individual will always be the guarantor of our progress; turning our backs on individualism will only lead to the kind of excesses we have, alas, seen in the past ten years and have proved to be detrimental for all mankind. One can always prove the opposite in theory, but reality forces more down-to-earth views. Therefore, my dear boy, study your languages diligently and we will all try to adapt as best we can to the new circumstances.

Isay wrote to Alfred in early 1943 that "every piece of news" from Amsterdam, even the most banal, "contained a tragedy." Friends reported that the authorities came looking for the Rottenbergs as well to (in Isay's cloaked language) "take us on a long car trip." At the beginning of March came the news that the elder Ptaszniks had been deported from Westerbork. Two weeks later, on 14 March 1943, Isay wrote to Alfred:

> I haven't much to report. More accurately, I'm not up to it and have no patience, which you will surely understand. Grandmother and Grandfather's deportation is a heavy blow to us. Mother is the worst off. She is unable to cope with it, her eyes are red from crying, and she can't sleep. Likewise, I've become anxious and gloomy. Aside from the family members in Holland, my mother, sisters and brothers and their families—23 people in all—who were shut up in various ghettos, have been missing for months.

Under Isay's typed letter, Lena added a few handwritten sentences. "My dear boy, we're so far away from one another at the moment, aren't we. I so look forward to seeing your handwriting and hearing all about what you're up to. I hope everything is going well for you. You would make us so happy with a snapshot."

In addition to Lena's elderly parents, two of her three sisters, their hus- bands, and a daughter were also deported. The third sister survived because when the war broke out, she was abroad and stayed there. Of Granddad's ten brothers and sisters, only two were still alive after the war: Hermann, who had moved to Sweden, and Maryla, who had emigrated to Palestine before the war. The others, together with their spouses and children, were taken from the ghettos of Warsaw and other Polish cities to the extermination camps. Isay's eldest brother Zacharias was deported to Auschwitz from France.

Isay, Lena, and their three children returned to Amsterdam soon after liberation. They had kept in touch by mail for nearly the entire duration of the war. When our grandparents were finally settled, they took over the role of the Ptasznik grandparents. On Friday evenings, everyone who had survived the war went to the Milletstraat to eat and be together. Isay assisted family members for years to come with legal restitution and the bureaucratic red tape of recouping their lost property.

He was unbowed and, at age fifty-six, still had the energy to start a new business—a modern factory making modern products with American-made machines. As soon as it was possible, he applied for permission to import them.

Back to the beginning of our scavenger hunt. When we first saw the notice from the Conference on Jewish Material Claims Against Germany, we assumed we would have to prove that our grandfather had been dispossessed and that we were his rightful heirs. This turned out to be unnecessary. And in any case, we would never have managed it in a month, the final deadline. All we had to do for the time being was register with the Claims Conference as the grandchildren of Isay Rottenberg.

We were eventually given access to a dossier on the Deutsche Zigarren-Werke at the Federal Office for Unresolved Property Issues in Berlin. Years earlier, the Claims Conference had amassed the evidence that Isay Rottenberg had been the owner of the Deutsche Zigarren-Werke. Already at the end of 1992 they had registered the factory with the Saxony government, listing Isay Rottenberg as its former owner. Later, some confusion arose as to who the present owner was. The Dannemann cigar company—which had taken the DZW over from the firm that had Aryanized it—lodged a protest and even claimed damages. A lawsuit between Dannemann and the Claims Conference ensued, resulting, in 2009, with the German government's awarding a hefty sum to the Claims Conference for Isay Rottenberg's shares in the company, plus interest.

All that time, we grandchildren were completely in the dark. The Claims Conference made no effort to locate us. They knew Isay Rottenberg came from Amsterdam; a single glance in the telephone book would have been enough to contact us. If we had missed that advertisement in the *Nieuw Israëlitisch Weekblad*, we would never have discovered the factory. It took us a year to hand over the papers to convince the Claims Conference that we were Isay Rottenberg's sole and rightful heirs. A few months later they paid us damages. It was a portion of the amount that the German government had paid as compensation for the DZW; the Claims Conference kept the rest for itself. It was a curious outcome, to say the least, and there was no possibility of appeal. When we submitted the claim, we had to agree to their opaquely communicated conditions. While disappointed, we took comfort in the realization that without the Claims Conference, we would not have found out about the factory at all.

The trove of materials that lay dormant until we dug it up provided an amazingly complete picture of our grandfather's cigar factory. We witnessed the National-Socialist takeover of a typical mid-sized German town, how local authorities operated during the first years of the Nazi regime, and their relationship with a Jewish entrepreneur. We gleaned much new information about our grandfather, and our view of him took on new dimensions.

Before the war, he must have felt more German than Dutch, much more than we had ever realized. Despite having lived in Amsterdam for more than ten years, he was drawn to Germany and envisaged his future there. He invested his savings in a factory, and lived and worked nearby, while his family stayed behind in the Netherlands. He would have preferred that his wife and children move to Dresden with him, closing his eyes to the simmering political troubles.

We were surprised by his willingness to continue living and working in Nazi Germany, but also by his determination, by his conviction that nothing could happen to him, and by his refusal to give in. Of course he couldn't have known what the Nazis were capable of, but he had heard and seen enough to take their anti-Semitism seriously.

When he got into trouble, his Dutch passport offered him security. Once permanently back in Amsterdam, he put his trust in the Netherlands' neutrality, as in World War I. So he did not flee the country and was, like so many others, taken by surprise by the German invasion. We can't be sure if that notion we had been raised with—that our grandfather's experience with the Nazis had taught him that the family had to get out, and spurred him to take matters into his own hands—is entirely accurate. True, he made sure his sons eluded the Germans. But even if he had had a plan for himself, his wife, and daughter, they waited too long and in the end were forced to make a hasty, ill-prepared exit. And during their flight he had temporarily lost track of his characteristic determination and courage, so our grandmother took control. His resilience was tested in Switzerland, and he regained his confidence and maintained his flexibility and optimism. After the war, back in Amsterdam, he was once again a pillar of strength for those around him.

Even now we can only guess why he never mentioned the Deutsche Zigarren-Werke. Perhaps he realized in retrospect that it had been a monumental mistake to buy and run a factory in Germany in 1932, and preferred not to be reminded of it. Besides, he never talked about his past anyway—not about his family, not about his youth in Łódź, not about his years in Berlin. The past, overshadowed by the murder of his close relatives, was too painful for him. He preferred to keep his emotions to himself. Look forward rather than back. Onward, and forget the rest.

AFTERWORD
BY ROBERT ROTENBERG

ON A SLEEPY SUNDAY MORNING LAST WINTER, I HOPPED ON THE mostly deserted subway train to head down to my office. Just before the doors closed, a well-dressed young man and his young daughter came in and sat near me.

Ask any of my three children, now in their twenties, about me and little kids. I can't resist doing magic tricks for them. I didn't make eye contact with the little girl. Instead, I took a quarter out of my pocket, put it between the forefinger and thumb of my left hand, slid my right thumb up inside and put my two closed fists out in front of me.

I had caught her eye. Slowly, I moved my hands toward the little girl and shrugged my shoulders as if to say: "which hand?" She gave a look up to her dad for his permission, he smiled and nodded, then she tentatively reached out with a tiny finger and touched my left hand. It was empty. She tried my right. Empty too. Then a surprise: I moved my left hand near her ear and pulled out the quarter.

I gave it to her, she smiled, and I said to the dad the thing that most parents with kids in their twenties say to younger parents. "Enjoy her while she's young, I have to warn you they grow up and move away."

"You have a daughter?" he asked. I could see him already projecting his daughter's future.

"Yes, she's twenty and away at university."

"Which school?" he asked. Something about his neatly-put-together appearance made me think that he was going to know the name I was about to tell him.

"Queen's," I said, naming one of Canada's top universities.

"Really," he said, his eyes lighting up. My suspicion was right. "What's she studying?"

Again, I sensed this was going to be a fit.

"Engineering," I said.

He nodded. "What's her name?"

My daughter is a real dynamo. A natural born leader. The type of young woman who on day one at school, camp, or university, comes home with a troop of new friends. She doesn't have an ounce of pretension about her, but simply exudes enthusiasm and confidence. Perhaps it comes from growing up with two older brothers—as I did. But I like to think she has a strong Rotenberg streak in her.

Even before I answered him I knew exactly where the conversation was going to go.

What I didn't know was that this conversation would echo back to me months later, as this remarkable book that you hold in your hand led me back to Germany in 1932, Holland in the 1950s, and my own family DNA.

It happened early in my reading of the book when Sandra, one of the authors, describes Isay, her grandfather. "Sometimes Granddad would do magic tricks for us, like swallowing his watch and retrieving it from his sleeve."

Here was this distant cousin who, just like me, loved to play with children and found joy in simple, fun magic tricks. Was this some kind of Rotenberg trait that I had unknowingly inherited? Years ago my oldest brother, a tax lawyer, opened a gelato shop. His greatest joy was serving children, his face lighting up as he handed them specially made cones.

I think of all the biographies I've read of famous people, strangers to me, and I realized that this was different. A part of this man had been passed down to me.

And how Sandra and Hella describe the clothes he wore: nattily dressed, in a suit and carefully chosen necktie, handkerchief in the breast pocket, gold cufflinks, elegant Italian shoes. I have only vague memories of my own grandfather, Max Rotenberg, but in every picture he's always impeccably dressed. Formal, yet, my mother once assured me, very warm. My father, Cyril, like his father before him—and his distant cousin Isay—was the same. I like to joke I never once saw him in a t-shirt or a pair of jeans.

But really, who was this man Isay, and beyond a ripping great story and a fascinating look at the interior workings of Nazi Germany in the 1930s, what kind of distant mirror is he to me? The Rottenberg family tree leads back to Ivansk, a small town in central Poland that I visited fifteen years earlier. In the late 1800s, the family left and went in many directions. My great-great-great-grandfather, Zecharriah, had seven sons and two daughters. One son, Naftali Hertz (my great-great-grandfather, if you follow), had a son, Elazar (my great-grandfather), who came to Canada. Naftali's cousin, the Isay of this book, eventually settled in Holland.

Growing up I had a vague knowledge that my family had come from a small town in Poland where they were quite successful, running the local inn, some kind of roundhouse. I've heard a few different stories of how we ended up in Canada. How my ancestors didn't want to be drafted into the Russian army for twenty-five years—as they understood Jews were conscripted. How they bribed an official who then decided to turn them in, forcing them to flee.

I distinctly remember years ago, when I was teenager, my father telling me and my older brother David—another Rotenberg writer—that his grandfather was on his way to South Africa when he left Poland. Apparently, at the last minute he happened to meet a friend in Vienna who said, "I'm going to Canada, why don't you come with me?"

My dad shook his head as he told us this story, the fickleness of fate. My brother and I were horrified to think we could have ended up living in such a racist county under apartheid. If we had, clearly we would have fought against the regime—the way our distant cousin Isay did against the Nazis. David turned to me and said, "It's a good thing we didn't end up in South Africa. They string up democrats and rebels like us."

That was years ago, and with a young family and career on the go, the Rotenberg family history was not at all in my mind. Then one day out of the blue I received an email from my cousin Lisa Newman. She is our keen and dedicated family archivist and an invaluable source for this brief afterword. She wrote to invite me to join a trip being organized by descendants of Jewish families from Ivansk who were re-dedicating a Jewish cemetery there that had been destroyed by the Nazis.

The trip brought together people from all across Canada and the US, including two distant cousins from New York who I'd never met, my father's uncle and Lisa. I have a picture of the five of us outside what was once our family compound, and it is stunning how much we all resemble each other. Especially me and my two never-before-seen cousins. Two families divided by space and time. History both divides us and keeps a common thread. It's a common story that has happened to every culture in the world. As a criminal lawyer in Toronto, perhaps the world's most multicultural city, I've met families from everywhere. So many have the same story—divided by history, various diasporas, and yet connected to their distant kin.

We were a Canadian family. The Rotenbergs who arrived in Toronto in the 1890s were a tremendous success story. Energetic entrepreneurs, a number of the brothers—including my grandfather Max and his brother Louis—started a company, Rotenberg & Sons, which brought in thousands of Jews from Russia and Eastern Europe. Their logbook that records all the names of the details of the passage, The Rotenberg Ledger (https://jgstoronto.ca/research/rotenberg-ledger/), is one of the most prized possessions of the Ontario Jewish Archives. Often, when I meet people I'll go online with them and look up their family name so they can see the actual signatures of their ancestors.

Like Isay, the Rotenberg brothers were savvy. They integrated quickly into Toronto society. There's a humorous and treasured letter from Louis about the need to change the family name. The rotten extra "t" was shrewdly dropped. For our generation of North American Rotenbergs, the Dutch Rottenbergs had been a mostly forgotten tale. I'm not quite sure why. In part my parents' generation had gone through World War II and clearly wanted to look to the future, not the past. And this was all a generation removed from them. I have vague memories of hearing about extremely distant relatives somewhere in Europe. But it always seemed remote, something that wasn't really a part of my sense of self. As a Jewish kid growing up in Toronto, I was very aware of the Holocaust, but it always seemed distant to me. Something that had happened to others. Many of my best friends to this day are sons and daughters of survivors. But not me.

Of course I had questions of my own. What happened on my mother's side, to Grandma's family in Poland? How about the Rotenbergs—were any of them left behind? I recall asking in my teenage years. My questions would provoke a knowing glance between my parents and I remember being told that they'd "disappeared."

Reading this book made them reappear. Not as concentration camp victims or survivors, but through the life and times of Isay Rottenberg, this formal, determined, affectionate man, and his equally determined and talented granddaughters. They went in search of their Grandpa Isay's incredible story, and, in finding out who he was, they found more about themselves.

A few years ago I introduced my cousin Michael Levine (his great-grandfather and mine were the two brothers who arrived in Canada from Ivansk) to another cousin of mine, Dr. Jan Ahuja. At that time Michael was growing fascinated with our family history, who we were, and what had made our ancestors pick up and leave, brave coming to this other world.

Branch Office: One Thirty-Six Agnes Street, Northern Crown Bank Building

L. Rottenberg & Sons

Bankers, Steamship & Insurance Agents

One Forty-one Queen Street West, Corner York Street

TORONTO, CANADA

Jany 1/12.

Cable Address: "BERGSON" Toronto

Dear Maggie:

I presume you are vexed at our not writing but you know the correspondents that we are. Anyway things are O.K. Thank God. Nothing to complain of financially. We have had the biggest month, I think, so far. Last night Harry + Pearl were at the house and we all decided that for the future our name should be "Rotenberg" with one "t" so as to eliminate the "Rotten" part of it. Don't you see. Govern yourself accordingly. M + I were at the Ball so was Harry + Pearl. They were very friendly indeed. Harry danced with Minnie and Pearl was quite nice. Really there is nothing new besides. Hoping you are enjoying the holiday and feeling well. Be sure to let me know re the letter will you? With love from your brother

Louis Rotenberg Jr

How had they had been so successful? I knew he'd find Jan fascinating. They clicked. It turned out that Jan had visited our Dutch cousins years ago. The spark was lit.

Michael made it a point to meet these cousins, the authors of this book, at a book fair in Europe. With his usual excitement, Michael, who loves to use the expression "you can't make this stuff up," brought me into this project. He was right: you can't make up a story about Polish-born Dutch Jewish businessman who in 1932 moves to Germany to take over the country's most modern cigar factory—six months before Hitler came to power. Add to this story his two granddaughters, who grow up adoring their grandpa but knowing absolutely nothing about all of this. Extraordinary journalists, they journey back to dig out an incredible tale. Not surprisingly, their book—this book—becomes a bestseller in Holland!

I never write with exclamation marks, but this book you are holding in your hand is just that.

As I read, I see my own family. Isay's industriousness mirrors my grandfather and his brothers who, after their travel business, turned to building office towers in Toronto. And the story of my distant Dutch cousins, the authors of this book, writers and journalists. As are so many Rotenbergs throughout North America. (Michael Levine says there are many of us).

But still, there is that distance between me and this history. After all, in my life I've really never encountered any significant anti-Semitism. This is something that happened elsewhere, a continent and lifetimes away.

Until I read:

It was reported in *Der Stürmer*, a virulently anti-Semitic German tabloid of the day, informing readers "with joy" that the Jew Isay Rottenberg was no longer in charge of the Deutsche Zigarren-Werke in Döbeln and the company had not a single Jewish employee.

That's not someone else. That's not another family's name in a ledger. Or on a shrine. That's my family. That's my name. That's me.

And that is the real point of this book.

It's not just a history of Isay's cigar factory. It's not just a story of his granddaughters' valiant quest to find him. This book is about all of our connections to a past that lives inside each and every one of us.

What comes through most clearly to me about this distant cousin of mine, besides his guts and his often pigheaded determination, is that whatever life threw at Isay, he was going to attack it with energy and zeal. He was going make the most of every day. He was going to be at the head of the pack.

I was getting near my subway stop. I knew the young father was going to know my daughter's name when I answered his question and I knew what he was going to say about her.

From the day she arrived at Queen's, my daughter took charge. She joined their well-regarded Engineering Society and by the end of the year was on the board of directors. At the end of her second year everyone asked her to run for president.

My father, Helen's grandfather, adored her, just as Isay adored his granddaughters, the authors of this book. My dad has passed away, but I know he would have been very proud of her. But not surprised. After all, she is a Rotenberg.

"You're a Queen's engineer, aren't you?" I asked the young father. I knew that Queen's engineering grads are extremely successful, and are a close-knit group.

"Yes," he said with evident pride. "I work for one of the biggest engineering companies in Canada."

"My daughter's name is Helen," I said. Little did I know that months later I'd be reading a book co-authored by her distant cousin Hella.

"Helen what?" he asked.

"Helen Rotenberg."

His face lit up. Even before he could reply, I could tell right away that he'd heard of my daughter. He knew her name.

"Helen Rotenberg," he repeated, greeting me with a wide smile as he put his arm around his daughter. "My company, we've sure got our eyes on her."

ACKNOWLEDGEMENTS

The assistance and co-operation we received in Döbeln gave considerable impetus to our research into our grandfather's cigar factory. From the very outset, city archivist Ute Wiesner was unceasingly supportive, and was tireless in tracking down the many Deutsche Zigarren-Werke dossiers. Ute introduced us to Stephan Conrad, Sophie Spitzer, and Judith Schilling from the Döbeln youth centre. They were fantastic guides, able to connect today's Döbeln with the Döbeln of the past. Their assiduousness in researching and drawing attention to the city's Nazi past made a deep impression on us. Up in Ute Wiesner's attic room, we also met the Döbeln Heimatfreunde: Horst Schlegel, who was able to tell us first-hand about Döbeln in the 1930s; Jürgen Dettmer, who offered us his chronicles of Döbeln during the Nazi period; and Karl Enzmann, who did the legwork in researching the history of the local cigar industry. Historian Christian Kurzweg was of invaluable assistance with his detailed knowledge of Saxony and local politics, enabling us to place the cigar factory in the proper context. Former diplomat Bernard Berendsen and his colleagues at the Ministry of Foreign Affairs, Bert van der Zwan and Lonneke Cruijsberg, did their very best to locate the dossiers on Isay Rottenberg's imprisonment.

Author Gert Mak's enthusiasm over the Döbeln story spurred us to write this book. Finally, we are indebted to Hans Driessen, Laura Starink, and Jozien van het Reve for their keen eye and critical commentary.

LIST OF PERSONS

APITZSCH: Board member of the Chemnitz Chamber of Industry and Trade.

ARNHOLD, ADOLF, HEINRICH, KURT, AND HANS (BROTHERS): German-Jewish banking family based in Dresden. Arnhold Bros. was the "house bank" of Salomon Krenter and Isay Rottenberg. Falsely accused of fraud, the Arnholds sold the main branch of the bank in 1935. Kurt Arnhold fled to the Netherlands in 1938; his brothers had already emigrated.

BEHR, RUDOLF: Nazi district leader in Döbeln since May 1934, succeeded Hermann Groine. Called up for military service in 1942, he survived the war and was prosecuted for crimes against humanity in 1947.

BIRKNER, KURT: Communist, one of the seventeen Döbelners arrested in 1933 on suspicion of high treason, and convicted in December 1934.

BLASE, AUGUST: Owner of a large cigar factory in Lübbecke. Purchased the DZW from the Deutsche Bank in 1937. In 1952, the East German state expropriated the DZW from Blase. The Döbeln building and grounds were returned to his legitimate successor, Dannemann, in 1990.

BÖKELMANN, ERICH: Communist, one of the seventeen Döbelners arrested in 1933 on suspicion of high treason, and convicted in December 1934.

BRÜNING, HEINRICH: German chancellor from 1930 to 1932 for the Roman Catholic German Centre Party.

BUSSCHE-HADDENHAUSEN, GEORG FREIHERR VAN DEM: Officer in Infantry Regiment 139, stationed in Döbeln from 1892 to 1908. Great-grandfather of the current Dutch monarch, Willem-Alexander.

BUSSCHE-HADDENHAUSEN, GÖSTA VAN DEM: Mother of Prince Claus von Amsberg, grandmother of King Willem-Alexander. Born in Döbeln in 1902.

CONRAD, STEPHAN: Works, alongside Sophie Spitzer and Judith Schilling, at the Treibhaus, a youth centre in Döbeln. These three are the driving forces behind the Nazi history workgroup.

DAMM, KARL: Took over the Döbeln clothing store previously owned by the Jewish shopkeeper Hugo Totschek in 1934, after Totschek died while in Nazi custody.

DANNEMANN, FRITZ: Cigar manufacturer, appointed director of the DZW by the Deutsche Bank in September 1935 after Isay Rottenberg was fired and expropriated.

DENECKE, HERBERT: Mayor of Döbeln from 1933 to 1935. Dismissed after a conflict with the NSDAP, whereupon he returned to his previous profession as criminal court judge. Appointed president of the district court in Freiberg in 1940.

DETER, ERNST: Cigar manufacturer from Frankenberg, member of the NSDAP, and board member of the Reichsverband Deutscher Zigarrenhersteller. After the war he was brought to trial for crimes against humanity.

DETMAR, JÜRGEN: Member of the Heimatfreunde, a society of history aficionados in Döbeln.

DRECHSEL, FRANZ: Communist, one of the seventeen Döbelners arrested in 1933 on suspicion of high treason, and convicted in December 1934.

ENDER, HERBERT: Factory director in Saxony, member of the Reichstag (national parliament) for the NSDAP, and economic adviser to Martin Mutschmann, NSDAP Gauleiter for Saxony. Supported Ernst Deter in his campaign against the Deutsche Zigarren-Werke.

FISCHER: Member of the Tobacco Workers' Union and lay judge at the regional court in Frankenberg. Beaten to death while in custody in 1933.

FRITSCH, THEODOR: Publisher and publicist from Leipzig; author of *Handbuch der Judenfrage* (1907), a follow-up to his *Antisemiten-Katechismus* (1887).

GASCH: Employee at the Deutsche Zigarren-Werke.

GLASBERG, MAX, KARL, AND RUTH (SIBLINGS): Jewish schoolchildren in Döbeln in the 1930s. An exhibition over their fate was initiated by Michael Höhme, principal of the Lessing Gymnasium in Döbeln.

GOTTSCHALK, WALTER: Mayor of Döbeln from 1935, succeeding Denecke. Fled the city in 1945, when the Red Army was poised to take the city.

GROINE, HERMANN: NSDAP district leader in Döbeln from 1931 to 1934; member of the Reichstag from 1933 to 1941. Killed during the German attack on the Soviet Union in the summer of 1941.

GRUNER, WERNER: Engineer at the metal factory Grossfuss in Döbeln, designer of the MG 42, the fastest machine gun used in World War II.

HAENSCH, WALTER: Worked for the municipality of Döbeln in 1935. Following a conflict with Nazi district leader Rudolf Behr, he was transferred to the Sicherheitsdienst (SD), where he worked under Reinhard Heydrich. After the war he stood trial in Nuremberg as the commander of special units that committed mass murders in the Ukraine.

HERTZ, PAUL: Jewish Social-Democrat member of parliament in the Reichstag. Left for Prague in 1933 to lead the SPD in exile. Stripped of his German citizenship by the Nazis in 1934.

HEYDRICH, REINHARD: SS leader Heinrich Himmler's right-hand man; Nazi leader of the protectorate Bohemia and Moravia; notorious for his ruthlessness. Killed in an attack in 1945.

ILLGEN: Chief prosecutor in Dresden, in charge of the 1936 bankruptcy fraud case against Isay Rottenberg.

KARIEL, GEORG: Jewish owner of the Wohlwert department store in Döbeln. The store was the last Jewish-owned business in Döbeln to be Aryanized in October 1938.

KILLINGER, MANFRED VON: Prime minister of Saxony, appointed after Hitler came to power. Lost his position in 1934 and became a diplomat for the Reichs government. He had been involved in the 1922 assassination of Walther Rathenau, then minister of Foreign Affairs. Committed suicide in Bucharest when the Red Army took the city.

KOLBE: High-level civil servant at the Ministry for Financial Affairs in Berlin.

KRENTER, SALOMON: Manufacturer, owner of the Bulgaria cigarette factory and founder of the Krenter Zigarren-Werke in Döbeln in 1930. Fled Germany in 1933; eventually went to Palestine, where he survived the war. Later settled in Italy, where he remained for the remainder of his life.

KRONSTEIN, ISIDOR: Salomon Krenter's business adviser. Accused Isay Rottenberg of bankruptcy fraud in 1935. His subsequent fate is unknown.

KUNZEMANN, THEODOR: SPD mayor of Döbeln from 1927 to 1933. Removed from his post on 9 March 1933. Died in poverty in 1944.

LENK, GEORG: Saxony minister of Financial Affairs from 1933 to 1943. Fought in the Waffen-SS from November 1944; was captured by Soviet troops and brought to Moscow, where he was tried and executed.

LESCHINSKY, EMIL: Director of the DZW after its Aryanization by
   August Blase in 1937.

LEWIN: Owner of the Bergmann Zigarrettenfabrieken in Dresden. Lent
   money to Isay Rottenberg to purchase the Krenter Zigarren-Werke.

LEY, ROBERT: Leader of the Deutsche Arbeitsfront. After labour
   unions were banned in 1933, this Nazi union represented labourers,
   employees, and employers alike. Ley was brought to trial for war
   crimes in Nuremberg. Committed suicide in his cell.

LUBBE, MARINUS VAN DER: Dutch Communist, sentenced to death in
   1934 for the arson of the Reichstag building in Berlin on 27 February
   1933.

MUTSCHMANN, MARTIN: Textile manufacturer from Plauen; NSDAP
   organizer in Saxony; appointed Gauleiter by Hitler in 1925 and
   governor of Saxony in 1933. After the war, Mutschmann was tried
   and executed in Moscow.

NITZSCHE, WALTER: Deputy mayor of Döbeln from 1933 onward.

NOURI, SALIM: Tobacco dealer from Bulgaria and business relation
   of Salomon Krenter. Lent Isay Rottenberg money to purchase the
   Krenter Zigarren-Werke.

NUSSBAUM, ELISABETH: Jewish-American wife of Johan Steenbergen,
   the Dutch consul in Dresden.

OEHMICHEN, ARNDT: Isay Rottenberg's legal adviser in Döbeln;
   member of the NSDAP and SA.

PAPEN, FRANZ VON: Chancellor of Germany in 1932; vice-chancellor
   under Hitler from 1933 to 1934.

PIPER, HELFRID: Son of shopkeepers with a business in colonial wares.
   Wrote about his youth in Döbeln.

RATHENAU, WALTHER: Jewish industrialist and politician; cabinet
   minister during the Weimer Republic; assassinated in 1922.

REUTHER, CURT: Director of the Döbeln Stadsbank.

RICHTER, FRANZ: Manufacturer of agricultural machines in Döbeln;
   sold his premises to the Krenter Zigarren-Werke.

RÖHER, OTTO: Deputy mayor of Döbeln (SPD) from 1927 to 1933. Stayed
   on under the Nazis as alderman until 1945; joined the SA in 1934 and
   the NSDAP in 1937. Turned the city over to the Red Army in May
   1945 and, despite his Nazi past, was offered a position in the new
   postwar administration. Was arrested in 1946 and jailed for two years.

RÖNNEKE: Döbeln police chief, appointed once the Nazis came to power.

SAUPE, FRITZ: Manufacturer, former submarine captain, acting mayor
   of Döbeln in 1933 following Kunzemann's ouster. Subsequently
   chairman of the city council and, in 1939, on the Deutsche Zigarren-
   Werke's board of commissioners. Volunteered to serve on the front,

was interned after the war, and died shortly thereafter while still in custody.

SCHACHT, HJALMAR: President of the Reichsbank from 1923 to 1930, and again in 1933. Minister of Economic Affairs from 1934 to 1937 and Hitler's key economic adviser. Was tried and acquitted in Nuremberg.

SCHILLING, JUDITH: Works, alongside Sophie Spitzer and Stephan Conrad, at the Treibhaus, a youth centre in Döbeln. These three are the driving forces behind the Nazi history workgroup.

SCHLEGEL, HORST: Oldest member of the Heimatfreunde, Döbeln's club of history aficionados.

SCHMITT, KURT: Minister of Economic Affairs in Berlin from 1933 to 1935.

SCHUBERT, HANS: Notary public in Dresden. Legalized the transfer of Isay Rottenberg's DZW shares to the Deutsche Bank.

SILVAN, VINCENZ: Trader in raw tobacco, business partner of Isay Rottenberg, initially codirector of the Deutsche Zigarren-Werke. Fled to the Netherlands in 1933.

SPITZER, SOPHIE: Works, alongside Judith Schilling and Stephan Conrad, at the Treibhaus, a youth centre in Döbeln. These three are the driving forces behind the Nazi history workgroup.

STEENBERGEN, JOHAN: Dutch consul in Dresden, director of Ihagee Kamerawerk, producer of the Exacta camera. Was tireless in his efforts to free Isay Rottenberg from jail.

STOCKMANN, EMIL: Cigar manufacturer from Döbeln, strident adversary of Isay Rottenberg.

STREICHER, JULIUS: Publisher of the anti-Semitic weekly *Der Sturmer* from 1925 to 1945 and NSDAP Gauleiter in Frankenland. Sentenced to death at the Nuremberg trials.

TAUBERT: Lawyer for the Reichsverband Deutscher Zigarrenhersteller.

THALER, URS: Swiss financial journalist; researched the Aryanization of Jewish cigar manufacturers in Nazi Germany.

THEERMANN, ARTHUR: Isay Rottenberg's accountant in Dresden.

TOTSCHEK, HUGO: Jewish owner of a men's clothing store in Döbeln. Arrested in the fall of 1933 and died shortly thereafter in prison.

TÜMMLER, ERHARDT: Döbeln metalworking industrialist, the city's largest single employer; member of Döbeln city council and on the board of the Reichsverband der Deutschen Industrie and the Verband Sächsischer Industrieller.

VEITH, HANS-JOACHIM: Lawyer for the Deutsche Bank, instigated the fraud case against Isay Rottenberg and had him arrested.

VLUGT, E. DE: Isay Rottenberg's Dutch lawyer.

WIESNER, UTE: Archivist at the Döbeln Municipal Archives.

WITTKE: Director of the Verband Sächsischer Industrieller.

WÖLFEL, ROBERT: Communist, chief suspect in the group of seventeen Döbelners arrested in 1933 on suspicion of high treason, and convicted in December 1934.

YOHAI, ALBERT: Isay Rottenberg's business partner in Amsterdam.

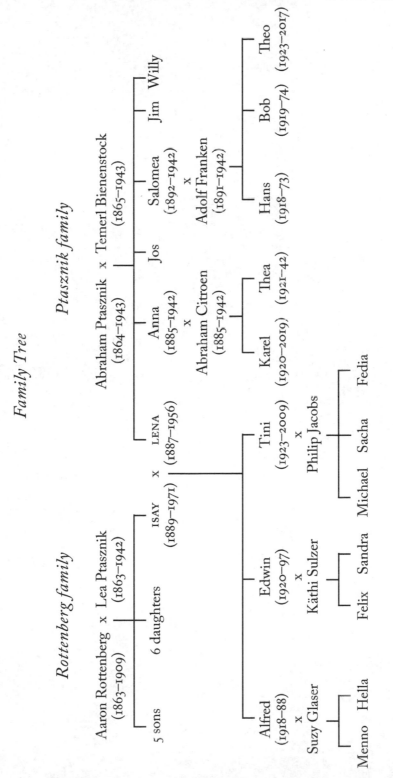

Family Tree

Ptasznik family

Rottenberg family

GLOSSARY OF TERMS AND ABBREVIATIONS

Political parties, entities, concepts, and terminology

DEUTSCHE ZENTRUMSPARTEI: German Central Party
DEUTSCHNATIONALE VOLKSPARTEI: German National People's Party
GDR: German Democratic Republic (East Germany), Deutsche
    Demokratische Republik, DDR
KAMPFBUND GEGEN DEN FASCHISMUS: anti-fascist organization of the
    Communist Party of Germany (KPD). It was founded in 1930 and
    was banned at the beginning of the Nazi regime in 1933.
KPD: Kommunistische Partei Deutschlands (Communist Party of
    Germany)
NSDAP: Nationalsozialistische Deutsche Arbeiterpartei (National
    Socialist German Workers' Party) = Nazis
REICHSTAG: Parliament (refers to both the collective body of
    representatives and the building in which it meets)
SPD: Sozialdemokratische Partei Deutschlands (Social Democratic Party
    of Germany)
WENDE: Peaceful Revolution (of 1989); German for *turning point*.

Nazi terminology

"BROWN": The SA were colloquially called Brownshirts (Braunhemden)
    because of the colour of their uniform. Sometimes used as an
    adjective for Nazi administrations or persons adhering to its ideology.
    Compare with Mussolini's "Blackshirts."

GAULEITER: The party leader of a regional area branch (*Gau*) of the Nazi Party.

HEIM INS REICH (BACK HOME TO THE REICH): A foreign policy pursued by Adolf Hitler beginning in 1938, whose aim was to convince all *Volksdeutsche* (ethnic Germans) who were living outside Nazi Germany to return "home" to Greater Germany.

OBERSTURMBANNFÜHRER: A paramilitary NSDAP rank used by both the SA and the SS, a higher rank than Sturmbannführer.

REICHSKOMMISSAR: Title given to Nazi-era governors, mainly in occupied territories as well as various other regions inhabited by ethnic Germans.

SCHUTZSTAFFEL (SS): Major Nazi paramilitary organization

SICHERHEITSDIENST (SD): Intelligence agency of the SS and the Nazi Party

STURMABTEILUNG (SA): Nazi Party's original paramilitary wing; see "Brownshirts"

Trade organizations

DEUTSCHE ARBEITSFRONT: German Labour Front; *labor* organization under the Nazi Party that replaced the various independent trade unions in *Germany* during Hitler's rise to power.

REICHSVERBAND DER DEUTSCHEN INDUSTRIE: Federation of German Industry

REICHSVERBAND DEUTSCHER ZIGARRENHERSTELLER: Federation of German Cigar Manufacturers

VERBAND SÄCHSISCHER INDUSTRIELLER: Association of Saxony Industrialists

VEREIN DEUTSCHER MASCHINENBAU-ANSTALTEN: Mechanical Engineering Industry Association

Other terms

ENGELANDVAARDERS: Literally "England sailer," a term given during World War II to men and women who attempted to escape from the Netherlands across over 160 kilometres of the North Sea to reach England and freedom.

VRIJ NEDERLAND: "Free Netherlands"; Dutch intellectual centre-left weekly magazine, established during the German occupation of the Netherlands in World War II as an underground newspaper.

WINTER RELIEF: *Winterhilfswerk*, an annual government drive (1933–45) set up by the Nazis to provide food, clothing, coal, and other items to less fortunate Germans during the inclement months.

PHOTO CREDITS

Photos 1 to 7: from the private collection of the Rottenberg and Jacobs
    families
Photos 8 and 9: Stadsarchief Döbeln
Photo 10: *Döbeln in alten Ansichten*, www.dobeln.de
Photo 11: Stadsarchief Döbeln
Photo 12: SLUB Dresden, Deutsche Fototek, photo Max Novak
Photo 14: *Stadsarchief Döbeln*
Photos 16 to 19: *Döbelner Anzeiger*
Photo 20: Sachsisches Staatsarchiv Chemnitz
Photo 21: *Stadsarchief Döbeln*
Photo 24: *Döbelner Anzeiger*
Photo 25: Archief Dietmar Bensch
Photo 26: *Döbeln in alten Ansichten*, www.dobeln.de
Photo 27: Private archive, Monica Norstrom
Photo 28: Museum Pfalzgalerie Kaiserslautern, photo Gunter Balzer
Photo 29: Steenbergen Foundation
Photos 30 to 38: from the private collection of the Rottenberg and Jacobs
families

SOURCES AND BIBLIOGRAPHY

Archives

BUNDESARCHIV, BERLIN-LICHTERFELDE
Reichsfinanzministerium
R 2/10394b, Bd 7. Verbot der Verwendung von Maschinen in der Zigarrenindustrie, Denkschrift 1933.
R 2/10397-10397a. Betriebsumfang der Zigarrenherstellungsbetriebe.
R 2/10430. Kartellierung der Zigarrenindustrie. Errichtung des Zigarrenkartells. *Deutscher Tabakarbeiterverband*
R 2/26733-267336. Verwertung von Zigarrenmaschinen. Durchführung des Gesetzes über die Einschränkung der Verwendung von Maschinen in der Zigarrenindustrie.
R 2/59117-59120. Einschränkung der Verwendung von Maschinen in der Zigarrenindustrie.
RY 37/2, 3, 19, 20. Berichte über die Lage der deutschen Tabakindustrie.

DEUTSCHE NATIONALBIBLIOTHEK LEIPZIG
Anklage 15J 250/33, 21 March 1934, charges of high treason against seventeen Communists from Döbeln. In *Datenbank Nazionalsozialismus, Holocaust, Widerstand und Exil 1933–1945*. Berlin: De Gruyter, 2015.
Urteil 2H9/34, 3 December 1934, verdict in the case of high treason against seventeen Communists from Döbeln. In *Datenbank Nazionalsozialismus, Holocaust, Widerstand und Exil 1933–1945*. Berlin: De Gruyter, 2015.

LEO BAECK INSTITUTE, NEW YORK

Arnhold Family Collection, Folder 8 AR 2920. Letter from Kurt Arnhold
from Park Hotel Amsterdam, December 1938.

NATIONAAL ARCHIEF DEN HAAG

Ministry of Foreign Affairs A-dossiers, 1815–1940, 2.05.03, dossier 197, inv.
no. 1656, Rottenberg imprisonment, 1935–39.
Ministry of Foreign Affairs, London Archive 2.05.08, inv. no. 2624,
"Thoughts on the Past and the Future" by J. Steenbergen, former
consul in Dresden, on the economic situation in Germany following
World War I, 1943.

NOORD-HOLLANDS ARCHIEF HAARLEM

Amsterdam Chamber of Commerce 1922–90

SÄCHSISCHES HAUPTSTAATSARCHIV DRESDEN

Bestand 11168. Ministerium für Wirtschaft, Nr. 2955 Wochen- und
Monatsberichte Gestapo Sachsen 1934–36; Nr. 752, 753 Industrieund
Handelskammer Chemnitz.
Bestand 13131. Deutsche Bank, Filiale Dresden, Nr. 264
Kreditkorrespondenz und Aktennotizen der Deutschen Zigarren-
Werke A.G.; Nr. 200 E. Stockmann Arisierung Fa. Fliegenheimer &
Co, Heidelberg.
Bestand 13471. NS-Archiv des Ministeriums für Staatssicherheit, ZM
1416 Akte 14 Ernst Deter; ZE 36684 Dr. Arndt Oehmichen.

SÄCHSISCHES STAATSARCHIV CHEMNITZ

Bestand 4539. Amtsgericht Frankenberg, Vereinsregister, Nr. 29
Reichsverband Deutscher Zigarrenhersteller, Bezirksgruppe Sachsen.
Bestand 30093. Personalakten, Nr. 51 Dr. Denecke.
Bestand 39074. NS-Archiv des Ministeriums für Staatssicherheit, Nr. 14
ZD 54/3363 Rudolf Behr.

SÄCHSISCHES STAATSARCHIV LEIPZIG

Bestand 20026. Amtshauptmannschaft Döbeln, Nr. 2409 Jahresberichte
1929–32; Nr. 2401 Sicherheitspolizei; Nr. 2508 Streiks 1925–33.
Bestand 20119. Amtsgericht Döbeln, Nr. 74 Handelsregister DZW;
Beschwerde Industrie- und Handelskammer Chemnitz; Nr. 948, Nr.
950, Nr. 573 Handelsregister Krenter-Werke.
Bestand 20206. Oberfinanzpräsident Leipzig, Devisenprüfungen,
Strafverfahren, Nr. 1866/1 DZW.

Bestand 20208. Finanzamt Döbeln, Steuerunterlagen Firmen, Nr. 66, 67, DZW, Blase, Verkaufvertrag Deutsche Bank-Blase.
Bestand 20925. Kammgarnspinnerei Stöhr & Co, Leipzig, Nr. 1058, 1059, 1060, 1061
Bestand 21116. NSDAP Kreisleitung Leipzig, Nr. 1 Stimmungsberichte 1934–37.
Protokolle und Vorlagen des Verbandes Sächsischer Industrieller, Dresden.

STADSARCHIEF AMSTERDAM
Family registry
Foreigner's register

STADTARCHIV DÖBELN
Akten I. 1. 19. Die nationale Erhebung im Jahre 1933.
Akten II. 2. 20. Die Niederschriften über die Ratssitzungen. Bd 88, 89, 1933–34.
Akten II. 2. 32. Die Niederschriften über die Ratsherrensitzungen. Bd 1, 1935–38.
Akten II. 4a. 305. Personalakten Theodor Kunzemann.
Akten II. 20a. 36. Massnahmen zur Behebung der Arbeitslosigkeit. Bd 2, 3, 1933–35.
Akten II. 20c. 51. Die Hitler-Volksspende, 1933.
Akten II. 22. 28. Die Verwaltungsberichte. Bd 5, 6, 8, 9, 1927–36.
Akten II. 22. 149. Bd 1–11 Die Bemühungen der Stadtverwaltung neue Industrien in Döbeln anzusiedeln, 1929–38.
Akten III. 5. 20. Akten des Rates der Bezirksstadt Döbeln, 1934–39.
Beilagsakten II. 22. 149. Bd 1 Die Förderung der Döbelner Industrie, 1930.
Endarchiv Personalakten, Nr. 544 Otto Röher.

Literature

Barkai, Avraham. *Das Wirtschaftssystem des Nationalsozialismus. Ideologie, Theorie, Politik, 1933–1945*. Frankfurt am Main: Fischer Taschenbuch Verlag GmbH, 1988.
———. *From Boycott to Annihilation: The Economic Struggle of German Jews 1933–1943*. Hanover, NH: Brandeis University Press, 1989.
Bäte, Ludwig. *Zigarren aus Lubbecke* (Brochure). Osnabrück: August Blase A.G., 1938.
Blasius, Dirk. *Weimars Ende: Burgerkrieg und Politik, 1930–1933*. Göttingen: Vandenhoeck & Ruprecht, 2005.

Feller, F. M. "Psychologisches Gutachten über die Indianerreklame der Krenter Zigarren-Werke in Dresden." In *Psychodynamik der Reklame*, pp. 223–32. Bern: A. Francke, 1932.

Friedländer, Saul. *Nazi-Duitsland en de Joden, Deel I. De jaren van vervolging 1933–1939*. Amsterdam: Nieuw Amsterdam, 2007.

Haase, Norbert. "Gedenkstätten und historische Orte.". In Clemens Vollnhals (ed.), *Sachsen in der ns-Zeit*, pp. 239–51. Leipzig: Kiepenheuer, 2002.

Haffner, Sebastian, *Het verhaal van een Duitser 1914–1933*. Amsterdam: Uitgeverij Rainbow B.V., 2001.

Halbertsma, E. H. *Johan Steenbergen, de lachende diplomaat*. Den Haag: Steenberger Stichting, 2000.

Held, Steffen. "Von der Entrechtung zur Deportation: Die Juden in Sachsen." In Clemens Vollnhals, *Sachsen in der ns-Zeit*, 200–224. Leipzig: Kiepenheuer, 2002.

Ilgen, Volker. "Bulgaria." In *Trodler und Sammler Journal*, no. 5 (2005): 168–75.

James, Harold. *The Deutsche Bank and the Nazi Economic War Against the Jews*. Princeton, NJ: Cambridge University Press, 2000.

Kurzweg, Christian. *Wirtschaftskrise-Strukturwandel-Kommunalpolitik. Auseinandersetzungen um die maschinelle Herstellung von Zigarren im sachsischen Dobeln 1929 bis 1934*. Leipzig: Magisterarbeit, 1995.

Lapp, Benjamin. *Revolution from the Right: Politics, Class, and the Rise of Nazism in Saxony 1919–1933*. Boston: Brill, 1997.

Lässig, Simone. "Nationalsozialistische 'Judenpolitik' und jüdische Selbstbehauptung vor dem Novemberpogrom. Das Beispiel der Dresdner Bankiersfamilie Arnhold." In Reiner Pommerin (ed.), *Dresden unterm Hakenkreuz*, 129–93. Köln: Bohlau Verlag, 1998.

Morsch, Günter. *Arbeit und Brot: Studien zu Lage, Stimmung, Einstellung und Verhalten der deutschen Arbeiterschaft 1933–1936/7*. Frankfurt am Main: Peter Lang GmbH, 1993.

Pfeifer, Werner. *Dobeln, aus Geschichte und Gegenwart*. Döbeln: Stadtverordnetenversammlung und Rat der Stadt, 1981.

Pieper, Christine, Mike Schmeitzner, and Gerhard Naser, Gerhard (eds.). *Braune Karrieren*. Dresden: Sandstein Verlag, 2012.

Reinmann, Wilhelm. *Mensch und Maschine in der deutschen Tabakindustrie*. 1935.

Schmeitzner, Mike, and Francesca Weil. *Sachsen 1933–1945, Der Historische Reisefuhrer*. Berlin: Ch. Links Verlag, 2014.

Schumann, Silke. "Die soziale Lage der Bevölkerung und die ns-Sozialpolitik in Sachsen." Clemens Vollnhals (ed.), *Sachsen in der ns-Zeit*, 57–72. Leipzig: Kiepenheuer, 2002.

Shirer, William. *The Rise and Fall of the Third Reich: A History of Nazi Germany*. New York: Simon & Schuster, 1960.

Smelser, Ronald. *Robert Ley: Hitler's Labor Front Leader*. New York: Berg, 1988.

Stockmann, Gottfried. *Die Stadt Dobeln als Standort der Industrie*. Borna-Leipzig: Universitätsverlag von Robert Roste, 1928.

Thaler, Urs. *Unerledigte Geschäfte. Zur Geschichte der schweizerischen Zigarrenfabriken im Dritten Reich*. Zurich: Orell Füssli, 1998.

Tooze, Adam. *The Wages of Destruction: The Making and Breaking of the Nazi Economy*. London: Allen Lane, 2006.

Uhlmann, Hans. *Die Entwicklung von Unternehmung und Betrieb in der deutschen Zigarren-Industrie unter der besonderen Berucksichtigung der Tabakbesteuerung*. 1934.

Vollnhals, Clemens. "Der gespaltene Freistaat: Der Aufstieg der NSDAP in Sachsen." In Clemens Vollnhals, *Sachsen in der NS-Zeit*, 9–41. 200–224. Leipzig: Kiepenheuer, 2002.

Wagner, Andreas. "Partei und Staat. Das Verhältnis von NSDAP und innerer Verwaltung im Freistaat Sachsen 1933–1945." In Clemens Vollnhals, *Sachsen in der NS-Zeit*, 41–57. Leipzig: Kiepenheuer, 2002.

Witteler, Hans. *Das deutsche Zigarrengewerbe. Entwicklung, Bedeutung und Tendenzen*. 1932.

Wünsch, Monika. *Die Geschichte Dobelns*. 1990.

Newspapers and magazines

Döbelner Anzeiger und Tageblatt, Volkszeitung fur das Muldental, Der Freiheitskampf, Der Sturmer, Dresdner Neue Presse, Berliner Tageblatt, Berliner Zeitung, Vereinigte Tabak-Zeitungen, Mitteilungen des Reichsverbandes deutscher Zigarrenhersteller.

Other sources

Dettmer, Jürgen, *Dobeln und der Nationalsozialismus in der Zeit von 1923 bis 1945*. [Chronicle of events, taken from the *Döbelner Anzeiger*, unpublished.]

Dobeln im Nationalsozialismus [Website Arbeitsgruppe Geschichte des Treibhaus Döbeln]. www.doebeln-im-ns.de.

Handbuch der deutschen Aktiengesellschaften. Berlin, 1932–42.

Höhme, Michael, *Schwierigkeiten mit der Wahrheit. Zur Geschichte judischer Burger der Stadt Dobeln in der Zeit des Nationalsozialismus.* www. judentum-projekt.de/geschichte/regionales/doebeln/.

Piper, Helfrid. *Ich uberlebte Workuta.* Hamburg, 1993.

Zum Beispiel die Glasbergs. Das Schicksal der judischen Familien Glasberg und Gutherz aus Dobeln. http://www.doebeln-entdecken.de/doebeln/ juedischen-familien.html.

CPSIA information can be obtained
at www.ICGtesting.com
Printed in the USA
JSHW042042071221
21060JS00002B/4